BARKERVILLE

AND THE
CARIBOO GOLDFIELDS

BARKERVILLE

AND THE

CARIBOO GOLDFIELDS

Richard Thomas Wright

VICTORIA · VANCOUVER · CALGARY

Heritage House Publishing Co. Ltd.
heritagehouse.ca

LIBRARY AND ARCHIVES CANADA CATALOGUING IN PUBLICATION

Wright, Richard, 1940–
    Barkerville and the Cariboo goldfields / Richard Wright.

Includes bibliographical references and index.
Issued also in electronic formats.

ISBN 978-1-927527-06-1

    1. Cariboo (BC: Regional district)—Gold discoveries. 2. Barkerville (BC)—History. 3. Barkerville (BC)—Biography. I. Title.

FC3849.B37W75 2013   971.1'75   C2012-907041-6

Edited by Lara Kordic
Proofread by Kate Scallion
Cover and book design by Jacqui Thomas
Cover photos by Major James Skitt Matthews, Vancouver City Archives
    AM54-S4-: Out P334 (front) and Richard Thomas Wright (back).
Frontispiece by Major James Skitt Matthews, Vancouver City Archives
    AM54-S4-: Out P165.
Unless otherwise credited, all interior photos are by the author or from the author's collection.

 The interior of this book was produced using 30% post-consumer recycled paper, processed chlorine free and printed with vegetable-based inks.

Heritage House acknowledges the financial support for its publishing program from the Government of Canada through the Canada Book Fund (CBF), Canada Council for the Arts and the province of British Columbia through the British Columbia Arts Council and the Book Publishing Tax Credit.

17 16 15 14 13 1 2 3 4 5

Printed in Canada

This book is for my sons, Richard Thomas Wright Jr. and Raven Carleton Wright, with whom I first hiked and biked these mountain trails, and for Amy Lee Newman, who has shared these goldfields stories with me for over a decade and who brought her talent and life to the Theatre Royal, Barkerville.

CONTENTS

INTRODUCTION

I ARRIVE HERE in the valley of Williams Creek on a sunny day cooled by clouds that hang over the Cariboo Mountains. A breeze rustles down the creek, shimmering the cottonwoods, quaking the aspens. The town is bustling, for this day marks the end of a depressing wet period. The warm air has dried the street, so I can walk the roadway rather than the boardwalk that fronts the buildings.

It was about 50 years ago that I first visited Barkerville, soon after it was designated a provincial park. Since then I have travelled the gold rush country often, caught up as the prospectors were 100 years ago. The prospectors, you see, unlike the miners, did not really go for the gold, but for the going. I did likewise.

The first edition of this book came out of those travelling years and several concentrated months of research and writing. This latest edition, more of rewrite, is influenced by a decade of producing shows at the Theatre Royal with Newman and Wright Theatre Company and decades of ongoing research around the world. It attempts to tell not only the story of Barkerville, but of the men and women who lived along Williams Creek. In particular, I have enjoyed telling the stories of little-known people: the miners who worked for wages, the dancehall girls, the Chinese shopkeepers, the men who died here or went home broke. For while the Camerons, Barkers and Begbies are significant, they did not exist in a vacuum. The aristocrat and the newly made millionaire lived and worked beside the unsung, dirty digger.

There is a danger in working on a book such as this. "Research is endlessly seductive," historian Barbara Tuchman says, and

I concur. Names from miners' records and store ledgers have frequently taken on lives and stories of their own. My regret is that not all the stories can be told in this book. But I cannot rebury these individuals, and if one is your long-sought-after great-grandfather, I would love to hear from you and exchange information. I can be contacted through my publisher, Heritage House.

A visitor once walked into the museum's visitor centre, had a quick look around and said, "Is this all there is?" A site interpreter explained that, no, there was a whole town just up the road. But there is even more than the town itself. If you travel to Barkerville, allow yourself time to walk the roads, hike the trails and talk to the folks who live here. Soon the Barkerville of long ago will come alive.

I hope this book brings you as much pleasure as I experienced researching and writing it. Enjoy these stories, and then go and find more.

NOTE ON MEASUREMENT, SPELLING AND LANGUAGE: Canada's transition from the imperial system of measurement to the metric system has often made the interpretation of historical measurements complicated and written history jarring. In an effort to make this guide easily understood and useful to the reader, we have used both the imperial and metric systems in the most logical manner possible. As a general rule, imperial units are used in historical context, whereas metric units are used in the walking tour chapters in Part 3, to better orient readers who are visiting the area.

Generally, the spelling of place names in this book follows historical spellings. For example, the Quesnel River was named by Simon Fraser for Jules-Maurice Quesnel, one of his party. When miners stumbled on this river they developed a settlement referred to as The Forks of Quesnelle (adding the "le"). This later became known as Quesnelleforks. Then, when the town at the mouth of the river developed, it was called Quesnellemouth, as opposed to Quesnelleforks or Quesnelle Forks. By the 1870s the town name was shortened to Quesnelle, and by the time the town was incorporated in 1928 it was further shortened to Quesnel. We have used the spelling that was prevalent during the time being discussed—in other words, Quesnelleforks, Quesnellemouth and Quesnelle prior to 1928, and Quesnel thereafter.

In a few instances quoted material and geographical location names contain racial slurs that most people today consider unacceptable or offensive but that were unfortunately commonplace in the 1800s. We have chosen to retain the original language to reflect the attitudes of the era covered in this book.

THE RUSH FOR GOLD

— PART 1 —

1 AN INTRODUCTION TO THE CARIBOO GOLDFIELDS AND WILLIAMS CREEK

Sunday, April 25, 1858, Victoria, Vancouver's Island.

THE SMALL COMMUNITY clustered around the Hudson's Bay Company's fur trading post, Fort Victoria, are on their way to church when an unscheduled steamer pulls into the tight harbour—the old *Commodore* out of San Francisco. Not far behind are the *Golden Age,* the *Stockholm* and the *Columbia.* The ships disembark 1,700 gold seekers into a population of less than 300 white settlers. During that summer more than 6,000 tents surround the pallisaded fort, and by autumn there is a permanent Victoria population topping 3,000. Over 30,000 men and women arrive in BC that summer. The fur-trade economy is yanked into the 19th century.

"Gold! Gold on Fraser's River." The news spread down the Pacific coast from port to port, swelling like an ocean wave until it crashed into San Francisco Bay. Rumour described miners washing a month's worth wages of ($25) in one day, and even First Nations women were said to be panning $10 a day.

"Where is Fraser's River?"

Miner Thomas Seward said no one knew, but word of a new strike hitting a depressed gold-based region "was enough to send hundreds of men into the wilderness to make their fortunes or to die in the attempt."

Fraser's River was north—in British Territory. Most miners "did not even know that Great Britain had possessions on the Pacific Coast." But they came by the thousands, an immense rush that emptied San Francisco. On April 20, 1858, an estimated 1,700 men left between 4:00 and 5:30 p.m. Montgomery Street "looked as deserted as on a Sabbath Day." The new El Dorado was north. The rush for Fraser's River was on.

The North American search for the Goddess of Dawn, the Gilded One, gold, had begun before Spanish conquistadores rode roughshod over the Native population in search of the Seven Cities of Gold. The first real rush in the Americas came in Brazil at Minas Gerais. Between 1695 and 1709 the population of a few Natives grew to 30,000 and in the next hundred years to 500,000. Then, in the early 1800s, gold finds in the US states of North Carolina and Georgia, both placer and lode, resulted in the Cherokee being pushed off their land and substantial foreign investments and immigrants coming to the eastern states.

But the real discovery, the discovery that would bring gold seekers from around the world, had to wait until 1847, when James Marshall found gold in the tail-race of a mill he built for self-styled feudal lord John Sutter. By 1848, 10,000 men scratched for gold in the Sierra Nevada. Then the '49ers streamed west until the creeks and rivers overflowed with diggers. There were men from Canada, James Wattie, John A. Cameron; men from England, Billy Barker, William Winnard; women from France, Fanny Bendixen, Julia Picot; and many others who would later become legends in the Cariboo rush. Gold recovery was enormous. On the Feather River, for instance, seven miners panned 275 pounds of gold in two weeks.

As men poured into California and depleted the gold, they spread east and north, over the next mountain. According to the British consul at San Francisco, the population of California was now over 250,000. Half were miners, waiting impatiently for the hint of a new strike. Only a whisper was needed, because when gold was there you had to rush; you had to be first.

Prospectors following wisps of reports had made their way into British Territory north of the 49th parallel by the early 1850s. Gold had been found on the Columbia River near Fort Colville, on the Similkameen River and on the Thompson River near Fort Kamloops.

On April 16, 1856, Governor James Douglas wrote to British colonial secretary Labouchere reporting "a discovery of much importance, made known to me by Mr. Angus McDonal, clerk in charge of Fort Colville . . . that gold has been found in considerable quantities within the British territory on the Upper Columbia."

Douglas suggested a tax levy placed on gold diggers, but noted that a military force would be required to police it. Labouchere replied on August 4 that an attempt at revenue "would be quite abortive" and that "Her Majesty's Government do not at present look for a revenue from this distant quarter of the British dominions, nor are they prepared to incur any expenses on account of it."

It was left to Douglas's discretion to determine the "best means of preserving order." In fact, Douglas reported on October 29 that the finds were not yet sufficient to attract large numbers, "in consequence of the threatening attitude of the native tribes, who, being hostile to the Americans, have opposed" their entrance. Hudson's Bay Company (HBC) men ignored the gold until Governor Douglas told them, "Acquire all the gold you can."

Douglas's "discovery of much importance" brought the fur-trade era to an end in New Caledonia and sluiced the young colony into the gold era. To say the Hudson's Bay Company entered this new era with reluctance is an understatement. The HBC had controlled the vast wilderness known as Rupert's Land and New Caledonia as the "true and absolute Lordes and Proprietors" for 200 years. They held a trade monopoly from the Canadian Shield to the Pacific Ocean and thereby ruled the population. This monopoly was based on the fur trade; any shift toward gold mining, settlement and agriculture would upset the delicate scales on which their profitable trade balanced. But as gold finds on the Fraser and Thompson came to light, this changed.

It was with mixed emotions that Douglas instructed his traders to accept gold. He anticipated that word would soon leak out and American miners would pour across the border, necessitating the establishment of British sovereignty over gold claims. There was no legislative body and no person of authority other than himself. To protect British territory, Douglas assumed that role.

On December 28, 1857, Douglas issued a proclamation stating that all gold mines on the Fraser and Thompson Rivers belonged to the British Crown. Basing his actions on the Australian experience and notes from the consulate in San Francisco, he announced a system of mining licences, with a fee of 10 shillings, or five dollars American. Anyone removing gold from the district without authorization would "be prosecuted, both criminally and civilly, as the law allows."

With these precautions taken, Douglas gathered 800 ounces (50 pounds) of gold from his posts and shipped the nuggets and flakes to the San Francisco mint on the SS *Otter*. The word was out—the rush was on. By March 1858, newspapers were spreading the gold excitement in sensational front-page stories. The British consul at San Francisco reported miners deserting California mines, boarding ships and emptying the town. Wages leapt as labour flowed north.

A second wave came as news reached the eastern seaboard. After initial hesitation, newspapers accepted the stories, and the British Colonial Office in London, England, realized that perhaps these gold finds were more important than previously imagined. Officials knew they must pay attention, for while the 1846 Treaty of Washington had set the boundary at the 49th parallel, it had not stopped the Americans' expansionist designs. The west coast, sparsely populated, unorganized and unprotected, was threatened by foreign immigration and American "sovereignty by occupation" or "annexation by occupation" claims. The Americans claimed that Oregon was theirs by right of occupation during the fur-trade era and dismissed Britain's claims on the basis of early boundaries.

In response, the new colonial secretary, Sir Edward Bulwer-Lytton, presented a bill to Parliament making New Caledonia a crown colony. Lytton's move was not solely a response to the tide of American miners, nor was it a result of his unbounded faith in the new colony's riches. Instead, Lytton saw his bill as a way to open free trade by ending the HBC monopoly. The bill was read on July 1, 1858, and a week later a temporary five-year plan for government was added. The name of the colony became British Columbia, which, in Queen Victoria's opinion, was "the best name."

The bill created two colonies—British Columbia and Vancouver Island. After 37 years with the HBC, James Douglas accepted governorship of the two colonies. A detachment of 150 Royal Engineers under Colonel Richard Moody was immediately dispatched from England to survey land for public sale, lay out the capital, construct roads and assist the governor in any way possible.

The gold rush that created the new colonies turned into a "humbug" for some as spring high waters drowned the gold-bearing sandbars. While thousands retreated to California, many more squatted on the Fraser's banks ready for further digging. Scattered along the river were experienced California miners such as William Downie, Ned Stout, Billy Barker, Dutch Bill Dietz, Doc Keithley, Richard Willoughby, John Cameron and Peter Dunleavy—and they knew that coarse gold, and perhaps the mother lode, was waiting for them upstream.

As early as 1858, Aaron Post was recorded at the mouth of the Chilcotin River. Then in the spring of 1859, Peter Dunleavy and some partners camped there. A Shuswap man named Tomah stopped for tea and told Dunleavy that his cousin Long Bacheese (also known as Baptiste) would lead them to bean-sized nuggets of gold. True to his word, Baptiste later led the miners to Horsefly River and the promised nuggets. His trail was still warm when Neil Campbell's party arrived, announcing that there were hundreds of miners hard on their heels.

2 THE CARIBOO REGION

SO BEGAN THE rush for "Cariboo," a corruption of the name of the mammal cariboeuf, or caribou, which roamed the region's alpine meadows. The name first appeared in the *British Colonist* in 1860 as miners moved up the Quesnelle River. The *Colonist* reported the name was "not of Indian origin but derived from a species of reindeer abounding in that section." Interestingly, the *Colonist* of November 11, 1860, commented even then on the caribou's decline, saying, "The cariboo [*sic*] is said to have been numerous in Canada West some years since, but latterly, as civilization has advanced, have become very scarce. It was from the killing of one of these animals on the North Fork of Quesnelle River, by some Canadian miners, early in the summer, that the name was first applied to that section, and it will no doubt be adopted by the government in case an official map is ever issued."

Sure enough, a year later Governor Douglas wrote to his office in London saying:

> The Gold Commissioners . . . represent the continued exodus of the mining population from their respective Districts towards the 'Cariboo' country, in speaking of which I have adopted the popular and more convenient

orthography of the word—though properly it should be written 'Cariboeuf' or Rein Deer, the country having been so named from its being a favorite haunt of that species of the deer kind.

Meanwhile a second approach was being made, this time via the Quesnelle River, by Benjamin MacDonald, a Prince Edward Islander. Prospecting out of Fort Alexandria on the Fraser, MacDonald found his first gold on the "Canal," or Quesnelle River, in June 1859. In response to the Dunleavy and MacDonald strikes, a multitude of streams were being prospected, and by 1860 the town of Quesnelleforks blossomed at the confluence of the Quesnelle and Cariboo Rivers. Only two years earlier most California miners had never heard of Fraser's River. Now a new river, the Quesnelle, was being mined a full 350 miles north of the border. The region was as remote as anything imagined, a country that only Natives and fur trappers knew. "It seemed as difficult of access as the Arctic regions," one miner wrote. And still, restless prospectors pushed farther east and north.

Quesnelleforks

Miners pushing upstream were quickly followed by their supply-line merchants and peddlers of all kinds. At a river confluence, a collection of claims stores in shacks and tents soon offered all manner of goods and services. On September 14, 1860, the *Colonist* reported miners on tributaries of the Quesnelle and Cariboo Rivers—Keithley, Harvey and Cunningham Creeks: "A town has started at the Forks of Quesnelle, and called Forks City. It is the distributing point for that region of country, and is filled with miners and others every Sunday buying provisions."

Quesnelleforks, as it came to be called, was located on the original route to the south slope of the Cariboo Mountains, on the trail that ran from Williams Lake to the forks and then over the Cariboo Mountains to Antler Creek. This was the common route in the early days, only bypassed by the Cariboo Road, which followed the Fraser River north to the mouth of the Quesnelle River and then east to Lightning Creek and Williams Creek.

Keithley Creek

On October 10, 1860, Gold Commissioner Philip Nind reported to his overseers in Victoria, "Gentlemen I take advantage of Mr. Batterton the Expressman going to the Forks of Q to forward to you three Mining certificates in favor of W.R. Keithley, Henry Wolf and I.P. Diller. I also beg to inform you that I have recorded three mining claims on the North Fork of the Q R to the above mentioned names and three claims to a water privilege in the same locality."

American lawyer William Ross "Doc" Keithley and his partner, Isaiah P. Diller, made a good strike above Cariboo Lake on a creek 20 miles north of Quesnelleforks that would later bear Keithley's name. By the time the best claims were struck a year later, a town called Keithley Creek was in full swing with three grocery stores, a bakery, a restaurant, a butcher shop, a blacksmith and several taverns. But Doc Keithley, George Weaver, John Rose and Benjamin MacDonald were hiking north again. From a high plateau they looked across alpine meadows sparkling in the autumn sun and saw creeks flowing north. Choosing one creek, the men made their way downstream, through a pass into a canyon. They found gold lying exposed—"sun-burned gold" that had begun to oxidize. From one pan they cleared $75, from another $100. They continued to prospect, staked the best land they could find, built a cabin and then headed back to Keithley Creek for supplies. They had found Antler Creek.

Antler Creek

Despite their efforts to "blind" their trail when they left Keithley Creek to cross the Snowshoe Plateau—now covered in several feet of snow—the Doc Keithley party was followed by Cariboo miners. At the new creek, 1,200 miners were at work in the spring of 1861.

Anglican Bishop George Hills wrote that the name Antler

came "from a fine pair of those of the Carribeau [sic] or Elk being found on the spot. These now adorn the entrance of a store." By July the canyon town was booming and the miners' wealth had brought in racehorses, theatrical troupes, women and dozens of whiskey mills. Antler was a strike to write home about. Newspapers had a headline heyday. "New Diggings—Great Excitement," the *Colonist* reported. "$75 TO THE PAN!"

Governor Douglas wrote to London confirming the find: "We are daily receiving the most extraordinary accounts of the almost fabulous wealth of the Antler Creek and Cariboo diggings. Mr. Palmer, a respectable merchant who arrived the other day from that part of the country with nearly 50 pounds weight of gold, assured me these accounts are by no means exaggerated."

When Judge Begbie visited that summer he wrote that Antler "may be considered as the head quarters of the Caribou; there were from 60–70 homes . . . many of considerable size . . . there is also a Saw Mill 1 ½ mile distant, the shops were well furnished and there were articles of luxury . . . e.g. Champagne at $12 per bottle."

Yet Begbie was "very glad to see the men so quiet and orderly; old Downie looked really almost aghast, he said they told me it was like California in '49, why you would have seen all these fellows roaring drunk, and pistols and knives in every hand. I never saw a Mining Town anything like this. There were some hundreds in Antler, all sober and quiet. It was Sunday afternoon—only a few claims were worked that day. It was as quiet as Victoria."

The Antler strikes drew headlines in the eastern press and once again lured men west. They came by sea; they came north through the US and they came overland across the plains and prairies.

Harvey Creek

In the spring of 1860, 38-year-old George Harvey, a Scot from the Orkney Islands, reached Quesnelleforks. The snow was still three feet deep, but he and three others struggled northward to Sellers Creek, where they managed to take out $2,300 in gold. As

JUDGE MATTHEW BAILLIE BEGBIE

Matthew Baillie Begbie, often mislabelled "the Hanging Judge," was a Scot, born in 1819 into a British Army family. When his father retired, the family settled in Guernsey, off the coast of France. Young Begbie was a brilliant student, with skills in map making, mathematics and law. He was called to the bar in November 1844 and soon gained the attention of the Lord Chancellor in the Court of Chancery. This attention led to Begbie's appointment as judge of British Columbia, the representative in all the courts of Her Majesty Queen Victoria. Begbie did not take his position lightly.

Judge Begbie's first circuit, in the spring of 1859, established him as a man who could debate, shoot, paddle, fight, camp and eat with any official, miner or criminal that circumstance dictated. He stood over six feet tall, a powerful man in all respects. Though he was not a hanging judge—he would sentence only two Cariboo men to the scaffold—he was not one to treat crime lightly, and fear of his sentences deterred outlaws and would-be thieves. As well, Begbie's presence on the creeks was a great satisfaction to those who "had heretofore felt beyond the pale of the law and protection and completely at the mercy of a few drunken desperadoes!"

On August 17, 1863, the *Cariboo Sentinel* remarked on the peacefulness of the creeks: "Everything is very quiet and orderly on the creek owing in great measure to [the magistrate] Mr. O'Reilly's efficiency and the wholesome appearance of Judge Begbie who seems to be a terror to evil doers and a sworn enemy to the use of the knife and revolver." Begbie's admonitions to the accused and to juries have become legend.

In one instance, after a jury brought in a verdict of manslaughter, Begbie roared at the accused:

> Had the jury performed their duty I might now have the painful satisfaction of condemning you to death, and you, gentlemen of the jury, you are a pack of Dallas horse thieves, and permit me to say, it would give me great pleasure to see you hanged, each and every one of you, for declaring a murderer guilty only of manslaughter.

To balance things out, Begbie also charged a man who had pleaded guilty to "go, and sin no more." He had a great sense of drama. When a dispute arose over a mining claim, he played the role of King Solomon and set up a foot race for the protagonists, from Richfield to the claim. The first man to run the distance and drive in his claim stake was declared the winner. In another instance he swore in a jury comprised entirely of men from the accused's country of origin—an apparent attempt to prevent the escalation of nationalistic tensions. Despite his sometimes questionable choices, Begbie was almost singlehandedly responsible for the sense of law and order that prevailed in the gold creeks of Cariboo.

Begbie became chief justice of British Columbia in 1870 and was knighted in 1875. Sir Matthew Baillie Begbie died in Victoria on June 11, 1894.

the river rose with spring melt, their claim was washed out, so he, Doc Keithley and a couple of others headed north. (The make-up of various parties of discoverers varies between accounts.)

Just beyond Cariboo Lake on the west side of the Swamp River (now the Cariboo River), they reached a creek, and, wrote the *Colonist,* "ascending this creek for some miles they found a falls 40 feet high . . . a good prospect was obtained at the foot of the falls." They left this creek and travelled farther up the Swamp River, likely to the canyon downstream of Cariboo falls, then east up the Clear River (Matthew River). Fifteen miles up the Clear River they came to "falls 200 feet high," which they likened to Niagara Falls. They may well have been the first Europeans to see what are now known as Ghost Lake Falls, where Ghost Lake empties into the Matthew River.

The *Colonist* records that Harvey and five others returned to Harvey Creek and set to work where he had staked out claims at the falls. By the autumn he was in Victoria with "a full purse," reporting returns of up to $140 a day per man. During the summer of 1861 eight companies had flumes and were reported to be doing well. The creek remained a small but consistent mining area.

George Harvey later suffered from smallpox in the 1863 epidemic. He died of pneumonia, in Victoria, at age 57 on March 29, 1879.

Cunningham Creek

No sooner had the excitement over Antler Creek abated than word of yet another rich strike seeped into the gold camps. Cunningham Creek takes its rise in the same mountains as Antler Creek but flows north past Roundtop Mountain then east to empty into the Cariboo River north of Harvey Creek and south of Matthew River. In the fall of 1861 Kentuckian William Cunningham and a small party made their way to this creek and found a bedrock outcropping at an elevation of 4,200 feet. They were soon producing $100 a day per man.

Cunningham Creek continued to produce for many years and was one of the sites in which Barkervillian Fred Tregillus had a particular interest. The Cariboo Hudson Mine operated on the creek's headwaters below Roundtop Mountain for many years but is now a derelict ruin. The road to Yanks Peak, a four-by-four road, travels up the valley to the alpine.

William Wallace Cunningham was a wanderer. Within a few months he had left Cunningham Creek to prospect to the west. He found gold on Lightning Creek and then had a success-ful claim on Williams Creek. High living, drinking and gambling kept the gold flowing out of his pockets, yet for a few years he was one of the most notable Cariboo miners.

Cunningham was one of the few miners to bring his wife to the goldfields. It is not clear when Louisa Cunningham arrived in Cariboo, but she gave birth to a son William, nicknamed the "Cariboo Nugget," on March 6, 1864, in Richfield. Her mother and father, David and Rebecca Sires, were also on Williams Creek, where they ran a boarding house.

Just three months after the birth of his son, the peripatetic William was once again prospecting when he contracted typhoid on the Swift River. He died at Soda Creek on June 1, 1864, just as new strike on Cunningham Creek was taking place. His family soon moved to Whatcom County, Washington.

Grouse Creek

In July 1861 the *Colonist* reported that "Grouse, or Salt Spring Island Creek . . . was struck recently by some men from Salt Spring Island. One company had prospected the creek. They sank down four feet and obtained prospects ranging from ten to twenty-five cents to the pan."

One of these men was John Ducie Cusheon, who came here with his wife, Margaret, his children and his mother-in-law, Mary Ann Webster, and became an active miner while Margaret ran Cusheon's boarding house. (Cusheon Lake on Salt Spring Island is named for the family.)

Grouse Creek soon became a small town, often called Kellyville for the Kelly family who later settled in Barkerville. While never the size of Barkerville, it was the site of the immensely rich Heron claim, still being worked in 2012.

Lightning Creek

Charlie Holtz came to the Cariboo as a mule packer. Born in Hamburg, Germany, in 1827, like so many he was enticed west by the California gold strikes. He dug for gold and then became a sailor on the USS *Active*, until he heard of Fraser River gold. There he bought a team of mules and became a packer. He was in the Cariboo when news of the Keithley Creek strike hit, so he wintered in Quesnelleforks. Then Antler Creek hit the headlines. Holtz told the *Colonist*:

He and some of his friends were at Antler when the strike was made, and they decided to do some prospecting. Besides Holtz, the party consisted of Dutch Bill, who afterwards struck William's [*sic*] Creek, Bob Davis, and some other Germans. The bunch ate noon-day grub at Tom Maloney's Flat, and packing about 150 lbs apiece, besides their picks, pans and shovels, they struck for new country. Leaving Maloney's Flat they separated, Dutch Bill striking off towards the valley of Williams Creek, while Holtz and Davis headed for Bald Mountain. Holtz and Davis had reached Groundhog Lake, and Holtz was beating through the brush quite a piece in the lead, when he turned and saw no sign of Davis. He called and fired his guns without any response. That was the last he saw of Davis for a long time.

Finding that Davis had strayed away, Holtz decided to camp for the night. At daylight he saw smoke from a campfire some distance away, and believing it to be Davis, he hiked over. Instead of Davis he found two well-known characters, Nate Campbell and Billy Farrell, otherwise known as Billy the Bladge, by reason of his oratorical powers. Holtz [was told] they were hiking in to Antler for grubstakes. Holtz proposed that as he had quite a bit of grub, he should grubstake the crowd, and they would 'go cayuse' on whatever they found. This was agreed to and the trio set out.

As a result of this hastily formed partnership Holtz was one of the finders of Lightening [sic] Creek, which turned out to be one of the richest. "We called it Lightening Creek," said Holtz, with a laugh, "because it made us see lightening [sic] getting down to it. Jiminy Crickets! But it was rough and rocky!"

Staking out the discovery on Lightening, Holtz and his pals were joined by others, each of whom got 100' frontage on the discovery. In this party were Holtz, Nate Campbell, Billy the Bladge, Jack Adams, Tom O'Brien and Jack Hughes. Holtz worked his claim for a short time to try it out, and turned up $7.50 to the shovelful. Afterwards however, he found that he had all he could do to run his mules, and he gave his claim to Johnny Burns.

Thomas Brown, an American citizen, told Governor Douglas that "Ned Campbell," (probably meaning Nate) with a company of 10 other miners, selected and recorded a claim on a newly discovered stream called Lightning Creek, a tributary of Swift River, which yielded about two ounces of gold to the pan full of earth. Prior to Brown's departure, a report reached Quesnelleforks announcing that the company had realized 1,100 ounces in one day almost as soon as they began to work.

It was July 1861, and another north-slope creek was yielding gold.

Lowhee

Richard Willoughby rode into the Cariboo gold rush like a character from the pages of a Louis L'Amour novel: Indian fighter, Texas Ranger, violinist, farmer and successful miner. A visitor to modern-day Wells can look south, across the head of Jack of Clubs Lake, to the hydraulic mining scar of Lowhee Creek. This creek was likely his biggest success.

Willoughby was born in 1833 in Boon County, Missouri. His father was a farmer and the captain of a police force, rangers raised to protect the border country. The story goes that when Richard was just six he accompanied his father on an expedition. The excitement was infectious, and before many years had passed young Willoughby headed for Texas to join the Texas Rangers. Before he was 20 he joined a party bound for the California gold rush. During the crossing he took command during a battle with First Nations and by all accounts was responsible for the survival of the wagon train. Richard Willoughby's legend was growing.

In California he mined successfully at Hangtown. He prospected in Arizona and New Mexico and opened a mine in Nevada. He was back in California when he heard news of the Fraser River.

Willoughby formed a party of miners and rode north through the Indian Wars in Washington Territory and Idaho. After several skirmishes the group reached the Fraser River, and Willoughby set to work near Emory's Bar, clearing over $20,000, which he soon lost.

He operated a saloon in Yale and took part in several musical productions as a singer and violinist, then prospected the Similkameen and Lillooet and wintered on the Harrison River.

In early 1861, presumably looking for another stake, Dick Willoughby headed for the Cariboo.

It has been said that Willoughby was one of the best prospectors and placer miners in the colony, and his success in the Cariboo proves this. After scouting the country he and his partner, Hanson Tilton, prospected around Burns Creek, between Williams Creek and Lightning Creek. Nearby they found surface gold and panned out enough for supplies. Back at Lightning Creek they traded for goods and tried to convince the gold buyer that the gold came from Williams Creek. He knew better. When Willoughby left, miners anxious to stake new ground followed him. The large strike became known as the Lowhee.

The creek was struck on July 13, 1861. Wash-up on the 28th produced 777 ounces—48 pounds—of gold. In one week in August they produced 430 ounces. By September 6 they had taken out $50,111—worth more than one million dollars today. All of this came from a strip 400 feet long, 12 feet wide and only 3 feet deep. Willoughby's claim unearthed a 16-ounce nugget, the largest in BC. Gold Commissioner Nind planned to take it to the World's Fair.

Lowhee's importance has been overshadowed by the town of Barkerville and the later wealth of Williams Creek. At the time Willoughby struck the Lowhee, Williams Creek was deemed a humbug. It had not proven up, but the wealth and success of Lowhee kept prospectors and miners in the area hopeful. Then Steele, Abbott, Barker and Cameron hit pay dirt in late summer of 1862.

The Lowhee was later the site of a large hydraulic operation that carved a long gulch south to the headwaters. For a short time the small town of Carnarvon perched at the top. The outwash gravel of the hydraulic operation, later augmented by Island Mountain tailings, filled in the eastern end of Jack of Clubs Lake. The south part of Wells is now located on these tailings, which are reported to be many feet deep.

Willoughby kept prospecting and developed a keen interest in photography. He took a few years out to farm in the Fraser Valley near Chilliwack, but farming was not his game. In 1876 he struck north to Alaska and once again made several good strikes. He never returned to British Columbia and died in Alaska in 1904. Unlike most miners, Richard Willoughby, the man from Lowhee, was still a wealthy man.

Williams Creek

The discovery of gold on Williams Creek and the man for whom the creek is really named has been wrapped in myth and conjecture since 1861. As recently as 1998, a "true story" suggested a group of seven men found the creek and named it for "Dutch Bill" Williams (usually referred to as "Dutch Bill" Dietz). For what is likely the real story we should turn to one of the discoverers, Michael Costin Brown, born 1838 in Dungarvan, Ireland. He arrived in California just in time to hear of the 1858 rush to BC, so he headed north. Three years later he was at Quesnelleforks when he heard word of Antler Creek, so he and his partner, Costello, walked north through heavy snow. After prospecting for several days without success they met William "Dutch Bill" Dietz and Mike Burns. In an interview years later, Brown told a story similar in detail to that of Charlie Holtz. Dutch Bill Dietz was an early Fraser River miner, with four claims on Prince Albert Flat just below Yale, but an Antler Creek latecomer. Luck had not been with him in this gold rush. His journey from California had netted him only a little Fraser River gold and a lot of trouble from Natives, who stole his supplies at Lillooet. Now he was late arriving at the Antler strike. Brown recalled the story in the *British Colonist* on December 24, 1913:

> While we were at Antler Creek, two men came into our camp, William Dietz, familiarly known as 'Dutch Bill,' and Mike Burns. They had been prospecting the neighboring country across the divide and Burns was discouraged and wished to leave that wild country, being short of grub and tired of gold hunting. On the other hand, 'Dutch Bill' seemed anxious to continue prospecting and offered to join us. This offer we accepted, and we crossed the

Divide, eventually making the headwaters of the creek, after some tiresome travelling, in which we travelled to a place near a little gulch or canyon, where we camped for the night, building a brush shelter. On the following morning we separated to prospect the stream agreeing to meet again at night to report progress.

The story of that day's prospecting, which we recalled over the campfire, has become a matter of mining history in British Columbia. 'Dutch Bill' made the best prospect, striking pay dirt going $1.25/pan. I and Costello had also done pretty well, finding dirt worth $1 or so a pan. You can well imagine we were well pleased with our day's exertions and each man in his heart felt that we had at last discovered very rich ground.

'I shan't readily forget,' said Mr. Brown, and his eyes glowed as the memory of the old familiar scenes was again brought up, 'the discussion that took place as the name to be given to the Creek, 'Dutch Bill' was for having it called Billy Creek, because he had found the best prospects of the 3. I was quite agreeable, but I stipulated that William Dietz should buy the 1st basket of champagne that reached the Creek. This appealed to Costello, and so the Creek was then and there named, not Billy Creek, but William's Creek. This was the most celebrated stream of Cariboo, called after William Dietz, who at least had an equal share with his partners in the discovery.'

Doubt is sometimes raised as to whether Williams Creek is indeed named for "Dutch Bill," but the evidence is overwhelmingly in his favour. For instance, as early as June 24, 1861, the *Colonist's* correspondent H.H.S. wrote, "Everything looks very encouraging up here at present, and great discoveries are being made . . . the latest of which is William's Creek called after Dutch Bill, a noted mountaineer and prospector."

Mining claim records at the BC Archives include a claim notice that reads:

This record was made with Const. H. Hose last summer and neglected being given to Mr. Nind [the Gold Commissioner].

    22 March 1862 Williams Creek. Recorded in favor of W. Deitze, [Mining License No.] 2159, M. Burns 1929; C. Good, 2108; F. Brumiller, 2138; J H Miller, 1903; five claims of 450 feet frontage running into the hill joining Smith and Co at the lower end, C. Brouse on the upper end.

Dietz was indeed the discoverer of the richest creek in Cariboo.

    The transformation this post-glacial creek underwent from its 1861 discovery to 1863 was explosive. Word soon reached Antler. Dissatisfied miners raced over Bald Mountain. While initial enthusiasm was high, the gold of Williams Creek did not give itself up easily. Miners who expected the easy diggings of Antler Creek dubbed it Humbug Creek. The diggings went down to a layer of hard blue clay that miners thought was bedrock; it was on this layer that most of the gold was found. Returns were mediocre.

    At the claim of miners Abbott and Jourdan, frustration was intense. Jourdan left for supplies, and Abbott decided to swing a few blows at the blue clay. Abbott's pick broke through, and when Jourdan returned he had 50 ounces of nuggets to show. No longer was this "Humbug Creek."

    Only 90 men and 7 women stayed during the winter of 1861–62; the rest went south and spread word of the strikes. Abbott assisted by scattering gold through Victoria's saloons. The gold sent to Victoria as winter fell on Cariboo was valued at $2.6 million. The next spring, few could resist the lure of gold shipments or the temptation to shoulder a shovel and head north; they were determined, or at least hopeful, to get their share of the gold they imagined was lying on the creek bottom.

    Bill Cunningham announced spring's arrival on the creeks with this letter on May 18, 1862:

Dear Joe,

I am well and so are the rest of the boys. I avail myself of the present opportunity to write you a half dozen lines to let you know I am well, and doing well—making from two to three thousand dollars a day! Times good—grub high—whiskey bad—money plenty.

Yours truly,

William Cunningham.

As he wrote, the trails crawled with men. On Lightning Creek a town called Van Winkle was already in existence; on Williams Creek, Richfield was taking shape. The word of gold was telegraphed around the world.

The *Colonist* ran news, rumours and reports that were picked up by *Times of London,* and the *Times* was picked up by papers around the world. In addition miners were writing letters home that fanned the flames. As far away as New Zealand and Australia newspapers announced gold.

"Astonishing Riches of the Cariboo Mines" headlined New Zealand's *Otago Witness* on February 8, 1862. It quoted the *Colonist* saying the *Otter* had arrived at Victoria with $250,000 in gold and went on to say, "If anybody here had entertained doubts as to the truths told concerning the enormous yield of the mines of our sister colony during the season just past, such doubts would have been entirely dissipated had he stood on the Hudson's Bay Company wharf last evening and saw the *Otter* come in with 70 passengers from Cariboo." Abbott and his two partners came in on this sailing carrying $80,000 in dust on their backs.

The *Daily Southern Cross* of Auckland, New Zealand, wrote on January 3, 1862,

Exciting news comes from the Cariboo country, where the mines are turning out very rich . . . Several lucky individuals have already left for below—amongst others, [Richard] Willoughby from Lowhee Gulch, with 11,000 dollars; two Pattersons, O'Rourke, Miller, Usher and

Davies with sums varying from 3,000 dollars to 7,000 dollars. Two packers, named [Stephen] Fellows and [Frank] Way, are said to have left here a few days ago with 40,000 in gold. The largest sum taken down by any one individual was 194 lbs weight—a regular mule load.

On May 24 the *Taranaki Herald* of New Plymouth, New Zealand, ran a report from February 7 of miners sluicing "100 lbs to 500 lbs a day for a company of three to six men." Similar reports were carried in the *London Times* and Australian newspapers. Anyone who had doubts about Cariboo's wealth was now convinced that here indeed was the road to riches. Who could resist when a good day's wage was one to five dollars in most places?

Downstream from Richfield was a small canyon. The claims below that gave little sign of being productive until Ned Stout and some partners tried a tributary gulch, struck gold and started bringing in $1,000 a day. Stouts Gulch, as they called it, proved there was gold below the canyon. But it was deep, not the usual eight feet.

One man who recognized the canyon's potential was an English waterman who had been scratching for gold since 1846. William Barker had arrived on Williams Creek in early spring 1861 and had a claim near Mink Gulch, above Richfield. The claim was unsuccessful.

In June 1862, Barker moved downstream, expanded his company to eight partners and claims and sank two shafts with no success. They tried again, and on August 17, 1862, hit the lead. In the next 10 hours they took out 124 ounces (nearly 8 pounds) of gold.

Gold Commissioner Thomas Elwyn wrote the colonial secretary that he considered this strike "to be of great importance for now the lead will in all probability be traced for a long distance down the creek." Elwyn was right on the mark. Claims, shaft houses, flumes, waterwheels and cabins sprouted along the creek like fireweed after a fire. And four months later John Angus "Cariboo" Cameron, another Fraser River miner, struck rich gravel just a mile below Barker and Company.

CLAIMS, COMPANIES AND FOREIGN INVESTMENT

What most prospective miners did not realize, unless they had been in previous rushes, was that "rush" was the operative word. Prospectors had to rush to get to a creek or lose out on finding workable ground. The claims were, after all, only 100 by 100 feet. A recently found 1862 map of the claims on Williams Creek shows only 160 companies, and there were approximately 600 individual claims on the creek from its headwaters to the meadows. If you were late you prospected for another creek, if you had the resources, or worked for wages if you didn't.

The next sticking point was that once the gold was deeper than a few feet, it took enormous technical and financial resources to keep sinking shafts and drifts. Most of the successful companies committed huge financial investments. John Cameron came with money he made on the Fraser, as did Billy Barker and many others. Isaiah Diller and company dug for 17 months, investing $8,000 ($200,000 today) before they hit the lead.

Investors bought into claims with funds to keep them going. Men worked for shares. And BC began its long association with foreign investment. The Hudson's Bay Company had begun with money from England's financial markets, which continued into the goldfields. Kwong Lee Company brought money from China. John Evans and his 4 and 20 Welshmen on Lightning Creek worked with British capital—which they lost. Others brought investment dollars from California or Canada's east coast. When Americans John Kurtz and Charles Lane tried to mine in the meadows, they looked south for capital and brought on financier Charles Hearst (father of newspaper magnate William Randolph Hearst), who invested in mines that covered over half of North America. But for the lonely, struggling miner with a few dollars and a hundred pounds of supplies, fortune was as distant as it had been on his home farm or apprenticeship.

By spring of 1863 two towns had grown around these two claims. With Richfield upstream and Cameronton downstream, the obvious name was Middletown. But that did not stick. Nor did Springfield, for the hillside springs. In July 1863 one miner wrote that this middle town was called Van Doulanville, after miner Charles van Doulan, but that did not take, nor did

Williams Creek. The name that eventually stuck, of course, was Barkerville. The first mention of Barkerville is found in the August 3, 1863, edition of the *British Colonist:*

Richfield Lower Town—Buildings going up.
This town has not yet been fairly named, some wish to call it Springfield, others, Barkerville; if we admire the trails which lead to it and the different springs which help to keep the same, in some places a complete puzzle from June to January. I should say it was an appropriate name, but it might, however, with propriety be called Barkerville, after Mr. William Barker, who, I am informed, was one of the first who began to work below the canon.

Everywhere the earth was being turned inside out for its wealth. By 1864 there were four towns in four miles on Williams Creek. Richfield, the "seat of Government," was farthest upstream. Below the canyon were Barkerville and Cameronton, forming one long main street of hotels, saloons, brothels, general stores, restaurants and numerous less important buildings.

Little mention is made of Marysville, but the town was scattered on the flats below Cameronton and on the benches of the creek's east side. Nearby were the rich Forest Rose, Prairie Flower and California claims, and Adam's sawmill. Based on the 1862 map of the creeks, it is possible that the original name of the town was Mayersville, based around the Mayersville Company run by R. Marcus Mayer.

3 ROUTES AND SUPPLIES FOR THE GOLDFIELDS

THE ANTLER CREEK strike opened up a vast new region to resource extraction and settlement and galvanized thousands into action. Miners poured north. The problem, as always, was not just where to find gold but how to get there and then how to establish a supply line. By 1862 an estimated 6,000 miners were on the north slope, creating an enormous demand for food and supplies. Food was scarce and prices were high. One miner reported that gold and flour were of equal value on a scale. Some miners were starved out. It was a rush into famine.

Miners used First Nations' trails, Hudson's Bay Company Brigade trails and new routes of their own making. Most of these were terrible, thrashed to the consistency of soup, broken by deadfall, over snow-covered heights and across creeks and rivers. Men like Timoleon Love, Captain Mitchell, the Barrys and someone known only as "Texas" soon built ferries and bridges, but the trails slowed the progress of supplies.

During this period pack trains came into the north-slope goldfields from Lillooet following a trail that incorporated old brigade trails. They branched northeast at Williams Lake toward Beaver Valley. At this bottleneck in early spring, thousands of men with horses, mules, oxen and cattle waited for the trail to dry out before they pushed into the new town of Quesnelleforks. Then they pushed upriver to Keithley Creek and over the hump into Antler Creek and Williams Creek. It was a total of well over 100 miles on a long, muddy, treacherous route, hard on men and deadly for livestock. Packers lost hundreds of horses and mules, and the supply lines bogged down.

The drovers' beef and sheep were sources of protein for miners, but there was not sufficient to feed thousands. All manner of goods had to be packed in on the backs of miners, Native packers, horses or mules, dogs or camels. Still, supplies were limited. Wages and returns on investment were marginal considering the price of food and supplies. In May 1862 George Eves reported that "on Williams Creek no grub [was] for sale excepting what was in the hands of Steel & Co. Flour, $1.20 per pound . . . We[']re drawing supplies from Antler, where there was a fair supply."

Merchants and freighters warned officials in Victoria that there were not enough mules in British Columbia to bring goods over the miserable trails. Only wagons could fill the great hungry maw—and wagons needed a road. Previously Governor Douglas had let a contract to widen the Harrison Douglas Trail into a proper 18-foot wagon road on the portages with a destination of Lillooet on the Fraser River. By the time they arrived, it was time to push north, so he let a series of contracts to build a road north from Lillooet to Soda Creek, then to Quesnelleforks and eventually to Barkerville. The great Cariboo Wagon Road had begun, and it would bring new life to gold rush camps along Williams Creek.

It is hard to imagine the logistics and number of animals and packers it took to keep the supply lines open. The miners were like an advancing army with their supplies, unable to keep up. E.T. Dodge and Company was one of several freight merchants and forwarders in New Westminster, 500 miles to the south, and in Lillooet. Their 1864 account books give an idea of the parade of animals necessary to move goods. In May 1864 the freight tallied from either New West or

Lillooet shows an average of 56 animals per day from just one forwarder. In the same month, 334,600 pounds (167 tons) of freight on 1,673 animals went north. Numbers from June through August were similar. In total, from May to September 1864, 836 tons were shipped on mule back—by one forwarder.

For some entrepreneurs, the never-ending shortage of supplies and high prices of freight presented an opportunity.

The Cariboo Camels

It seemed like a good idea at the time. Bavarian-born Frank Laumeister, a merchant in Yale, had read in California newspapers about a new beast of burden that could out-pack a mule, out-walk a horse and live longer without water and food than a desert snake. Camels—dromedaries and Bactrians.

The United States government had been experimenting with dromedaries for several years, using them for army explorations in Texas and in locating a desert route to California with a certain degree of success. American packers also began using the animals along the Colorado River near Yuma, Arizona, and from the Carson Valley to Virginia City, Nevada. Laumeister was a frontier optimist. He put together a syndicate, including Adam P. Heffley and Henry Ingram, and commissioned John C. Callbreath to travel to San Francisco to investigate camels and check out the beasts' potential.

It was the beginning of a story that would create more myths, tall tales, folklore and general misinformation than anything in BC history except the gold rush itself. But the real story can be found. It has always been there, overlooked, misrepresented, diluted with fantasy and illogical fiction.

The success of the US Army camels had prompted private companies to consider importing them for use in pack trains. The catalyst came in 1859 in Nevada when silver was struck on the Comstock. Bavarian-born Otto Esche, a San Francisco merchant, reasoned that as camels weighed 600 pounds to a mule's 250, they might make better pack animals. He decided on Bactrians, which were heavier, more compact camels with stout legs and two humps and were better suited to the Sierra Nevada's cold climates than the taller, lighter dromedaries. Bactrians came from Mongolia, the rocky Gobi Desert in particular.

Esche chose a herd from the cold, mountainous area along the Amur River, near what is recorded as Nicolaessky, Russia (most likely Nikolayevsk-on-Amur). The camels had already been used for packing. He brought in three shipments, and on March 1, 1862, an advertisement appeared in Victoria's *Colonist:* "To Packers. Twenty-Five Camels for Sale."

John C. Callbreath, an American with a roadhouse at Seton Lake and the owner of the SS *Lady Seton* side-wheel steamer on the Douglas route, ignored all the negative stories about the husbandry of camels and horses' alleged dislike of the beasts and focused on the successes. His vision was about to enter the folklore and myth of British Columbia.

Callbreath, along with Gustavus B. Wright, Frances Laumeister, Adam Heffley and Henry Ingram, were not idle dreamers or schemers. Callbreath and Wright had a contract to build a section of the Cariboo Road from Lillooet to Clinton. Frank Laumeister, a Bavarian, a California 49er, a merchant-entrepreneur, came to BC in 1859. Americans Adam Heffley and Henry Ingram were no slouches either and later became successful ranchers.

Callbreath purchased 23 Bactrians for $6,000 from Otto Esche in San Francisco, the largest sale made from Esche's imports, and loaded them on the steamer *Hermann*. The *Alta California* newspaper wrote, "The Bactrian camels have left for British Columbia. Many are anxious to know whether the experiment of using them will succeed or not in that climate."

Early BC historians have mixed fact and fantasy in telling the Cariboo camels' story. We now know that the camels did not come from herds used by the US Army; there were 23, not 21; they were used for two seasons, not one; and, most importantly, they were not a failure.

Their arrival at Esquimalt on the *Hermann* on April 14, 1862, was chaotic. "Mr. Callbreath's twenty-three Bactrian camels arrived . . . They are singular looking animals, and when driven from the steamer frightened the horses at Esquimalt out of their propriety and a week's appetite," wrote the *Colonist*.

By the middle of May, six camels were carrying freight between Port Seton and Lillooet, one of the most difficult trails in Cariboo. P. Smith, a correspondent with the the New Westminster–based *British Columbian*, reported,

> Several trains had left for Quesnelle river, loaded with goods for miners and merchants. The camels are employed in packing over the Pemberton portage, and are found to answer admirably.
>
> While they carry from 500 to 600 lbs, at a load, being double that of a mule, their keep costs little or nothing as they pick up all they require by the way side, no small consideration when feed is from 6 to 7 cts per pound.

The remainder were put to work following the old Hudson's Bay Company Brigade trail to the Cariboo mines.

Laumeister was responsible for the camel train, and he took them through Quesnellemouth, not Quesnelleforks. Twenty miles east on July 22, 1862, Bishop George Hills encountered the camels and recorded the event in his journal: "Reached Cottonwood River at 2 p.m. Here the strange sight of Camels presented itself and I crossed my horse at a spot somewhat away from the usual place lest I should have my shy animal take fright."

Harry Guillod met them a little farther along the trail at Lightning Creek, just a few miles from Barkerville, on August 20. He wrote, "Was bothered today by the camels, of which there are a dozen here, who have a neat idea of walking over your tent and eating your shirts."

There is no record of the camels reaching Williams Creek at either Richfield or Barkerville, but it is possible they did, as there was no *Cariboo Sentinel* newspaper at that time to report on their movements. The last mention of camels in this area by journalists was September 17 near Cottonwood. We can't be sure which direction they were travelling, but it appears to be down the trail, or west. Then in mid-October 1862 the *Colonist* reported, "The Camels. About a dozen of these animals are all that survive. They are turned out to graze at the Forks of Quesnelle River, and are considered the greatest failure of the season."

The camels could pack, no doubt about that. "They beat any transit we have, either ox, mule or cayuse ponies. They are so well acclimatized they will eat anything from a pair of pants to a bar of soap," wrote a reporter from Lillooet. Yet by all accounts, the camels lasted only two years in Cariboo. Would they have been more successful with proper care and management? And what became of the camels when the Cariboo pack train ended?

By figuring the trips the camels made, the goods they packed and the cost of freight, we can calculate that by the end of the first trip to Cariboo Laumeister and his syndicate had broken even. In 1863 they made at least two trips, more likely three, before the syndicate sold half the camels. So we have an income over two years of approximately $24,000 after expenses—a 400 percent profit after two years. And they still had at least half the camels left. This does not sound like failure.

A factor unrecognized by many writers is the profound difference in travel to Cariboo from 1858 to 1865. In the early years the route struggled over First Nations' trails as a pack trail was hacked out of the timber. The Cariboo Road began at Yale in 1863, but did not reach Barkerville on Williams Creek until 1865. There is clear evidence that life on the creeks changed dramatically with the coming of the road. Freight rates dropped considerably—from 75 to 90 cents per pound to 15 cents per pound—as did the cost of goods. Where once foot travel or horseback were the only means of travel, sternwheelers churned up the river, stagecoaches galloped the road and wagons freighted goods. Society on the gold creeks shifted in population, cost of living and lifestyle.

When the road reached Barkerville in 1865, the days of high freight rates were over. The camels were a financial success doomed by technological change. They packed for two years on the Cariboo Road and then on the Dewdney Trail as far east as Fort Steele and south to Walla Walla, Washington. Some were sold to other packers, a few died and the remainder lived in retirement on Ingram's Westwold ranch. The last one died in 1904.

The Cattle Drovers

Fresh beef, pork and mutton were so important to carnivorous miners that they were willing to pay the outrageous price of 50 cents a pound. Men with ranching backgrounds found selling cattle a quicker way to prosperity than digging in cold gravel.

Six such men were the Van Volkenburgh brothers, Benjamin, Abraham and Isaac; the two Harpers, Jerome and Thaddeus; and Edward Toomey, a butcher with a Barkerville store and abattoir. The Harpers were experienced cattle drovers with grasslands in the interior already preempted by the early 1860s. The Van Volkenburghs, Americans of Dutch extraction, added manpower to run several stores in various gold camps.

The Harpers hailed from Tucker Company, West Virginia. Jerome, born in 1826, left Tucker Company with three brothers in the late 1840s to try their luck in California. Seeing opportunity in South America, they sent Jerome to open a store in Chile. He was doing a good business when a rebellion erupted. Jerome had backed the rebels and was banished to Patagonia, where his brother Captain Harper rescued him and brought him back to California.

By 1852, Jerome and Thaddeus, then aged 23 and 22, respectively, were farming in Santa Clara Company, California. In 1858 they came north, and by 1859 they were operating a sawmill at Yale, BC. In the 1860s they were associated with a scheme taking place in Victoria to outfit a ship to take part in the US Civil War on the side of the Confederacy. The plan failed, and the Harpers settled into business, bidding on a road contract and gathering land.

As the Cariboo rush created a demand for supplies, they drove cattle from Washington and Oregon. Dr. Cheadle, in his 1863 *Journal of a Trip Across Canada*, says, "Jerome Harper arrived on Horseback; he was bringing in a drove of 500 cattle from Oregon; a Virginian and staunch supporter of the South he said he was bitter because his mother and family had been driven out of their homes in Virginia where they had nice estates and left penniless."

Soon the brothers had ranches at Cache Creek, Harper's Camp and in the Chilcotin country. They started another sawmill at Quesnellemouth, a flour mill near Clinton and a partnership with Toomey and the Van Volkenburghs. To satisfy the need for fresh meat, the Harpers, Toomey and the Van Volkenburghs formed a company, Messrs. Van Volkenburgh and Company, with shops in Richfield, Barkerville, Cameronton and other camps, advertising "a large supply of the best Meat always on hand." The partnership virtually monopolized the cattle industry for over a decade, and in various forms started the largest ranches in the province.

In December 1869 the *Cariboo Sentinel* noted, "Van Volkenburgh & Company, the enterprising butchers, have slaughtered 360 sheep, and stored them in a clean and airy place, in the storehouse just above the gorge. Messrs. V. [Van Volkenburgh] intend to bring more to the knife, so that we shall have a plentiful supply of fresh though frozen, mutton during the winter."

Things began to fail in the early 1870s when Jerome was kicked in the face by a horse, suffering a broken skull. He retired to California, where he was described as being insane, and drowned in his bathtub in Santa Barbara on November 27, 1874. Thaddeus fought with his family and eventually gained the land and businesses and carried on. He started a cattle drive to Chicago but diverted to California. In the 1880s he organized what eventually became known as the Gang Ranch and gradually increased the acreage to over one million. Thaddeus also became active in mining again, with claims near Stanley and on the present-day Horsefly River, which was then known as Harper's Camp.

By 1890 Thaddeus had sold out his mine leases and the ranches, but the JH brand, one of the first to sear a hide in BC, is still being heated in branding fires today. Thaddeus retired to Victoria and died there in 1898. (The Barkerville archives have in their collection an *aparejo*, or pack saddle, with the JH brand.)

While the Harpers managed to corner the market, there were many other drovers. General Joel Palmer was the first. He brought a cattle herd and several wagons of merchandise north in 1858 and again in 1859. The Jeffrey brothers of Alabama came through in 1859 or '60 with cattle, and in 1861 Major Thorpe of Yakima, Washington, Ben E. Snipes, William Gates and William Murphy all brought herds north. Lewis Campbell joined John Wilson to bring in 300 head. Wilson had already been to the gold-fields and was gathering land at Grand Prairie, where he would become the cattle king of the Thompson country.

Daniel Drumheller brought a herd west from what became Alberta, and Aschal Sumner Bates bought cattle for his Thompson River and 150 Mile House spreads. By the height of the Cariboo rush in 1862, drovers were bringing in over 4,000 cattle per year, a total of over 21,000 by 1868, when the province began to gain self-sufficiency in the beef market.

As well as the cattle trailed in from the south, the Williams Creek area was the site of at least four "milk ranches." These were situated along the meadows toward Wells and east in the Pleasant Valley area. In 1867 the *Cariboo Sentinel* reported that these ranches totalled 80 cows, producing enough milk for the whole of Williams Creek and Lowhee Gulch, at "the moderate price of $1 per gallon."

Ranchers and farmers were attracted by the fortunes of the goldfields, but many of them stayed and settled the rich grasslands of the province, starting a thriving industry that continues today.

Phases of Development

The gold towns along Williams Creek went through three phases: the Discovery Phase of 1860–63, when individual miners prospected their way north and mined with the simplest of methods; the Mature Phase of 1864–78, when more sophisticated shaft and tunnel mining techniques removed deep placer deposits; and the Hydraulic Mining Phase of 1879–85, when shaft and tunnel mining declined and the emphasis shifted to large-scale, heavily capitalized hydraulic mining that left the hills and valleys laced with water systems. It was during the Mature Phase that long-term operations financed by companies of men were

THE NASON FAMILY

Ithiel Blake Nason was born in Maine on April 24, 1839, and as a young man swallowed the lure of California gold. In 1858 he drifted north and turned to another occupation, operating Jerome and Thaddeus Harper's sawmill in Yale. In 1861 he arrived on Antler Creek with enough money to allow him time to prospect. Near Wolfe Creek he sank three shafts with moderate success. Within a few years, Antler was waning and the sawmill there was put up for sale. Nason and W.A. Meacham, an American, bought the equipment and had it moved to Williams Creek, where miners constantly needed lumber—not only for buildings but also for the miles of flumes and sluices that criss-crossed the creeks.

Business boomed and they upgraded their operation to a steam sawmill. The *Cariboo Sentinel* of August 27, 1866, carried their announcement:

> Williams Creek Sawmill Company. The undersigned lumber merchants beg to inform the inhabitants in general of Williams Creek that they have now in operation a Steam Saw Mill located at the mouth of Mink Gulch above Richfield, capable of manufacturing 1000 feet of lumber per hour, any length, any width required in the market, and of a Superior Quality. MEACHAM, COOMBS & NASON.

In 1870 the partnership dissolved, but Nason carried on. He also kept an interest in mining as one of the six original shareholders in the Waverley Hydraulic Mining Company, continued work on his two Williams Creek claims (the mill was located on one these claims, at Deadwood) and began a new mill on Jack of Clubs Creek.

Nason had two families—his first was with Nellie Bouche, a Metis woman from Fort Stuart with whom he had several children from 1864 to 1872 and who later married William Favel, a Barkerville teamster. In 1875 Nason married Mary A. Watson in Victoria and began a family of eight children at their home in Richfield. (Interestingly enough, he gave the children of his second marriage the same names as the children of his first marriage.) Nason was a member of the Cariboo Hospital Board of Directors for 15 years, a school trustee for 6 and a British Columbia MLA for 4 years beginning in 1889. In 1891 he was re-elected in a by-election caused by the death of Barkerville merchant Joe Mason.

During his fourth year in office as MLA for Cariboo, on May 27, 1893, Nason died of cancer in Victoria. He was just 53 years old. His widow and children moved from Cariboo to Victoria, but this was not to end the Nason influence along Williams Creek.

In 1904 Oliver and Blake Nason, two of Ithiel Nason's sons from his second marriage, returned to Barkerville, where they worked mines until enlisting for the First World War. Upon their return they again mined at sites such as Beggs Gulch and Canadian Creek. Oliver Nason was also hydraulic foreman for the Lowhee Company for a time.

the norm. The stability of these operations and the completion of the Cariboo Road in 1865 provided the opportunity to use better technology and created a base for merchants.

While gold held out and miners' riches filled merchants' tills, the area prospered. But soon there was not enough business for all four towns. Marysville faded early on, then Cameronton and Richfield—though for years the government tenaciously hung onto Richfield's offices and courthouse. The face of the creek changed radically in 1868 when most of Barkerville burned down to be replaced by a less crowded, more orderly town site. This new town likely played a part in the demise of the surrounding towns.

By the late 1880s, what remained of Cameronton had merged with Barkerville, which, as times became tough, emerged as the permanent town on Williams Creek. Even at that, Barkerville's life ebbed. Strikes on Lightning Creek drew miners away. As the placer gold that opened the country dwindled, men drifted to other towns, to pioneer ranches, to homes in the east or on the coast. A few stayed to wash huge hydraulic pits or tunnel into the mountain and kept some life in the old town.

With its heyday past, Barkerville slipped into relative obscurity at the turn of the century, then surged briefly to life again when a second wave of miners came looking for wages in the 1929–39 Depression years. The Second World War ended the brief revival and pushed Barkerville toward ghost-town status.

GOLD RUSH SOCIETY

PART 2

4 MOVING SOCIAL ENTITIES:
A PORTRAIT OF GOLD RUSH LIFE

RESTORED BARKERVILLE ILLUSTRATES not only a time and a place, but also gold rush society. The deeper we look into Barkerville personalities before and after the Cariboo gold rush, the more we find that the gold rushes were moving social entities. A mere 40 odd years separated the Georgia rushes in 1828 from the Omineca interest in 1871. The California (1848), Australia (1852) and Montana, Nevada, Idaho and Cariboo (1862) rushes all occurred within a span of fewer than 20 years, and they were soon followed by the silver strikes of the 1870s in Arizona and Nevada. The first and most successful men were often those with previous mining experience. They had the knowledge, often the capital and frequently the friends to make successful forays into the mother lode creeks.

Through police and court records, newspaper reports and later biographies we find that many people who flocked to Cariboo during the rush encountered familiar faces there. Many of the men who owned or worked in mines were friends or acquaintances, and many appeared in court as witnesses for others. For example, in 1872 James McMillan testified in court that 15 years earlier he knew Eliza Ord in California by the name of Mrs. Christian. Similarly David Williams testified that he knew Mary and Samuel Nathan in Australia in 1852. At least 20 other Barkervillians had been in the Australian goldfields around Sovereign Hill and Ballarat. Half a dozen men who found themselves in the Cariboo around the same time had served in the Royal Engineers together; another half-dozen had been in the Crimean War and a few had been in India together.

Close to 70 people are recorded as mining or working in California before they moved to the Cariboo, including Billy Barker, John Cameron, Doc Keithley, Charlie House, Fanny Bendixen and Jessie Heatherington. Major William Downie had the town of Downieville, California, named for him. John Kurtz, a Mason, best known for the Kurtz and Lane claim, was a California vigilante, as was James Pollock, so they no doubt knew many of the California circle. One member of that circle was John Thompson, known as Liverpool Jack, who was banished from California and sent to New York in 1856 by the Committee of Vigilance, a militia group intent on cleaning up San Francisco. He returned to the west, to Victoria and Barkerville, where he was widely known and reported as an outlaw and petty criminal.

Many who arrived in Barkerville moved on quickly, whether they found success in the mines or not. White Pine near Elko, Nevada, attracted many Cariboo miners according to reports in the *Sentinel*, as did the Kootenay strikes at Wild Horse Creek. Florence Wilson went to Idaho for a summer and met friends there. Francis Laumeister, the camel entrepreneur, successful miner John Adams, and Colonel John van Houten all ended up in Tombstone, Arizona, where Houten was murdered and Adams shot a constable. Saul Wolfe committed suicide in Virginia City, Nevada, and Barkerville miner William Pendray also died there. Outlaw Boone Helm, who murdered three merchants near Quesnelleforks and others in Idaho and Montana, was hanged and buried in Virginia City, Montana. And we find "Doc" or "Judge" Keithley in Deadwood, South Dakota, in 1876, along with Barkerville clothing merchant Abraham Hoffman.

Many Cariboo miners kept in touch by moving to the

Kamloops region, the Okanagan and Victoria, where we see them reappear as pallbearers for their old cohorts. Even as they were filed away in the Kamloops Old Men's Home, they maintained the friendships and kept the stories. The Cariboo goldfields and the miners and merchants who populated the creeks were not a distinct population. There were all part of a revolving, interwoven social structure that circulated between gold rushes over much of the world.

Walking down Barkerville's main street, you might imagine that all the town's residents had been homeowners or merchants. In Barkerville itself the majority were merchants, but the main population of Williams Creek was miners, always hard at work, often poor and unhealthy. Debt chained men to the creeks. Without money they could not leave, and there was always the chance the next shovelful would bring gold or the next claim pay better wages. The buildings of Barkerville can be seen as windows or touchstones to the many people who came here to find wealth, whatever form that took. There were winners and losers.

Williams Creek often yielded its gold in immensely rich pockets. For example, from 120 feet of ground, the Steel Company took $120,000; from 500 feet the Cunningham Company took $270,000; from 50 feet the Diller Company took $240,000 and from 80 feet the Burns Company took $140,000—at a time when the average wage in eastern Canada was 1 dollar a day, and on Williams Creek 4 to 10 dollars a day.

Far more common were the men who came to Cariboo poor and desperate and left destitute and despairing. Mining was difficult. If you arrived on a crowded creek too late, the ground was staked and you had to buy a claim or shares with any available capital. Otherwise, you earned a living for meagre room and board by working for another company in a deep, cold, wet shaft. If your claim did prove up, it was difficult to work on your own. To raise money for equipment and labour, you had to sell shares. And the profits, if there were any, would be divided. More often, a man went home wiser rather than wealthy. And then there were those who remained in the cemetery on the hill.

Details of a miner's hard life are recorded in the letters of Robert Harkness, an Overlander of '62. Writing to his wife, Sabrina, Harkness speaks of two things—his love for her and his day-to-day struggle.

Richfield, June 10, 1863 . . . You must pay well for everything you get here. Flour is $1.12 a pound. This is at the rate of $225 per barrel. Beans & rice are each a dollar a pound. Sugar is $1.75, nails $2, Tea (very poor) $3, Tobacco $5. It may seem extravagant to pay $5 a pound for tobacco but I do like to sit & smoke & think of my far away Nina. Salt is $1.25 a pound, equal to $17.50 for such a little sack as we used to sell for ninepence. Potatoes are $1.25 a pound or $75 a bushel. A clay pipe or a box of matches, such as we get at home for a copper, costs half a dollar here.

Gilbert Munro, Aus McIntosh & I came up together & we still live in a brush tent together. Munro was lucky enough to get work the first day he came at making shingles & has been at work every day since. Aus has not had work to do. I have been working at whatever I could get to do but have not got steady work. I expect to go to work for the Brouses next week & work steadily. As soon as I can save a couple of hundred dollars I'll send them home to you. Wages are ten dollars a day, out of which you must, of course, board yourself. We live on bread, beans & bacon, with an occasional mess of very tough beef ($0.50 a pound) & manage to subsist for from three to four dollars a day each . . . I worked pretty hard today carrying stones to a man building a chimney . . .

Williams Creek, May 31, 1864. Very many have left & are leaving every day, unable to earn enough to procure grub. I am very comfortable compared to what I was last summer. For two summers past, I have been "pitching my tents" but this year I have a good cabin to live in . . . There are two other men living in the same cabin but each cooks & eats by himself.

Williams Creek, June 28, 1864. I worked for the "Bed Rock Drain Co." up to last Saturday, but had to take all my pay in stock, except about 60 dollars. The stock is unsalable now, money is very scarce, work hard to get and times dull. I am doing nothing at present but hope to get work again soon.

Harkness and his friends wintered in New Westminster doing odd jobs, returning to Barkerville each spring to try again. By the time he wrote his last known letter from New Westminster, in the spring of 1865 (he returned home the following year), he had turned into a pessimist. "Gilbert Munro intends starting direct for Cariboo in a few days," he wrote. "He persists in thinking there may be 'luck' for him in the mines, but I consider it is a matter of serious doubt whether he ever gets home at all or not." Monro was still there in the 1890s.

Another pessimist, Alexander Allan, owner of the *Cariboo Sentinel,* wrote home after selling his business in 1868:

There are, it is true, many who have made and are now making their fortunes, but it is also too true here that the far greater number rank as unfortunates, those whose lot . . . is worse than the most miserable and poverty-stricken person in the Old Country—many of these poor fellows brought up in luxury and wealth have to live in hovels here of a description even worse than the barns into which beggars used to be put in old times—and this too in a climate where the mercury freezes (which it did, not 3 weeks ago) and they often have to go to their laborious toil (pursued in holes where they are continually drenched to the skin with water) with but scantily filled stomachs.

Disenchanted miner William Mark wrote a bitter letter in 1862 to Donald Fraser, who had been promoting the Cariboo in the *Victoria Times* newspaper:

There had been a great deal said about the richness of this creek [Antler Creek] and the quantity of gold taken out from time to time; but not a word was said on the other side of the question, and there had been several companies ruined at this creek. One company, a party of eight Cornishmen . . . were on ground adjoining this rich claim . . . The day we left Antler they abandoned the place, and left it ruined men. This was the case with every other creek; some struck it rich, and this was blazed in every paper. The many lost all they had, and were completely beggared. This was never named but hushed down.

The goldfields population is one of the most discussed and exaggerated numbers along Williams Creek, next only to the total amount of gold produced. One Barkerville guide recently began his tour by saying, "Imagine this valley filled with 20,000 19-year-olds." Other estimates range in the tens of thousands. All would be a gross exaggeration.

Population figures are elusive as no official census was taken until 1881, and by then, of course, the population was significantly lower. Figures must come from the number of gold mining licences, brief estimates by government officials and the general reports of the day. Barkerville curator Bill Quackenbush has done more research into tracking this number than anyone. He estimates that the population for the north-slope mines, Antler Creek to Lightning Creek, during the height of the season, was up to 6,000. This figure closely matches my highest estimates and is based on mining licences, contemporary estimates and what little information the government gathered. The population decreased by tenfold in the winter and in the years after the major rush. However, in 1865, a report in the *Sentinel* said there "is not in the aggregate a white population of 6000." In his January 1865 report, Gold Commissioner Peter O'Reilly said, "the largest population in the mines at any one time during the past year probably amounted to 4000, at least 1500 of who left again before the close of the season." In 1867 the *Sentinel* reported that the "average population [is] less than 2000 miners."

Contemporary population figures were often flights of fantasy fuelled by the government's desire to convince officials in London to send more money; merchants overestimated to show an interest in their particular camp and ensure that there were enough supplies; successful miners lauded the country while destitute losers cried humbug and reported miners flocking south.

A rough government Cariboo tally taken in 1869 counted 919 white males and 69 white females, 720 Chinese males and 6 Chinese females, and 27 "coloured" (presumably African-American) males and 4 females—for a total of 1,666 males and 79 females. By 1876, when an accurate count, but not a census, by the Gold Comissioner was made on Williams Creek, there were 295 white males, 208 Chinese males, 25 white females with 25 children and 12 Chinese females with 1 child. That number could have been doubled when surrounding creeks were counted.

So the population was between 2,000 and 6,000, depending on the time of year, and much lower by the 1870s. Certainly there was never the 10,000 or 20,000 that some have estimated. The resources to support those numbers simply did not exist.

The belief that all miners were young is another goldfields myth. Estimating the ages of gold rush participants requires even more statistics. However, my Gold Rush database of some 7,000 individuals (with up to 118 fields per record), minus a few unknowns and duplicates, allows some reasonable estimates. If we know a person's birth date and when they applied for a mining licence, for instance, we can calculate the age at which he was on the creek. There are 445 such records.

The average age of men and women combined in 1865 was 33.2. There were only 17 (out of 445) under the age of 20, including 7 women (but not including infants). Seventeen were over 50; 37 were over 45. So, of 445 known ages calculated for 1865, 388 were between the ages of 20 and 45. The low number of women and infants affects the age range.

If we have enough birth dates and death dates we can calculate the average death date in, and outside, the goldfields. There are 561 such records, approximately 8 percent of the database. The average death age of all those gold rushers whose death records have been found shows an average death age of 56. For those who died outside the goldfields, the average is 66. The average death age in the goldfields up to 1881 is 37.6 and from 1881, until 1920, it is 58.6. One causal factor is the almost complete lack of infant deaths; another is the fact that miners comprised the highest percentage of the workforce. After the 1881 census, the population was much smaller and older.

The folks who came to the gold rush were not teenagers searching for a new home. They were men and a few women, well past apprenticeship age, many of whom had mined previously, most of whom had had previous careers or employment. These people were skilled, middle-aged, often married, looking for wealth for investment and retirement. The databases show that 416 miners are recorded as married, and we know that most left their wives behind. These numbers do not include Chinese or First Nations residents because of a lack of comprehensive birth and death records.

The causes of death from 1861 to 1881 are as expected, given the prevalent occupation and the state of medical practice at the time. Of 205 recorded deaths on the goldfields prior to 1881, the most common cause was mining accidents, totalling 39. Heart problems accounted for 17 deaths, non-mining-related accidents accounted for 12 and drowning other than in a mine for 9. Stroke, pneumonia and typhoid claimed seven lives each, though it is likely that more people died of these illness but were misdiagnosed. Seven deaths each are attributed to suicide and exposure, and another seven were child or infant deaths. There are a total of 40 causes of death listed, some specific, some vague and 34 unknown. Many illnesses would be curable today with a prescription drug.

It has been said that if we were to walk down the street in any gold rush what we would notice most is the number of bearded faces and the variety of accents. It was a cosmopolitan mixture. There were men, and a few women, from all parts of the globe.

Of 1,700 individuals with known nationalities in the 1860s, the bulk were from the United Kingdom: 345 from England, 101 from Scotland, 65 from Ireland and 181 from Wales, totalling 692, and 164 categorized as other "British Subjects," which could have included Canadians. So approximately half were native English speakers.

There were 93 Germans, 34 French, 26 Scandinavians, 16 Mexicans (plus several more Mexican packers whose residence was in the lower country), 8 Italians, 3 West Indians and 14 identified as "Black" with various birthplaces. There were many Chinese, whose lack of records and poor transcription of names by colonial officials make them much harder to tally, but who, by some accounts and in some towns, totalled over 50 percent of the population. First Nations and Metis were present in significant numbers but, again, difficult to identify as they were usually known or recorded by nicknames only. In Barkerville there were over 30 First Nations people identified during the first decade.

This cultural mélange created a town and community unlike anything more settled regions experienced. Social structures gave way to convenience and necessity, former cultural barriers between nationalites and colour tended to blend and social status became less defined.

WHAT WAS YOUR NAME IN THE STATES?

Nicknames tell their own story of goldfields society and give us a window into the individuals who made up this cosmopolitan life. There is a story, a piece of folklore, told in every gold rush, of a young easterner searching for his brother. He goes from camp to camp, stream to stream, asking if anyone has seen his brother, but no one has. Finally he turns and heads home, not knowing that in the last camp he was only yards from his brother's claim. The problem was that no one knew him by his real name.

So common was the mining camp use of nicknames that it even inspired a song:

What was your name in the States?
Was it Thompson or Johnson or Bates?
Did you run for your life,
or murder your wife?
Oh, what was your name in the States?

Anglican bishop George Hills travelled to the Fraser River in 1860 and wrote in his journal about nicknames and the folklore of the missing brother:

The appellation of all miners is 'boy.' Their chief is 'Cap.' All are called 'Dick, Tom or Henry.' Men are not known by their real names. You inquire, as I have often done, the name of someone. Nobody knows his name, only he is called so & so of such & such a bar.

I was speaking to a miner. He said he had just come from California & with him had come a miner who had sold his claim there for 1800 dollars. I asked what the man's name was. He said he went by a nick name, 'Bam.' He knew not his real name. He had known, in California, instances of considerable difficulty arising from this.

In his 1865 book *Vancouver Island and British Columbia*, Matthew Macfie wrote,

If any delicacy is shown by men at the diggings in regard to disclosing their real names, no impudent questions are asked on the subject; but a name is extemporised by the miners, arising out of some eccentricity of person or character, some notable expression at any time uttered by the individual, or event that may have occurred in his experience . . .

If a man seems educated, the company in which he may be working or travelling, in ignorance of his true appellation, will usually designate him by the laconic title of 'doc,' for doctor, or 'cap' for Captain. If tall, his associates, should his family-name not be forthcoming, may dub him 'Big Bill.' Should he have a weakness for frequently referring to some town, creek or country from which he has come, he may expect to have the name of the place united by his won, such as 'Rattlesnake Jack,' 'Oregon Bob' etc. A gentleman who was fond of displaying an array of initials before and titles after his name was significantly called Alphabet McD . . .

In keeping with Macfie's findings, we have "Oregon Jack" Dowling, a packer with a roadhouse south of Cache Creek; "Long Abbott," who stretched to six foot four on Williams Creek; "12-foot" Davis, or Henry Fuller Davis, who staked a miscalculated 12-foot section of gravel near Abbott and took out $8,000; "Two-Man Brown," named for his size; and William "Doc" Keithley, a law-yer turned miner. There was "Ottawa Smith," who prospected the Quesnelle River in 1862; "Dutch Bill" Dietz, the Prussian miner who discovered and gave his name to Williams Creek; packer Jean Caux, known throughout the Cariboo as "Cataline," after his place of birth; and outlaw "Liverpool Jack" Thompson.

When Dr. Cheadle visited in 1862 he had dinner with Billy Farrell—a former sailor and "successful miner, from his loquacity nicknamed 'Billy the Bladge,' rough, noisy, breaking forth into shouts and laughter"—as well as "Scotch Jennie," "a Scotchwoman, fair fat and forty."

Wellington Delaney Moses, the scribe of Williams Creek, had trouble keeping track of all the Annies on the creek, so he added descriptors. There was "Gentle Annie," perhaps named for Stephen Foster's song, "Big Annie," "Hyda Annie" and "Albino Annie." Moses used no punctuation and it took years to learn that Albino Annie's nickname did not refer to her colouring but was in fact a possessive, "Albino's Annie," meaning she was the wife of Albino Resendes, a Mexican brick maker.

The two major discoverers of gold on Williams Creek, Billy Barker and John Cameron, each had nicknames. Cameron was dubbed "Cariboo Cameron," while Barker was known as "English

Bill" for a ditty he frequently sang, accompanied by a little shuffle:

I'm English Bill, English Bill
Never worked and I never will,
Get away girls or I'll tousle your curls.

Poet James Anderson was "Scotch Jimmie" on the creek, but when he returned to Scotland he was given the sobriquet "Caribou Jim."

When Sir Hector Langevin, Canadian Minister of Public Works, arrived he realized the significance of nicknames and made a diary list, including some of those mentioned above, plus a few more:

Black Jack [John Smith], Wild Goose Bill, Roaring Bill, Hog John, Dancing Bill [Latham], Pike, Dutch Pete, Pilgrim, Dirty feet Pete, Delaware, Flap Jack Johnny, [Mary Sheldon] Peanuts, Long Cock Dave, Bit to the Pass (woman), Slippery __ Kate (woman), Gassy Jack, Poker Jack (woman), Six Foot Pete, Blue Mud Bill, Oregon Hilley, Bill in Hell, Limber Jim, Sleeping Jesus, Norman Bill (de Cosmos), Wake up Jesus, Bill the Bug, Gum Boots Sally (woman), Set Him Up, Wake up Jake (gentleman) Waving Jack, Red Head [Miles] Davis, Swamp Angel, [Neil Wilson] Red Attick, Cotton Vest Smith, Kelly the Pirate, Kelly the Smuggler, Bloody Edwards (son of a gentleman in Somerset House, England).

It is not too hard to figure how "Six-Toed Pete" or "Dirty-Faced Pete" got their appellations, but it would be a brave man who asked "Blue Dick" Berry how he came by his name.

5 THE DISCOVERERS

William Ross "Doc" Keithley

Doc Keithley and his friends were the discoverers of Keithley Creek, Harvey Creek and Antler Creek, and pivotal in opening up the Cariboo Mountain gold creeks. Keithley appeared on the scene in 1859 at Quesnelleforks. We don't know if he prospected or mined on the Fraser.

Unlike many miners, Keithley was not an inexperienced youngster. He was 34 years old when he came here in 1857, born in Missouri and a practising lawyer in Sacramento. No doubt his education gave him the honorific "Doc."

In the Cariboo he is associated with George Harvey, Isaiah Diller, George Weaver and a few others, all determined, experienced, successful middle-aged miners. Reports tell us little about Keithley, but he mined on the south slope, crossed to Antler Creek and then was a partner in the Peter claim.

He spent three winters in Cariboo and in June 1862 went to New Westminster, likely to seek medical help as the *British Columbian* reports that in March he had something "like dumbague accompanied by a distressing cough, the symptoms of consumption." He had, by some accounts, "skedaddled," left the country owing money, despite his wealth. He owed board of $70 at Quesnelleforks and was taken to court. He had issues with merchants Boas, Levi and Hamburger, for they were advertising that the public should not accept a note in their names from Keithley for $2,400. On May 27, 1862, he sold half his interest in the Peter claim on Williams Creek for $3,000 to these merchants.

Keithley does not appear to have returned to Cariboo but moved south, as did many Cariboo miners, and next appeared in Idaho City in 1867 as an attorney. He kept moving. He turned up in Ogden, Utah, in 1870; Salt Lake City in 1874; and then to the roughest gold rush town around—Deadwood. Here in 1876 he was pegged as "Judge" Keithley. He dabbled in politics, running for mayor against well-known E.B. Farnham, and bragged that he had been in every mining camp and was known as "Old Necessity" for his proverbial supposition that "necessity knows no law."

By 1880 Keithley had left Deadwood (three or four years seems to be his usual term of residence) and moved to Buena Vista, Colorado, where he lived until 1884. Butte, Montana, was next, where in 1888 he slowed down long enough to marry Emma Scott. He was listed as being 54 (though he was over 60 at the time) and his wife as 29. Just a few years later, in 1894, a nephew wrote to the Salt Lake paper looking for him, saying he had "last heard of [Keithley being] in Dakota," i.e. Deadwood. By 1900, Keithley appears to have been living with another nephew, Joseph Keithley, in Carterville, Missouri, though another source puts him in a home for destitute men in Butte. Whatever the case, like so many gold rushers, Keithley drifted into anonymity.

William Barker

There are numerous myths associated with the Cariboo gold rush: Barkerville's being the "largest city north of San Francisco," few women on the creeks, a crime-free gold rush society and many others. Perhaps the greatest myth was the story of Billy Barker, one that began at the time of his death. It said Barker was a Cornishman, a potter by trade, a British Naval deserter who jumped ship in Victoria to follow the Fraser rush, who married when he struck it rich and whose wife ran off when he ran out of money. The crack in this legend came in 1984 when Barkerville curator Ken Mather unravelled the true story. Barker was a waterman from Cambridgeshire who left a family in England and reached North America just before the California gold rush and continued mining all his life. His second wife had died, not run off. Further research has fleshed out the profile of this gold rush pioneer.

When Billy Barker and his company struck the lead on Williams Creek in August 1862, he was 48 years old. Given the average life expectancy of the era, he was on his way to old age. This strike was the culmination of years of prospecting and mining.

Baptized on June 7, 1817, in March, Cambridgeshire, England, William was the sixth child and fourth son of Samuel and Jane Barker. Samuel was a waterman, and William followed in his father's footsteps. In his 21st summer William met Jane Lavender, a 27-year-old widow.

Jane had led a hard life. At 18 she had a child out of wedlock; the following year she married boatwright Robert Lavender; six months later she had a child who only lived four months. Four children followed, but in April 1839, when the last child was only a few months old, Robert died, followed two weeks later by Jane's father. Thus, she was likely desperate, perhaps destitute, when she met William Barker a short while later. As the story goes, the two met when Billy stopped at the pub that had been owned by Jane's late husband. In August 1839 they conceived a child, and they married that October, at Bluntisham-cum-Earith, an inland port for barges.

Emma Eliza (named for William's sister) was born on May 3, 1840. A year later Barker's father died. Changes were in the wind. By 1850 the Great Northern Railway had knocked the bottom out of barge freighting. Sometime between 1842 and 1846, William Barker left the fens of England and came to North America.

Barker's early years in America are vague. Many William Barkers immigrated, but there is a matching signature in

Pennsylvania for 1845, which likely belonged to our man, and we know he mined in California. In the meantime his wife and daughter were in the Doddington, Cambridgeshire, Union Workhouse. Jane died there May 25, 1850, of secondary syphilis. Emma stayed in the workhouse until going to live with relatives.

Barker and partner John Butson were on the Fraser and issued licences on September 29, 1859, at Lillooet. He and some other Californians were working on Canada Bar and dealing in water rights from nearby creeks. He met Bishop George Hills, who recorded the meeting in his journal, which Ken Mather read 125 years later. Barker had not contacted his family for 14 years, he said. He promised Hills he would.

When Barker arrived in Williams Creek, he was 47 years old, short (about five foot nothing) and heavily built with slightly bowed legs, a bushy greying beard and an easily inflamed temper. Barker arrived in the spring of 1861 and, with five other men, staked the Barker and Company claim near Mink Gulch, above Richfield, next to Major William Downie's claim. The claim was unsuccessful. Early the next summer, in June 1862, Barker moved downstream and, in partnership with four other Englishmen, staked a second claim, contrary to the Mining Act. Barker was thus forced to sell his shares in the upper claim, just before it began producing.

At the downstream claim Barker and Company expanded to eight claims and sank two unsuccessful shafts. They began again, and on August 17, 1862, they struck rich gravel at 52 feet. In the next 10 hours they took out 124 ounces of gold, a share of $20,000 each.

Bishop Hills wrote, "Head of the lead having been struck on Barker's claim . . . all for some days after having been 'on the Spree' that is more or less intoxicated & off work, excepting one . . . a very worthy young Englishman & well brought up." The one Englishman well brought up was Charles Hankin, the only member to overwinter and caretake the claim. A story circulated that Judge Begbie financed the Barker Company. In fact Begbie, through a man named Walker, invested after the strike, which was an extreme conflict of interest. Begbie did not admit to the deal for many years, though newspapers editorialized over the rumoured breach of conduct.

Here again Barker met Bishop Hills and told him he had contacted his family and was considering returning home. But gold was burning a hole in Billy's pocket. He and six partners headed for Victoria. Within a couple of months, on January 13, 1863, he married another widow, Elizabeth Collyer, who had arrived on the brideship *Rosedale*. Elizabeth and Billy partied the winter away, then headed back to Barkerville. The claim was worked continuously, with three shafts and a Cornish wheel going full tilt. Barker left at the end of the summer with even more money.

When he returned in the summer of 1864, the claim was not producing well. By July he had sold all his interest. In total Barker had likely taken in close to $500,000 in today's money. It appears that by the end of the summer of 1864, he may have been broke. Not only did he sell out his interest in the claim, but also he defaulted on a loan to Robert Burnaby and Edward Henderson, and gave them land he held as security for a loan to William Winnard, the Barkerville blacksmith who was facing bankruptcy.

In May 1865 Elizabeth left him, though not by choice. She died on May 20 in Victoria. Barker wrote again to his daughter in England.

Barker's money was certainly invested, at least in part, in other mining ventures. He was a partner in the Never Miss Company in 1864 and '65, and by the late '60s he was working at a claim called Barker No. 2 on Valley Creek. In 1873 he led a prospecting expedition to Horsefly country and continued working there through the 1870s.

Billy's last hurrah has been unrecognized by official biographies. In the early 1890s he had a partnership of old prospectors, all of whom would die in the next decade, in a claim on Donovan or Poor Man's Creek near Beaver Pass. Unfortunately it was unsuccessful.

Barker often wintered in Clinton where several of his old partners—John Chenhall, John Butson, John Pollard, John Westley and Robert Walker—had settled on ranches. It was there that his friends suggested he go to Victoria and have a cancer on his jaw attended to. In January 1894 he went to the Old Men's Home in Victoria. Doctors found the cancer too far advanced to operate. Billy Barker, Cambridgeshire waterman and Cariboo miner, died on July 11, 1894. He was 77 years old.

John Angus "Cariboo" Cameron

John A. Cameron, nicknamed "Cariboo" Cameron, was descended from a long line of stalwart Scots who came to British America in 1745. Cameron was raised on the family farm near Cornwall, Canada West, the United Empire Loyalist settlement to which his family retreated during the American War of Independence. In 1852 Cameron headed for the goldfields of California, then in 1858 he and two brothers went north to the Fraser gold rush. From the two strikes Cameron made $20,000 and returned home to marry his childhood sweetheart, Sophia Groves, a farmer's daughter 12 years his junior. Soon after the wedding, news of Cariboo filtered east and John, Sophia and their one-year-old daughter, Alice, headed west by way of Panama.

The Camerons arrived in Victoria on February 27, 1862, after a long trip that weakened the child. Before John and Sophia could leave the coast, 14-month-old Alice died. Saddened but determined, John and Sophia Cameron headed north to Antler Creek and then over Bald Mountain to Williams Creek, where they staked their claims.

Like Billy Barker, Cameron had staked claims on the upper part of Williams Creek but was attracted downstream by Ned Stout's success. A company was formed of John and Sophia Cameron, Allan McDonald, Richard Rivers and Charles and James Clendennin. Three weeks later a claim owned by Robert Stevenson was added, but after a week Stevenson transferred all his interests to Sophia Cameron. Years later Stevenson said he and John Cameron had quarrelled over the location of the claim. Cameron wanted single claims on the left (west) bank of the creek a half-mile or so below the Barker shaft, and Stevenson wanted to stake two, abreast, on the right bank. Cameron won, and it was called the Cameron Claim.

The shaft did not pay off quickly, and as the winter of 1863 approached the miners began to wonder if this was the right location. The shaft was not the only concern. Typhoid was raging along the creek. Sophia became ill. Dr. Wilkinson tried to help her, but she was evidently a difficult, complaining patient. On October 22, as the thermometer dropped to –29°F, Sophia died. Cameron was heartbroken and vowed to carry out her last wish and bury her at "home" in Canada West, away from the tragic creek. Her body was placed in a tin casket inside a wooden coffin and buried temporarily beneath a deserted cabin. There had been 5,000 miners on the creek during the summer—only 90 men and 7 women remained to attend Sophia Cameron's winter funeral.

The digging was hard. The first shaft failed, and with the onslaught of a heavy snowfall, the Clendennins abandoned the claim and joined the migration of miners heading south. The rest of the partners continued to dig, then hired Overlander William Halpenny and several others to help.

Two months after Sophia's death, on December 22, 1862, Stevenson and Halpenny struck gold; Santa Claus had arrived early. Bedrock was struck at 38 feet, but the richest gravel was at 22 feet. The claim was rich enough that by the end of January a grieving but wealthy Cameron offered $12 a day and a $2,000 bonus at Victoria to any miner who would help him haul out Sophia's coffin. Twenty-two men started out, several turning back at each roadhouse until only Cameron, Stevenson, Dr. Wilkinson, Richard Rivers, Rosser Edwards, Evan Jones, French Joe and Big Indian Jim were left. Eventually they left the snow behind, and Cameron and Stevenson bought a horse and continued on their own to Port Douglas and by steamer to Victoria.

The difficulty of hauling the coffin (and by some accounts 50 pounds of gold) through winter snow is an indication of Cameron's dedication and determination. Sophia was buried in

Victoria in March 1863. Yet Cameron had not forsaken business. In Victoria he bought out the Clendennins and two adjacent claims, giving him five full shares of the company, then headed back to his claims.

The Cameron Company mined vigorously throughout the summer of 1863 while the burgeoning town of Cameronton—named in Cameron's honour—grew up around their claims. In July Cameron was hiring as many men as he could: 60 were already at work and that number was expected to rise to 150. Three shafts were producing. The gold was pouring out—not in ounces, but by the pound.

In autumn Cameron went south again, ready to fulfill his promise to Sophia. He took $300,000 in gold and shares that would later net him another $40,000, a total of over five million in today's dollars.

At home in Canada West, Cameron's money was gratefully received by a number of beneficiaries. Two brothers got $20,000 each, and the two brothers who had been with Cameron in Cariboo got $40,000 and a farm each. Cameron married Christianne Wood in 1865 and made investments in timber, the construction of the Lachine Canal and even some eastern mines. The investments were not as successful as the Cameron Company on Williams Creek.

Meanwhile, rumours rumbled. Why had Cameron taken the trouble to bring Sophia's body home? She had been sold into "slavery"—the coffin was filled with gold, they said. No one could accept that Cameron had simply, but with difficulty, fulfilled the dying wish of the woman he loved. When a New York paper reported Sophia's return from slavery with an Indian tribe to Cameron's new Cornwall mansion, the infuriated man reluctantly agreed to exhume his wife's body and end speculation. The coffin was raised and, surrounded by family, friends and curious onlookers, John A. "Cariboo" Cameron poured out the alcohol that had preserved young Sophia. Sophia was identified, the casket was closed and the rumours were laid to rest. And grass never grew again where the alcohol had drained.

"Cariboo" Cameron did return to the goldfields. In 1886, his fortune reduced, he and his second wife made another try for the gold, but it was too late. The easy-to-reach gold he had known was gone, and he was an old man. Soon after he arrived in Barkerville, he suffered a massive stroke and died. On November 7, 1888, he was laid to rest in the same cemetery he had located on his claim when he buried young Peter Gibson in 1863. Welsh miner Harry Jones wrote: "I went over from Van Winkle to attend his funeral. There was a big crowd. But there would have been more had he been rich. It is that way."

The Diller Company

Finding gold was not a matter of luck. Letters, journals and mining documents show time and again that gold was found by men who had three attributes—experience, capital and determination. The story of Isaiah P. Diller and Company is an example.

Diller was a farmer's son from Pennsylvania, born on March 16, 1830. When he heard of Fraser gold, he borrowed money from his widowed mother and was among the first to test the bars of the Fraser River. By November 1858, Diller was in Yale, chairing a miners' meeting and asking for the removal of corrupt Commissioner of Crown Lands Richard Hicks. In June 1860 he sold his rights in the White Mill claim, "consisting of 75 feet of ground to Ah Sun (Chinaman) for the sum of $25. Also one small cabin." Diller was on his way north.

Diller "threw in" with Doc Keithley and Henry Wolf. They staked a claim on the North Fork of the Quesnelle River, near Quesnelleforks, in October 1860. But they kept moving and staked another claim near Wolf Gulch, above Keithley Creek. This proved a rich find, which provoked a minor rush and subsequently the town of Keithley Creek. Diller now had experience and capital.

Diller moved north again, and by October 1861 he and James Loring of Boston had two claims near Richfield. They were joined by Hardy Curry, a Georgia boy known as Hard Curry. They moved down the creek and staked a claim on the right bank across from

Stouts Gulch in September 1861. It was known as the Hard Curry or Diller claim. This is where the determination came in.

For 17 months they dug with no results. Despite sinking two shafts, moving tons of rock and gravel, employing 21 men and investing close to $8,000 (about $200,000 in today's terms), they had no encouraging results. Then on February 18, 1863, they began their wash up, and in three days brought in 25 pounds of gold worth $4,720—they had hit the lead. In eight weeks they produced 10,653 ounces at a value of $170,448. The net profit was $135,976, or $43,325 per share, close to one million dollars each in today's money.

Diller, all 240 pounds of him, had said he wouldn't leave until he had his weight in gold. He left with his weight and his 120-pound dog's weight in gold. In July, as production lagged, the partners hired an armed escort and headed south. According to the *British Columbian* newspaper, Diller had already brought down $130,000 in April. The claim continued to produce but not to the extent it did the first season. The three partners suffered varied fates.

As the Diller myth goes, he arrived at his Pennsylvania home as the family farm was being auctioned off to pay taxes and a mortgage. Unrecognized after so many years' absence, Diller was the high bidder. He revealed himself to his aging mother and gave her the deed. He later moved to Oregon, where he married for the second time and then to Seattle with a third wife, then built the Diller Hotel, the first Seattle hotel with an elevator—at least that's the popular myth (it is incorrect).

The fact that his family farm was at the centre of the Battle of Gettysburg is likely what drew him back. He returned in 1864, married and settled, then in the '70s purchased "a magnificent estate" on Chesapeake Bay, Virginia. He died there on June 13, 1877, of an aneurism after helping a neighbour.

Hard Curry lost his fortune in unsuccessful mining ventures and died in California in the 1870s. James D. Loring opened the "Go-at-'em" Saloon with hurdy-gurdy girls and brought one of the first pianos into the Cariboo. He died on April 29, 1874, of tuberculosis.

The Overlanders

"Gold in the Cariboo." The 1861 headlines of a new Cariboo gold strike on Williams Creek attracted would-be miners and fortune hunters from the mines of California, the rough coast of Scotland, the slums of London and the farms of British Loyalists in Canada West.

In eastern Canada, men banded together in home-town groups to begin what was purported to be an easy five-week journey across the prairies and through the Rocky Mountains. This route was chosen because it was much cheaper than the long, uncomfortable ocean voyage by Panama, and there was the feeling that establishment of a western route through "All British Territory" would stop US expansionist moves.

From Canada, the Overlanders travelled by rail and steamer to Wisconsin, then by Mississippi riverboat to St. Paul, Minnesota, on the frontier's edge. By stagecoach, foot and sternwheeler they moved north through a country about to erupt in a bloody war with the Sioux. As the sternwheeler *International* pulled into the Fort Garry dock on her maiden voyage, the people of Red River Settlement (now Winnipeg, Manitoba) gave a hearty cheer for the "Overlanders." Thus began a trek destined to become a legend.

Only at Fort Garry did the 250 Overlanders realize the extent of the vast and harsh country they were about to enter and how ill-equipped and inexperienced they were. Men who had never spent a night under canvas, ridden a horse, harnessed an ox, walked more than a couple of miles, been hungry, or even cooked their own meals or washed their own clothes were about to embark on a journey across half a continent. The journey would take four to five months; seven men would die.

At Fort Garry the many small home-town groups formed into three major parties based on religion, temperance, friendship, nationality and, finally, leadership and route. Fortunately, there were men among the 250 with the experience and leadership qualities to pull them together. The main party under Thomas McMicking left Fort Garry on June 2, 1862.

The route they took is paralleled today by the Yellowhead

Highway. Week after week, month after month, the Overlanders trudged westward: across the hot, flat plains, through rivers, over hills, through muskeg, then over the mountains to Tête Jaune Cache on the Fraser River headwaters. By this time they were short of provisions. Some of the men were showing symptoms of scurvy; all were hungry. The Overlanders divided into two parties—one going south by way of Albreda Pass and the Thompson River to Fort Kamloops, the other larger party building rafts and dugout canoes to float the Fraser to Quesnellemouth and, with luck, the goldfields of the Cariboo.

By the time they reached Quesnellemouth, autumn leaves were dropping and miners were heading south for the winter. A few Overlanders persisted and went on to Barkerville. Most wintered on the coast and returned the following spring.

The arrival of 200 Overlanders in 1862 can be likened to 80,000 young, hardened craftsmen arriving in present-day British Columbia by some new means of transportation (based on the 1862 provincial population of approximately 20,000 and a present-day population of 4.4 million). Contrary to reports of historians from the 1930s to the 1950s, most of the Overlanders *did* go to Cariboo to search for gold; however, they did not go directly to Williams Creek in the fall of 1862. They were exhausted, starving and broke. Winter was sweeping in over the coastal mountains. Mining was over for the year.

Many of the pre-1862 Overlanders disappeared from documentation, their small parties absorbed in the anonymity of the goldfields or the Pacific west. However, of the 250 known Overlanders of 1862, we know the following.

Sixty stayed in Edmonton or went south into the plains. Five were guides. Ten died en route, leaving 175 to reach BC in the fall of 1862. Ten or 20 went south to the United States or home to Canada immediately. Of those remaining, close to 100 are documented through mining licences, letters, journals and mining records as going to the Cariboo for the 1863 season. A few who had wintered in California returned to the Cariboo. The prevalent myth that they scurried home, lost interest or took up other work is clearly wrong. Many stayed in British Columbia and became influential provincial pioneers, while several such as John Bowron, Sam Rogers, William Rennie and John Pinkerton stayed in Barkerville, operating businesses, mines and nearby ranches.

Despite the effect the Overlanders specifically, and the gold rush as a whole, had on the development of British Columbia and Canada, little can be found in academic journals or general history books, which tend to leap precipitously from the fur-trade era to Confederation. Aside from being featured in grade school curricula, the eastern lust for western wealth and the fact that Canada clearly wanted "the golden fields of British Columbia" and was willing to give a railway in return are generally ignored. It is difficult to find more than a passing reference to the Overlanders or the Cariboo goldfields in any contemporary history of the west.

Over and over again the *Cariboo Sentinel*, the *British Colonist*, the *Toronto Globe* and others argued for the need to connect the newly formed country of Canada with the other British North American colonies. For example, on September 9, 1867, the *Sentinel* passionately editorialized on the budget approval for a road that would form the final link in a route from Halifax to Fort Garry. "It only remains to open the road from the Upper Fraser through the Yellowhead Pass, as proposed by Sir James Douglas, and over the plains . . . in all 230 miles, to have a communication with Fort Garry."

Their frontier optimism was misplaced. It was 20 years before the railway would reach the west coast in July 1886. The Trans-Canada Highway was years away, and the Yellowhead route even further.

Despite the efforts of Overlanders such as Thomas McMicking, who wrote eloquently and frequently on the need for east–west routes, the main routes of commerce were north–south. There were fervent arguments by Overlanders and other westerners that not only did British Columbia *not* need links with Canada, but that the Cariboo did not need British Columbia. A railroad would only draw wealth *out* of BC, they argued. Goods, cattle, sheep and horses from Washington and Oregon, and California merchandise, came from the south. "You need us; we don't need you," was a common 1860s sentiment. It is an argument still echoed in the 21st century, an argument rooted in Cariboo gold and Overlander journeys.

Those Overlanders who stayed in BC became a part of the literature, the myth, the folklore of pioneer British Columbia. Their journey marked them. Their obituaries recorded that this man, this woman, was "an Overlander." They began businesses on the coast such as the Morrow's Overlander restaurant and Heron's saddlery. John Bowron and George Tunstall became gold commissioners and government agents. Robert McMicking was a pioneer of the BC Telephone Company; his brother Thomas was a town clerk and deputy sheriff.

John Jessop founded the *New Westminster Times* and *Victoria Press*. He helped frame the BC Education Act as the first superintendent of education. John Mara was elected to the BC legislature and became speaker of the house.

The Mickles, McQueens, Cooneys and Moores became leading interior stockmen, and the Schuberts were prominent settlers in the Okanagan. Shoemaker John Fannin wrote music and used his love of natural history to found the BC Provincial Museum, now the Royal BC Museum. William Fortune began the first flour mill in the Interior of BC near Kamloops. Dan Williams explored the Peace Country and became a legend in his own right. Alfred Perry kept exploring and led Walter Moberly to Rogers Pass for the CPR route. Moberly is remembered, Perry forgotten.

In the Cariboo, George Wallace founded the *Cariboo Sentinel* newspaper in Barkerville and was followed by editor/publisher Robert Holloway. William Rennie was a shoemaker; Colin McCallum had a tailor's shop; Archibald McNaughton and Andrew Fletcher were merchants. The Wattie brothers were successful miners and donated significantly to the cultural life of the creek. Dr. Edward Stevenson practised medicine in Barkerville.

Many others stayed in Cariboo as miners, including John Pinkerton, Samuel Rogers, John Malcolm, Sam Kyse, Archibald McNaughton, Andrew Fletcher, W.H.G. Thompson, Andrew Weldon,

THE RENNIES—AN OVERLANDER STORY

On the walls of the Masonic temple hangs an 1869 photograph of members of Cariboo Lodge #469, bedecked in lodge finery, standing on a rugged, half-cleared hillside. On the extreme right, a man with a hard countenance and a look of bitterness, perhaps anger, faces the camera. His name is William Rennie, and his expression reflects a story of terror and tragedy. His story is one of the grand and classic tales of the Cariboo gold rush.

Long after the main group of Overlanders reached Quesnelle-mouth or Kamloops and dispersed to their winter retreats, five men still trekked west, victims of procrastination. They were brothers William, Gilbert and Thomas Rennie, along with John Helstone and John R. Wright, all natives of London, Canada West. They left London late, on May 15, 1862, reached Fort Garry on July 7 and Fort Edmonton at the end of August, when good travelling weather had long passed. Returning Metis guides conveyed the news that the vanguard Overlanders had reached the Fraser River headwaters with few problems other than a shortage of provisions.

The temptation was to winter at Fort Edmonton, as a few other Overlanders had done, and work the North Saskatchewan River for gold. They were warned—an autumn crossing was dangerous. But weighing heavily on their decision was the desire to reach the Cariboo. As winter closed in they pushed west. On October 4 they reached Tête Jaune Cache on the Fraser River. The headwaters camp had been trampled, littered and cleared by the 200 men who passed through a few weeks before, so it was with difficulty that the five located two cottonwoods large enough to make dugout canoes. While a couple worked with axes, adzes and fire to hollow the canoes, the others killed the four oxen, their walking larder, and jerked the meat. Eleven days passed. On October 17, as cold winds whistled winter up the Fraser, they lashed their two canoes together and pushed into the current.

The water was low and fast, and the five men paddled hard, not stopping to prospect bars and creeks along the way. On October 29, in the Giscome Rapids, several miles of rock-studded river two days out of Fort George, disaster struck. The two canoes wrapped broadside around a half-submerged rock. No matter what maneouvre they tried, the canoes remained firmly stuck. Hours passed and the sun sank, drawing the cold curtain of night around the five men huddled in the middle of the river.

For three freezing days they were stranded until William Rennie carved thongs from a moosehide and braided a rope with which one man swam and pulled the others to shore. Frostbitten fingers could not light a fire, so they spent another night huddling together. On the fourth day John Helstone and Thomas Rennie woke with frozen feet. In desperation they lit a fire with gunpowder, and their hopes soared with the flames.

On the sixth day they attempted to reload the canoes. When this failed, they decided that Gilbert and William Rennie would walk to Fort George for help. On November 4, one week after striking the rock, the two men set off, anticipating a journey of a couple days. A storm blew in, snow fell, ever deeper, ever more difficult to push through. A river crossing took three days, and still there was no sight of the fort. They shot a mink, a squirrel and a few grouse and ate a handful of rosehips. Williams Rennie's feet became frostbitten; his pace slowed to a shuffle. The days grew into an agonizing blur. The journey through winter to the safety of Fort George did not take two days or two weeks. It took 28 days.

At Fort George, Hudson's Bay Company factor Thomas Charles told them he could not send help. The trail was impassable and the river not solid enough for travel. Without a rescue party, a slow, cold, certain death awaited Thomas Rennie, John Helstone and John Wright at the upriver camp. Gilbert and William assuaged their consciences with the belief that, given their own difficulties, the other three could not have survived. They were wrong. Ninety miles upstream the three men were living a winter hell.

The three men at the river camp had 10 days' food and plenty of firewood, so there had been no immediate sense of dread. Soon a rescue party would arrive. Then the storm came. Their frostbitten limbs screamed in agony. They were unable even to search for firewood. By the time Gilbert and William Rennie reached Fort George, the three stranded men were in terrible pain and dreadful condition, but they were alive. They waited, and as they waited the fire burned out. They could not relight it.

Factor Charles pressured the two Rennie brothers to move on. Provisions were short. On January 26, 1863, they headed south for Quesnellemouth.

Incredibly, after two months, two of the three men upriver still clung to life, still waiting for rescue. When a wandering band of

Carrier Natives stumbled on their camp they found two men eating the flesh of the third. The survivors drove the Natives away at gunpoint. Two weeks later the Natives returned to the river camp, this time to kill the devils who ate human flesh. As the sole survivor struggled on rotting limbs to escape, he was killed by repeated hatchet blows.

Months later the whole story unfolded when trapper John Giscome found the camp. His Native companions, frightened of "whiteman's justice," showed him where all the belongings were. Giscome buried the grisly remains of the tragedy.

The two surviving Rennies worked the winter near Williams Lake and then travelled to Williams Creek. Gilbert suffered from rheumatism so they left on June 17, 1863. Not for some months would the Giscome story reach the two men. Gilbert returned east to his wife and family. William was back in Barkerville by June 6, 1867, where he advertised in the *Cariboo Sentinel* as a boot and shoemaker.

In the Great Fire of 1868, William Rennie lost his shop and goods, valued at $1,000, but reopened on September 22. He stayed in Barkerville, running his store and investing in the Murtle Company and the Proserpine Gold and Silver Company until about 1879. On August 29, 1880, the Reverend Sexsmith married William Rennie and Catherine Evans at the home of lumber merchant Ithiel Blake Nason. Catherine was the widow of Captain John Evans, of Welsh Adventurers fame, who died at Stanley almost exactly a year before.

By 1881 they had left Barkerville and the rest of their lives, and their deaths, passed unnoticed and unrecorded. Of William Rennie all that remains is a likeness in a Masonic lodge photograph.

James Kelso and many more. Some died within a year or two such as D.F. McLaurin, John Jones, William Hugill, David Byers, E.W.W. Linton, Thomas McMicking. Pivotal miner and guide Timoleon Love lies in an unmarked grave in Cranbrook, BC.

They were farmers, merchants, musicians, husbands, artisans, teamsters, artists, tailors and labourers who built the province.

John Bowron

John Bowron, the son of William Bowron and Sarah Odell, was born in Huntingdon, Quebec, on March 10, 1837. He was a tall, slim young man of 25 studying law when news of the BC goldfields reached him. He took only a moment to pack up and join the Huntingdon party of Overlanders heading west.

The party of more than 25 men became an integral part of Barkerville's life. It included men like the Wattie and Sellars brothers, *Cariboo Sentinel* founder George Wallace, Peter McIntyre, William Gage, blacksmith William B. Cameron, George Tunstall and William B. Schuyler, the latter two being schoolmates of John Bowron.

Bowron wintered at Victoria, and in the early spring he and partner Bill Schuyler trekked north to the gold creeks, where they were issued mining licences on May 11, 1863. John Bowron did whatever work he could—carpentry, cleaning out sluice boxes, separating gold from sand and digging in a shaft—until he found an opening in the government service.

While maintaining an interest in certain gold claims, Bowron took on an increasing number of responsibilities: he became a librarian in 1864, a postmaster in 1866, a mining recorder and constable at Richfield in 1872, a government agent in 1875, and a gold commissioner in 1883.

Bowron firmly believed that the true wealth of Barkerville would be found in the "mother lode" or gold quartz veins, and although he was scoffed at he persisted and eventually convinced the government to put some effort into exploration. When Bowron's belief in the gold quartz veins proved justified, there was a flurry of excitement. But costs were too high and capital investment money was short, so no major attempt was made to retrieve the gold until the opening of the Cariboo Gold Quartz Mine in the 1930s.

In 1869 John Bowron married Emily Penberthy Edwards, an American woman 13 years his junior. They had five children—John, William, Alice, Lottie and Archie. William built his house across the street from the family home and then moved away, as did all the others, though Lottie frequently returned and for many years was an important member of the self-professed Barkerville upper crust. Both John and Emily were active in the Cariboo Amateur Dramatic Association. John Bowron rode through several changes of government and, as a courteous, kindly, generous man, was a most respected citizen and government official.

Barkerville was a mature mining town when the Bowrons lived here. The population was stable, though the economy was still based on gold, and miners and prospectors still came and went. Lottie's schoolmates included Nettie House and Johnny Houser, long-time residents. In Lottie's later years she had vivid memories of the town and its life:

> I used to waken in the morning to the sound of rushing Williams Creek and the song of the anvil from the O'Neill blacksmith's shop across the street and the sound of Billy Hodgkinson's pack horse with a bell carrying milk up town from the milk ranch down the road.
>
> Another cheery sound was the water dripping into the water barrel in the wood shed. This had to be brought from the springs on the hillside in overhead wooden troughs, and to the backs of the various homes by smaller troughs.
>
> I recall the anxiety lest the snow should not have gone by May 24th so that we girls might wear our summer dresses for the usual picnic at Joe Mason's meadows up at Jack O' Clubs Lake.
>
> The exciting arrival of the stage on Thursday evening and its departure Saturday morning—everyone was excited when the stage came in—the children watched for it behind the church—then the cry being carried from one child to another—"Here's the stage, here's the stage."
>
> If to others in the outside world we seemed to live in a queer place we as children knew nothing of this, and to us our lives were quite natural and complete.

Emily Bowron died in Barkerville in 1895, and in 1897 John Bowron, then 60, married 33-year-old Elizabeth Watson at Victoria. The couple had one child, Aileen Genevieve Leone. John Bowron died in Victoria on September 6, 1906, shortly after he retired. His second wife, Elizabeth, died in 1922 and his daughter Lottie in 1964. John Bowron's name is remembered in Bowron Lake Provincial Park, a few miles east of Barkerville.

The Company of Welsh Adventurers

Cariboo gold attracted many interesting men, and Captain John Evans of Machynlleth in North Wales was certainly one. Evans was employed at a cotton factory and had invested in quarries and became inspired to organize a Cariboo expedition of 24 Welsh Adventurers. While Evans took a shortcut via Panama to scout their prospects, the other men travelled to Victoria via Cape Horn.

While awaiting their arrival on the *Rising Sun*, he went up the Fraser to Quesnellemouth, then arranged with Governor Douglas for the lease of a large mining claim on Lightning Creek. The lease was unusual, for by regulation miners had to work their own claims or a combination of claims. Evans used the threat of all British capital being withdrawn if allowances were not made.

Evans's 24 Welshmen arrived in Victoria in June 1863 after a six-month sea voyage, and proceeded to their crown-lease creek, a laborious five-week journey. The Adventurers mined here for two seasons with expenses of over $26,000 and retrieved only $450 in gold. For some time men had been deserting, and when the venture finally failed in the fall of 1864, all but Evans and a few others scattered. A few of them, such as Harry Jones, are buried in the Stanley cemetery just a few miles west of Barkerville.

Captain John Evans was a pious puritan who once said that he would like to find just one good mine so that he might give all the proceeds to the Booth Street Welsh Congregational Chapel in Manchester, which he had helped found. He came from a country with sharp religious divisions and was surprised to find these divisions were blurred in the colonies and the community lacked his brand and level of morality. Evans deplored the fact that on Sunday, the Lord's Day, gambling, swearing and other vices continued at an uproarious level. To counter this immorality, Evans and a few of his men built a small hall in Barkerville on a lot granted by Gold Commissioner Cox. This Cambrian Hall served as a meeting hall and a place for religious services until it was burned in the 1868 fire.

Many coveted the valuable property near the Methodist church. With the hall's destruction, there was a rush for the land. When unauthorized building began, Evans appealed to Magistrate Chartres Brew in March 1869, stating the offer from Cox and explaining,

> Some have gone so far as to commence building in such a manner as to completely block up the entrance to the Hall, thereby rendering it nothing less than back premises to a saloon and something worse.
>
> The building [the old Cambrian Hall] was the only Protestant place open for religious purposes throughout Cariboo during a period of two to three years, it was also entirely unsectarian.

The land title was granted, the claim jumpers evicted and a new Cambrian Hall was built.

In 1875 Evans was elected to the Legislative Assembly of British Columbia, and in 1877 he was married (for the third time) to Catherine Jones, a woman who brought him great happiness. Unfortunately, the happiness was short-lived. In June 1879 he wrote to his children that his rheumatism was bothering him. On August 25, he suffered inflammation of the bowels and kidneys and died at Stanley. His friends wrote on his grave marker, "Blessed are the dead who died in the Lord . . . "

While these adventurers were the best known of the Welshmen on the creek, they were only a small percentage. Ongoing research here and in Wales is uncovering the stories of many Welshmen, mostly miners, who migrated to the goldfields.

6 FALLEN ANGELS, BUSINESSWOMEN AND COMMUNITY BUILDERS

A WELL-KNOWN RIDDLE asks "Who was born, lived, but had no name?" The answer is Lot's wife. It would be equally correct to answer the women of Williams Creek. They were born, lived on the creeks, had children and ran businesses, but with few exceptions, their names remain unknown. The newspaper items, the pioneer profiles, the obituaries, even the birth announcements are all male dominated. On June 18, 1866, the *Cariboo Sentinel* announced, "Birth, at Barkerville, 15 inst., wife of William A. Meacham, a son." And on November 27, 1869, it reported, "Mr. Fick, the proprietor of the New England Bakery, has returned . . . with his wife." Hurdy dancers and prostitutes were referred to by their first name, or a nickname, if at all. Madams and business-women were known by their last name, when mentioned.

Despite beliefs to the contrary, the creeks were not devoid of women. There may not have been many, but they were here, and as individuals they had greater influence on the social and eco-nomic structure of the region than any one man, John Cameron and William Barker aside. By compiling enough records, it is pos-sible to paint a faint portrait of women on the creeks.

In the two decades following 1862, close to 400 women can be accounted for by name. Women were close behind the first men who reached the creeks. Harry Guillod found miners' wives and children on Lightning Creek in 1862. Nine prostitutes paraded Williams Creek that summer, and women opened saloons, whiskey shops, boarding houses and restaurants. When winter came they headed south. Mrs. Mary Ann Webster and her two daughters, one of whom was Margaret Cusheon, a saloonkeeper's wife, were lost in a snowstorm on Bald Mountain for several days. Johanna Maguire, a prostitute, was here in 1862.

That said, there was a "want of women" in the Cariboo, as was reported in the *London Times:* "There is not 1 to every 100 men at the mines; without them the male population will never settle. A large number could obtain immediate employment as domestic servants, at high rates of wages, with the certainty of marriage in the background. The miner is not very particular— 'plain, fat, and 50' even would not be objected to."

Colonel Moody of the Royal Engineers wrote that "Maids of all work" would be snapped up, but that farm girls would do better than town girls. Women in England read the report and responded. Maria S. Rye, who worked with an emigration society, wrote to the *Times* that in the summer of 1862, she was receiving 100 letters a day from women ready to embark. And embark they did. At least two brideships, the *Tynemouth* and the *Rosedale* arrived in Victoria and, as was expected, most of the women were quickly offered jobs or marriage. Florence Wilson, the Barkerville actress, librarian and saloonkeeper, was on the *Tynemouth*.

The first winter following Barker's strike, only 90 people stayed on Williams Creek, 7 of whom were women. They deserve recognition: Rosa Donnelly, wife of a miner; Anna Cameron, wife of hotel keeper Richard Cameron, and her sister Lizzie Roddy, who later married A.D. McInnes; Sophia Cameron, wife of John A. "Cariboo" Cameron, who died that winter of typhoid; Scotch Jenny, a.k.a. Mrs. Janet Morris, a merchant's wife; Mary Winnard, wife of blacksmith William Winnard, and an unnamed French woman.

The following season a steady influx of women began. Eliza Barker came with her new husband, Billy; Eliza Bailley opened a whiskey shop; Lizzie Boardman, Louisa Cunningham and Jessie Heatherington came with their miner husbands; the Brown family opened a hotel in Richfield; Mrs. Samuel Nathan, a.k.a. Mary Boyle, opened a brothel, as did Mary Sheldon, Fanny Bendixen and likely Julia Picot; Mrs. F.W. Dustin began a boarding house on Conklin Gulch; Rebecca Gibbs, a black woman, had a laundry; Florence Wilson, Mme. Lamon and Mme. Lawrent all opened saloons.

Many of these women were active socially. Florence Wilson started a public library; Jennie Allen, Johanna Maguire and others were known for nursing sick and injured miners. Catherine Parker, her daughter Minnie and Florence Wilson were also active in the Cariboo Amateur Dramatic Society, and Mrs. Tracey sang at church.

Women also applied for mining certificates, though whether they mined or took an active part in the claim is debatable. Certainly Margaret Cusheon and Eliza Ord appear to have been active in claim affairs, but most women's licences were likely just a way for their husbands to hold an extra share or work another claim in their name.

Many, if not most, women who came to the creeks married here. Often marriage certificates hinted at past lives, while obituaries were edited for refinement and respectability. A former dancehall girl was remembered posthumously as a midwife; a prostitute's past was forgotten.

Many of these gold rush women bore children here in this rough land with its primitive medical facilities. Anna Cameron was the first. When Allan Richfield Cameron was born on October 25, 1862, at the Pioneer Hotel in Cameronton, miners stood in line waiting their turn to hold the child. Wellington Moses made frequent notes in his diary about women like Mrs. Frances Lee, Mrs. Fred Rose and Eleanor Edwards losing a child or having stillbirths.

When their men died, as men in the goldfields frequently did, no woman remained a widow long, except by choice. Shortly following the required year's mourning, they were remarried.

Catherine Parker became Mrs. Austin; Catherine Evans married William Rennie when Captain Evans died; Ellen Peebles remarried, to William Wormald; Scotch Jenny Morris became Janet Allen. Subsequent census records show the blended families of Cariboo.

Divorces appear to be uncommon but are also poorly recorded. Anna Cameron divorced Richard and married Benjamin van Volkenburgh, and Margaret Waddell went to court to have Florence Wilson pay a bill, pleading her position as a divorced woman. Often these women were referred to politely as widows or grass widows. Williams Creek women died of old age, heart attacks and, as in the case of Mary Wintrip, of suicide following a bout of depression.

The Demimonde—Women of the Town

Whiskey dealers, gamblers, thieves, prostitutes, madams, pimps and barkeeps followed hard on the heels of any rush for frontier wealth. When miners flocked to BC from Oregon, California and beyond, the parasites poured in to suck miners dry.

Not all the women on the creek were kindly and respectable. Jane Snyder got Joseph Shearer drunk and had him sign over all his claims to her. The court had little sympathy and awarded each of them half. Mme. J.B.A. Reviere, perhaps a prostitute, fell in lust with Cariboo sheriff Daniel Chisholm. They fled Williams Creek, abandoned her child in Victoria and escaped to California. Chisholm was married, with children in the east. Another unknown woman abandoned her newborn or stillborn child to the waters of Williams Creek.

And there is no doubt that Williams Creek had plenty of brothels and individual prostitutes, for where there were men and money, prostitution was sure to flourish. The role of madams, prostitutes and brothels in Barkerville is poorly documented— not surprising, given Victorian morality—but a few references appeared in newspapers. One such reference appeared in the *Colonist* of September 10, 1862, and was copied later in the San Francisco papers, reinforcing an image of Barkerville as a coarse, rough mining town.

THE PROSTITUTES: on the creek—nine in number—put on great airs. They dress in male attire and swagger through the saloons and mining camps with cigars or huge qwids of tobacco in their mouths, cursing and swearing and look like anything but the angels in petticoats heaven intended they should be. Each has a revolver or bowie knife attached to her waist, and it is quite a common occurrence to see one or more women dressed in male attire playing poker in the saloons, or drinking whiskey at the bars. They are a degraded set, and all good men in the vicinity wish them hundreds of miles away.

Viscount Cheadle refers to two Cariboo women at Lillooet Lake in October 1863: "Steamer brought in 2 prostitutes, white woman and negress, having spent the season in Cariboo (made fortunes)." And in the summer of 1862, a Williams Creek miner wrote, "There is a great deal of gambling and drinking carried on by the lucky miners and on fine days you could see Cypreans [prostitutes] promenading about in long boots, britches and fancy hats." These women were likely categorized as street-level prostitutes. They were followed by the madams who ran the parlour houses—saloons with extra rooms for sexual dalliances. The line between a respectable and a disorderly house is blurred by time.

Prostitutes' success relied on keeping a low profile, so they remain hidden, except when dragged into the public eye. Hattie Lucas was one such case. She threw stones at the house of Mary Sheldon, a madam. Then she was in court and fined for sticking a pistol in a butcher's face and whacking him with a "shooting stick" (a cane gun), after an argument. Lucas was described as, "a tall and graceful young woman, having considerable personal attractions, but unfortunately a passion so uncontrollable that even the gravity of the court could not restrain its outbursts." Then William Williams, a miner who made a habit of assaulting women, pulled her off her horse and knocked her down three times. Williams got three months. He later assaulted Elizabeth Thurber, a hotel and saloonkeeper.

Mary Sheldon, alias Slap-Jack Johnny, had had a tough time with the law in Victoria and headed to Barkerville, where she opened a brothel. She was described as "a buxom middle-aged woman of matronly appearance," whom the Court characterized as "being of sober steady habits." Obviously the court was willing to overlook a few indiscretions. Sheldon often travelled to Yale by stagecoach with other single women and may have been running a brothel circuit, like those that were common during the California gold rush.

Mary Nathan, also known as Mary Boyle, was married to Samuel Nathan in Australia, had a child and moved to California. The couple then set up shop in Victoria, where Mary was a prostitute who went by the name Judy, and Samuel was the keeper of a disorderly house, or brothel. After a falling out, Mary divorced him, sort of, came to Barkerville and was involved with several men who helped her get started in a saloon. Moses notes in his diary that she died at her house in Barkerville on November 12, 1878: "Late Mrs. Mary Nathan was buirried [sic] from her resident to the grave yard at Cameronton." Her grave is unmarked.

Johanna Maguire is perhaps one of the most recognized of early Barkerville prostitutes. In August 1862, Bishop George Hills described her as follows: "She was a notorious keeper of a house of ill fame and, moreover, on this occasion the wretched woman proved to be intoxicated and I was obliged to request her to go away.

"Yet she had done several acts of kindness to the invalid," Hills added. There was the angel in Johanna Maguire, the miners' nurse and daughter of great Irish liberator Daniel O'Connell. She epitomizes the gold rush "fallen angels," the women who sold whiskey and their bodies to lusty miners, then nursed them through smallpox and typhoid fevers.

Bishop Hills simply could not understand the gold camp's complex social life:

The fact is these men, worthy men as miners, are so accustomed to life in the transits of vice, and to hear blasphemy and evil discourse of immorality, that they have sunk to a lower level, depraved . . . [and they] pronounce excellent and praise to the skies a keeper of a house of ill fame, a drunkard and blasphemer and a prostitute, a wretched woman who happened to show a kind disposition to the sick.

The point of Hills's private tirade is that goldfields life was not as refined as history would have us believe. The social rules and barriers that made Bishop Hills and his congregation comfortable had been cast aside.

Johanna Maguire left Williams Creek in September 1862, after one season, with $3,000—over $50,000 in today's money. She didn't earn it washing clothes or by being unpopular. On her way out of Williams Creek, she got lost and was reported dead. Days later she stumbled into the safety of a Chinese miner's cabin, but she had lost her horse and all of her earnings. In Victoria she moved in with Edward Whitney. He was not a good man and beat Joanna regularly. She died on December 3, 1864, after a particularly vicious beating, though the inquest said she died of over-drinking. Whitney went free.

Eliza Ord came to view when she went on a rampage and broke all the windows in the home of James Bruce. She came to Barkerville as the "wife" of an unknown miner and and kept a variety of establishments after leaving him. She was in and out of court, often as plaintiff. Later, presumably divorced, she sued Robert Drinkall for breach of a contract to marry, but it was thrown out of court. Eventually she moved to California but came back 10 years later to re-establish a share in a claim. She charged a judge with pocketing the money and was committed to an insane asylum, but was released by New Westminster doctors who claimed she was quite sane. Back in Barkerville she found her house ransacked and destroyed. She died in New Westminster in 1893 of emphysema.

This was not an easy life for women, as law was on the side of men. Assault was not uncommon. Consider Sophia Rouillard, one of several French women in town. She came to town at age 25, likely for only a summer. She loaned Nelson Creek miner Caeser Cassia $500, and when she asked for payment a third time he punched her hard in the stomach. She reportedly remarked, "That blow will be the death of me." Her stomach was "on fire" for days, but even the doctor couldn't help, and 10 days later she died in her house. The inquest jury of 12 men, 4 of whom held liquor licences, found she died by "the visitation of God in a natural way, accelerated by the use of strong drink, and not otherwise." Her obituary noted that she was "a lady familiarly known to many in the colony"—a euphemism for prostitute.

It was a case that was repeated over and over. Jessie Heatherington was found dead in her Richfield cabin in 1864. Despite strong evidence against the accused, John Baumgarter, he was released and her death was atrributed to alcoholic misfortune. The juries were consistent. When a Chinese prostitute died in a "house of ill fame," with Solomon-like wisdom, a jury returned a verdict of "found dead." And when Chinese prostitutes were sold or hustled to another town, the only concern was whether a colonial law had been broken.

On May 18, 1872, the *Sentinel* reported, "Ah Moye, madam of Chinese brothel that claimed to have ten inmates, stated that a man named Charley tried to extract license money from her." In June, Soo Lang was charged with obtaining licence money under false pretences. He was acquitted.

These women's invisibility continues. They are buried in Cameronton or Richfield cemeteries—but their graves are unmarked, unrecorded.

Hurdy-Gurdy Girls

The hurdy-gurdy girls were dancing girls, "terpsichorean artistes," the *Sentinel* newspaper called them. They were brought from Germany, "direct from Baden-Baden," usually via California, by an entrepreneurial saloonkeeper. While Barry and Adler of Barkerville's famed Fashion Saloon are credited as the first to bring hurdy dancers to the Cariboo, it is at best a doubtful claim. Also doubtful is the suggestion that French madam Fanny Bendixen was in charge of them. No contemporary documentation links her with the dancers.

In fact, James Loring of Diller claim fame may have been the first to bring in dancing partners for miners. In 1865, perhaps sooner, he was employing Native women at his Terpsychorean [sic] Saloon in Cameronton. From that time on, Native women were a part of the underside of Barkerville's social life, most often surfacing as prostitutes such as Lucy Bones or Gentle Annie.

In North America the hurdy-gurdies are known primarily as dancehall girls in mining communities. "Hurdies" is an old English term for the buttocks or the hips; however, in this context the name comes from a musical instrument played with buttons and a wheel that rubs a string, creating a distinctive drone. The hurdy-gurdy and the bagpipes were the most popular instruments for dancing in the rural areas of Europe for centuries and were particularly popular in western Germany in the 19th century, where many of the players were young women. In Barkerville they were also accompanied by fiddle.

At this time, a relative lack of war, famine or epidemic in parts of Europe, and the resulting increase in population meant that farm families could no longer support all their children. The dispossessed wandered and sold wicker products, and found that music increased sales. In autumn these Landganger, or pedlars, returned to their communities. The Landganger broom girls travelled throughout Europe and went on to Australia, North America and other lands, under an agent called "the seller of souls." Often called hurdy-gurdy girls, they were forced by their agents to work in dancehalls and coffeehouses of seaports, and later in mining camps.

While not all Barkerville hurdies were German, my research has shown that at least 15 had German birthplaces. Not all were from Baden-Baden, but many, including Elizabeth Feiling, were from the state of Hesse. Rebecca Fick was from Hanover,

Rosa Haub from Nieder-Weisel, Elizabeth Ladd from Frankfurt, Martha Pendola from Bremen, Georgianna Nachtigall from Hamburg, and Margette Braun from Langenhain.

It appears the hurdies first arrived the summer of 1866, dancing in their celebrated style at the Fashion Saloon and Martin's Saloon. By the next summer they were also enticing miners into Jacob Mundorf's Crystal Palace Saloon and soon to Sterling's Saloon. One dance cost a miner one dollar. The girls got a percentage of the sale of any drinks they enticed miners to buy. And entice they did, for some miners were reported to be broke, having spent all their earnings on the hurdies. They were not prostitutes, according to the *Cariboo Sentinel*. But judging by hurdy houses in California, prostitution was certainly part of the business. In 1866 the *Sentinel* ran a letter describing the hurdies:

HURDY GURDY DAMSELS. There are three descriptions of the above named "Ladies" here, they are unsophisticated maidens of Dutch extraction, from "poor but honest parents" and morally speaking, they really are not what they are generally put down for. They are generally brought to America by some speculating, conscienceless scoundrel of a being commonly called a "Boss Hurdy." This man binds them in his service until he has received about a thousand per cent for his outlay. The girls receive a few lessons in the terpsichorean art, are put into a kind of uniform, generally consisting of a red waist, cotton print skirt and a half mourning headdress resembling somewhat in shape the top knot of a male turkey, this uniform gives them quite a grotesque appearance. Few of them speak English, but they soon pick up a few popular vulgarisms; if you bid one of them good morning your answer will likely be "itsh sphlaid out" or "you bet your life."

The Hurdy style of dancing differs from all other schools. If you ever saw a ring of bells in motions, you have seen the exact positions these young ladies are put through during their dance, the more muscular the partner, the nearer the approximation of the ladies' pedal extremities to the ceiling, and the gent who can hoist his "gal" the highest is considered the best dancer; the poor girls as a general thing earn their money very hardly.

James Anderson, the bard of Cariboo, wrote a song about the hurdies, sung to the tune of the popular folk song "Green Grow the Rushes Oh!" and published in the *Sentinel*, July 23, 1866:

Last simmer we had lassies here
Frae Germany—the hurdies, O!
And troth I wot, as I'm a Scot
They were the bonnie hurdies, O!

Chorus: Bonnie are the hurdies, O!
The German hurdy gurdies, O!
The daftest hour that e'er I spent
Was dancin' wi' the hurdies, O!

They left the creek wi' lots o' gold,
Danced frae orr lads sae clever, O!
My blessin's on their "sour krout" heads.
Gif they stay awa forever, O!

Clearly James Anderson was not one of those who wept when the hurdies left for warmer climates in the fall.

There may have been a language barrier, as most of the girls were German, and some townsfolk may have questioned their morals, but that did not deter many of them from staying each fall to marry merchants and miners. Elizabeth Ebert, known as "dumpy little Lizzie," married Edward Dougherty and moved to the Clinton area. Elizabeth Feiling married Samuel Walker, who kept a boarding house at Centreville on Mosquito Creek. Jeanette Ceise, a German girl who married John Houser in San Francisco, was a hurdy, as was Martha Pendola, the German wife of Italian merchant Angelo Pendola. Jacob Mundorf of the Crystal Palace Saloon fell under the charms of a dancer he hired, Katrina, nicknamed the Kangaroo. He married her, but not before she had several children. (She later divorced him on the grounds of cruelty.) Carpenter Joseph St. Laurent, later of Quesnel, married Georgianna Wilhelmina Henrietta Nachtigall. And when the dancehall closed, Mrs. "Hurdy Billy" Hodgkinson, Isabella Irvine, married a miner and took in laundry. Charlotte Millington tried to forget she was a dancing girl. After she and husband R.H. Brown moved to Victoria, she was known as a former governess and midwife. Doubtless there were others. Martha O'Neill (later Boss), who was raised in Barkerville said, "Of course there were other 'Hurdy's' in the town too, all married and mostly with large families." Each of these women accepted the challenge of a new land and stayed to pioneer.

John Milross appeared in early Barkerville as a bartender who supplemented his income with sign painting. He is one of the few men identified as a "boss hurdy." By the 1870s he was "boss" of Milross' Hurdy's, whom he hustled between Barkerville and Lightning Creek when neither town could support a full-time dancing set. The Austins, Catherine and John, also "bossed" a set of hurdies at the Stanley Hotel in the early '70s.

The last mention of the hurdies in the *Sentinel* appears in 1871. By that time Rosa Haub was in change of the dancers and would go down to Victoria to bring new girls north. But Barkerville was fading and gold was scarce, so the "lady professors of the terpsichorean academy" drifted south to California. Rosa got only as far as Victoria, where she found eligible bachelor Ephriam Langell, married and moved to Orcas Island in Washington.

Madam Fanny Bendixen and the Lottery of the Gold Ingots

The enigmatic Fanny Bendixen came on the world stage in San Francisco at about age 25, as the California gold rush waned. According to pioneer journalist D.W. Higgins, she was the mistress of notorious underworld figure Ned McGowan, who was banned from California by the Committee of Vigilance, and who later became a figure in Yale. McGowan knew Fanny in San Francisco and Victoria, and described her as a beautiful and elegant woman dressed in furs, jewels and silks. Inexplicably, she became a virtuous woman overnight, began attending church every Sunday, shunned her former underworld companions and announced her marriage to Louis Bendixen, a German born in 1825. The change was not accomplished without difficulty, for her former suitor reacted violently. When gifts did not have the desired effect, he resorted to severe beatings and had his henchmen throw acid on her gown. Supposedly her resolve to reform intensified.

Fanny Bendixen may have been part of the great migration from France following the Lottery of the Golden Ingots, under Napoleon III. This French government scheme dumped 5,000 supposed French revolutionaries into California in 1850. The Lottery was supposed to offer a way for French citizens to immigrate, but the government, in choosing those to be exported, made a special self-serving effort to choose undesirables and common criminals. As the great exodus of 1858 took place from California to BC, British consul William Lane Booker in San Francisco wrote:

A great many French have left this city and it is believed that five to six thousand will start during the next two or three months—a large proportion of these belonged formerly to the "Garde Mobile" and were sent here, their expenses being defrayed from the proceeds of a Lottery established in France with the sanction of the Government entitled "Le Singut d'Or"—It was understood that they were people the French Government was anxious to see emigrate being generally imbued with the most violent Republican ideas, however in this country they have been quiet and orderly. The appear extremely anxious to leave California.

Ingots had been unpopular in California. The Fraser and then the Cariboo rushes offered a door to another future. At least 30 and likely more former French citizens made their home in the Cariboo—people like Eude Aime, Josephine Columb, Marie Coulon, Marie Laurent and Julia Picot, the hotelier. Perhaps the discrimination and a desire to start their own business prompted the Bendixens to move north to another coastal gold rush boomtown—Victoria. Here they built a modest two-storey brick hotel, the St. George's, which became known for its accommodating host and hostess. Gold rushes came and went, as did the prosperity they produced, and in a few years Victoria felt the effects of a recession. Business declined, and the Bendixens' marriage collapsed. Louis returned to California by the time of the census of 1866. He lived in San Francisco where he died on January 8, 1874.

Fanny held onto her dream of opening a successful saloon. She saw that while Victoria was momentarily fading, there was money to be made in the high mountain creeks of Cariboo. She was in Barkerville by June 1865, occupying a house on the main street next to Moses's barbershop. She borrowed or raised money and in June 1866 opened her first of several saloons, as reported in the *Sentinel:*

> Parlour Saloon, Barkerville. Madame Bendixon begs to announce to her friends that she has refitted this well-known Saloon, where she invites the public to give her a call. The bar is stocked with the best of LIQUORS and SEGARS that can be procured.

In California the term "parlor saloon" was understood to mean a saloon/brothel. By November 1866 the saloon was empty, but Fanny was not to be kept down. A year later she announced a second establishment:

> Belle Union Saloon, kept by Mrs. Fanny Bendixen, Barkerville. This Saloon, which is fitted up in the most elegant style, has just been opened to the public. None but the best brands of LIQUORS and CIGARS served at the bar. This is a PRIVATE SALOON for the accommodation of customers.

Again, what a "private saloon" entailed in Barkerville is unclear, but to Californians it meant a place with a doorman who only admitted those known to the establishment. The accommodation was taken care of by young women.

This saloon was lost in the fire of 1868 but rebuilt by contractors Bruce and Mann in November 1868. In 1869 there was a county court case involving Fanny Bendixen: James Burdick vs. Bruce and Mann. The court records indicate that Bruce and Mann built a "house" for Burdick on a lot owned by Fanny Bendixen, "with whom Burdick is in partnership." Fanny held the liquor licence of this house, where the gross receipts of the bar were from $15 to $20 a day, rising to $25 and $50 a day around Christmas. "The house is also a hotel or boarding or rooming house—it has beds." There is a possibility that this "house with beds" was a brothel and that Burdick was the traditional male partner of a madam.

This establishment met with some success. Bendixen took advantage of the 1870s strikes in Van Winkle by opening the doors of the Van Winkle Saloon, then selling it in 1874 and opening the Exchange Saloon in Stanley, a stone's throw from Van Winkle. The Stanley saloon featured a reading room "with the latest periodicals and newspapers." The 1871 Barkerville Directory also connects Bendixen with the St. George Saloon, a name she brought from Victoria. Perhaps Fanny was in business with a number of Barkerville entrepreneurs who knew her success at saloon keeping.

By 1880 Fanny was back in Barkerville with a saloon and boarding house. In this last business, next to the Masonic lodge, she became a fixture of the town, the subject of reminiscences. Charles O'Neill's daughter remembered her as a "fat and good-looking French woman; must have weighed some 300 averdupois [sic] and there she sat on two chairs amid her glasses and bottles, She had nothing but smiles for the children (and often gave them 'British Sweeties') and called them 'cherie' but let an adult enter her shop and the air became blue with curses."

When Judge Matthew Begbie made a visit to Cariboo in 1889

he wrote, "Madame Bendixen is here in great form, indeed enormous, vast, of undiscoverable girth, though she was always of goodly diameter."

Fanny maintained some contact with her family, for in 1897 she brought her grandniece Leonie Fanny Perrier to live with her, likely as a companion in her declining years. Leonie's mother had just died, and her father was living in San Francisco. In Barkerville Leonie married Hugh Cochrane. They soon had a daughter, Clara Frances Leonie Douglas Cochrane, and on January 6, 1899, a son, Robert Hugh Cochrane.

In January 1899 Fanny was ill and realized it was time to make a will. She left Hugh Cochrane all her real estate in Barkerville and appointed him executor and trustee for the benefit of the Cochranes' daughter. She left her friend Frank Meyer $200 and gave her earrings to Mrs. Elizabeth Kelly, wife of Andrew Kelly. She left nothing to Leonie, with whom she did not get along. Leonie was not happy with the arrangement. She wanted the earrings, so she concocted a codicil to the will and had Fanny sign it in April, by which time the older woman was barely coherent.

Fanny died on May 1, 1899. Her death registration listed her age as 80—though in the 1881 census she was 44. No sooner had she died than a court case began. Elizabeth Kelly wanted the earrings and sued. It was found that Leonie had not acted in good faith. Judge Clement Cornwall decided only Fanny's first will would be recognized and awarded the earrings to Kelly.

Even in death Fanny Bendixen was a woman who captured the imagination of many and likely the hearts of many a miner and businessman along the creeks. Her grave in Richfield is unmarked.

Catherine Parker

Catherine Parker—boarding house keeper, saloonkeeper, boss hurdy, mother and wife—is a good example of a woman who came with her husband and stayed to make the rough mining camp a community.

Catherine was born to Michael and Elizabeth Dunn in Dublin, Ireland, on April 14, 1841. When she was about 20 she moved to England, where she met Samuel Parker of North Wellingborough, Northamptonshire, four years her senior. Their marriage record is elusive, but by 1859 they had a daughter, Minnie, and in 1861 they had another daughter, Kate. About this time the family moved to British Columbia, where they ran a trading store in Douglas, at the head of Harrison Lake. A third daughter, Sarah, was born here. They moved to Barkerville after Douglas was bypassed by the Cariboo Road. Their exact arrival date is unknown, but in June 1867 Mrs. Parker announced a "Grand Ball and supper at her new house . . . the very comfortable Mrs. Parker's Boarding House" in Upper Barkerville, next to Fulton's large bowling alley and saloon. She offered meals at all hours, "as the culinary department is under the direct surveillance of the proprietress."

The ball elevated the Parkers into Barkerville's social life. Soon they were both singing and performing with the Cariboo Amateur Dramatic Association, so much so that in July 1868 the organization gave a benefit for Mrs. Parker.

Catherine Parker was eight and a half months pregnant when the fire of 1868 struck. Just two weeks later, on October 4, son William was born. They rebuilt a sizable house with 10 bedrooms, a parlour, a bar room and a kitchen, all "most comfortably furnished." "Beds, Beds, Beds," she advertised, referring to the fact that most boarding houses and hotels were only offering rude cots. Samuel invested in a few mining claims.

In March 1872 they listed their saloon and lodging house for sale, then auctioned it off on July 3. Like many folks, they left the economic depression of Barkerville and bought the Stanley Hotel on Lightning Creek from J.J. Robertson. Interestingly Catherine is never referred to by her first name in written records. She is always Mrs. S.P. Parker.

On January 31, 1873, Samuel Parker's heart gave out and he died at age 37. He was buried in Cameronton. Left with four children and a hotel, Catherine immediately put the hotel up for sale, but records show that it was still on the market in 1875. It did not take her long to accept the proposal of Cornish miner and widower John Austin. They were married on August 23, 1873, and a year later, on July 24, Catherine gave birth to a daughter. Leaving no one out of his social commentary, Wellington Moses, in March 1875 noted, "Mr. & Mrs. Austin and daughter came over from Lightning Creek this afternoon and got drunk." Moses also records that in 1875, the Austins brought in four hurdies to the Stanley Hotel for Mrs. Austin, and that they also had a set of hurdies contracted to dance at Forest and Cunio's in Barkerville, so she was clearly a boss hurdy.

In an odd move, given the economic climate, the Austins sold the Stanley Hotel to John Fleming and started the Austin Hotel in Richfield. Judge Crease and his wife, Sarah, made a trip here in 1880, and she refers to Mrs. Austin as "a good-looking, tall, fair, lively woman with a large family." Catherine was now 40.

In 1881 Mrs. Austin moved from her hotel in Richfield and took over John Knott's "large saloon," what is now called the Barkerville Hotel. We do not know much about the Austins' remaining years in the Cariboo, but we do know that they moved to Vancouver in the 1880s. Catherine contracted pneumonia at age 50 and died on October 28, 1890. John survived her until 1903. They are buried side by side in Vancouver's Mountain View Cemetery. While some of the children married in the Cariboo others moved to Vancouver, where some of their descendents still reside.

In 2009 Newman and Wright Theatre Company at the Theatre Royal in Barkerville presented *Firestorm*, a drama about the fire of 1868. It featured Catherine Parker and attracted the attention of Parker relatives in Vancouver, who had just found the only known photo of Catherine and presented it to the theatre for the summer.

7 WILLIAMS CREEK MULTICULTURALISM: A GOLDFIELDS MOSAIC

MINORITIES WERE THE norm during gold rush days. In fact it wouldn't be too much of an exaggeration to say that there were as many accents in Barkerville as there were shovels. Men and women came from all over the world. Only the Chinese—who at times formed half the population—and the English, the colonial power, were not true minorities, though the Chinese were sometimes treated as outsiders.

The Chinese

The Chinese called North America *Gum Sahn*, or "Gold Mountain." The lure of wealth brought people to any gold rush, and the Chinese were no exception. During the California gold rush they came from poor farms to a land that was, in their eyes, uncivilized and populated by "barbarians" and "round-eyes." They came with pride in their ancient, rich culture that had bloomed while most Europeans were still living in caves. Chinese heritage included a language, customs, traditions and knowledge that in many was surpassed that of Western civilization and certainly that of rough, crude North Americans.

The Chinese were some of the first to rush to the sound of gold rattling in pans on the Fraser River. On July 3, 1858, the British consul in San Francisco, William Booker, wrote to London: "I have to report the arrival at this Port of the British Ships 'Caribbean,' 'Mooresfort,' 'Leonidas' and 'Carntyne' with Chinese passengers from Hong Kong." The *Caribbean* had 378 Chinese passengers, the *Mooresfort* had 573, the *Leonidas* had 299 and the *Carntyne* had 419—for a total of 1,669.

With an average sailing time of just under 60 days, the ships would have left Hong Kong around the middle of May, just after the first news of gold in British Columbia leaked out and raced around the world. Before the summer was out, these men were mining on the Fraser River.

Chinese who left Guangdong province for the new land were called Gold Mountain men. Poems and songs were sung about them:

If you have a daughter, don't marry her to a Gold
  Mountain boy.
Out of ten years, he will not be in bed for even one.
The spider spins webs on top of the bed.
While dust covers fully one side of the bed.

To the whites of California and British Columbia, they were "Celestials," "slant-eyes," "Chinees," "Chinks" and, in the view of most miners, came only to take the gold and rush back to China as wealthy men. In that desire the Chinese were no different from most miners, who came not to settle but to tear out the gold and retreat. The Chinese dealt with these cultural and racial conflicts by keeping a low profile when it came to mining and by forming associations of friends and neighbours called *tongs*. Records show, for example, that 77 percent of Quesnellemouth Chinese came from K'ai-p'ing. Of the population of 400, over half were members of the Chou clan from K'ai-p'ing.

The British government encouraged Chinese immigration to British Columbia, aiding large merchants like the Kwong Lee Company to import indentured labourers from the poorer Chinese provinces—a system similar to the Hudson's Bay

Company's importation of young Scots to serve in the fur trade. Chinese immigration presented the government with a body of easily controlled people who helped offset the enormous influx of Americans, who might make a move toward "annexation by occupation." In turn, the Chinese preferred what they called the British government's "square and equal rule" to Californian influence on Williams Creek. An example of Chinese preference for British rule was seen at a Fraser Canyon Cariboo Road toll gate, operated by a Chinese man. He posted a notice that "King George Men" were to pay one price and "Boston Men," Americans, double.

At the same time, Governor Douglas, taken aback by the influx of thousands of Chinese from California to the Fraser River rush, wrote to London in April 1860: "A great number of Chinese miners were also arriving and taking up mining claims on the River Bars, in the Lytton district, who are reputed to be remarkably quiet and orderly." Miners such as I.P. Diller and William Dietz were also selling their claims to Chinese as they rushed north to word of coarser gold in Cariboo. Douglas added, "They are certainly not a desirable class of people, as a permanent population, but are for the present useful as labourers, and, as consumers, of a revenue-paying character."

Judge Begbie took a different tack: "The Chinese are here. There is nothing in British Constitution to say they should not be, and while they are here we should protect them as we would any white man, and sometimes better."

By the early 1860s, over 1,000 Chinese were working on the construction of the Cariboo Road, and others were being hired to augment the Antler Creek labour force. In Barkerville the Chinese formed a large and important segment of the community. They did not restrict themselves to labouring jobs. Many saw this new land as an opportunity to move ahead and formed the new merchant class, the social elite of the new world. And although Chinatown was their business centre, Chinese shops were scattered along the length of the creek. Chinese merchants in the north end of town lost heavily during the Great Fire of

1868, but most of Chinatown (at the south end) survived and retained the character of the pre-fire town: crowded, dirty and unsafe.

While a few Chinese women came to the mining grounds, they were the exception. The fare to the new world was prohibitive, and the Chinese commitment to family, clan and village remained strong. The men intended to return to support this connection with gold. This commitment, and later the immigration restrictions and head tax, resulted in a primarily bachelor society.

By the close of the 1870s, most mining ground was either in the hands of large companies or individuals who patiently worked small claims. Unemployment became a problem. And the Chinese, though they struck for higher wages in Barkerville, were still being paid only half to two-thirds of the wage of white miners. Sentiments against Asians increased with unemployment. But scattered along the gold creeks of BC, Chinese mined and gardened, smoked a little opium (legal until 1908) and lived their solitary bachelor lives.

The next decade was a difficult one for immigrants, relieved only by work on the transcontinental railways and the vast labour force required. By the end of construction, the Chinese population of British Columbia exceeded 20,000. Over half the population of Cariboo was Chinese. Quesnelle Forks, Dog Creek and other camps were over 95 percent Chinese. By now the BC government was charging Chinese $10 per year for a licence to live in the province. In 1884 a head tax of $50 was levied on Chinese immigrants. It was raised to $100 in 1900 and $500 in 1903. No other immigrant group has had to pay a similar tax. The 1924 Asian Exclusion Act barred all Chinese, except consuls, merchants and students. The act was repealed in 1947, but not until 1966, 109 years after the first Chinese miners arrived at Fort Victoria, were nationality and race removed as criteria for selecting immigrants.

Blacks

"Africans," the official records called them. "Coloured" was carved in graves markers, lest we forget. Some, like Dan Williams, were former slaves. But they had a variety of backgrounds and occupations. Wellington Moses was a British sailor–cum-businessman, his neighbour David Lewis was a barber and many were miners like the men of the Davis Company.

In 1865 author Matthew Macfie wrote, "The descendants of the African race resident in the colonies are entitled to some notice. About 300 of them inhabit Victoria, and upwards of 100 are scattered throughout the farming settlements of the island and British Columbia. The chief part came to the country some time previous by social taboo and civil disabilities. They invested the sums they brought with them in land."

Black immigration to BC was a result of increased pressure on minorities in California, including a move to prohibit "negro" immigration. Two of this group were John K. Giscome and Henry McDame, who pre-empted land on the west side of the Fraser near Quesnellemouth in September 1862. John L. McLain pre-empted land on Bouchie Creek, which was then known as Henry's Creek or (unfortunately) Nigger Creek. McLain is buried in Barkerville. His headboard reads "J.L.B. McLain (coloured)."

The black community in Barkerville included Dr. William Jones, a dentist, and his brother Elias, both of whom were educated at Oberlin College in Ohio. Their father had purchased his freedom in North Carolina. Another brother, John Jones, taught school on Salt Spring Island, where many black immigrants settled.

Other Cariboo blacks included I.P. Gibbs, a barber who worked with Wellington Moses for a time, and Rebecca Gibbs, a washerwoman and one of Barkerville's poets, and possibly related to I.P. Gibbs. John Anderson was a correspondent for the *Elevator*, a San Francisco newspaper for Blacks. Harris Greenbury was a charcoal burner after whom Mount Greenbury near Wells is named. Mrs. Ann Wheeler lived in Richfield; Aaron Skank worked on the Dutch Bill hydraulic claim and broke his leg in a mining accident; Henry Steele kept a restaurant; Miss Amy Hickman kept a lunch house; Isaac Dickson or "Dixie" had a "Shampooing Establishment" and contributed to the *Cariboo Sentinel*. There were miners such as Charles Gray, William Port, Henry Knight and Henry Allen (who hanged himself in his cabin in April 1868). In all we have found records for close to 50 Blacks on Williams Creek.

Reporting on the Great Fire of 1868, John Anderson wrote in the *Elevator*, "Sufferers include our friends W.D. Moses, I.P. Gibbs and Miss Hickman. Mrs. R. Gibbs saved her things but lost her house." One day after the fire Amy Hickman advertised, "Forest Hill Restaurant. Miss Hickman has opened her old stand again at Richfield and is prepared to furnish Single meals at one dollar. Board $12 per week."

Like the Cornish tin miners so prevalent here, the Masons and the Canadians, the Blacks of Barkerville took strength in their ties with those of similar background. In doing so they contributed to the mosaic of the goldfields and the development of Barkerville.

Wellington Delaney Moses: 30 Years a Sailor

Like most people who came to the gold rush Wellington Delaney Moses had a life and career before Barkerville. He was 50 years old, 30 years a sailor, when he packed his bags to move north. Moses was born on Grand Cayman Island to Levant Moses, a mariner, on May 7, 1815. It is likely Levant had been a slave and doubtful, according to the records of slaves and owners, that Wellington was. There is no record of Wellington's mother, though he notes in his 1870s journal that he dreams of his mother and grandmother on Grand Cayman. In the census of 1805 his family is not listed under "free people of color" on the island.

According to British Merchant Marine records, Moses went to sea as a ship's steward in 1830 when he was 15 years old. At age 29 he was still in the Merchant Marines, was five feet seven inches tall, had black hair and black eyes and could write. His records note that for three years he was in the American "foreign service," but never in the navy. This might be when he appeared on board the *Jane*, which had departed from Matamoros, Mexico, and docked in New Orleans on May 5, 1836. He was recorded as a cook and a "Black." When not at sea he was residing on Mile End Road, in London.

Records show that five years later Moses was living in Liverpool, and on February 25, 1841, he married Rebecca Montgomery, daughter of tailor William Montgomery, at the Church of St. Martin in the Fields. They had a child, Rebecca Jane, on March 12, 1842. Strangely they do not appear among the 22 people with the last name Moses in the 1841 or '51 Liverpool census, so they may have moved back to Mile End Road in London, where there are several Moseses recorded with no first name. Or they may have moved to New York.

They next appear in California in the 1852 census, where Wellington was listed as a 38-year-old black cook, born in the West Indies, with a previous residence of New York. Rebecca was listed as being 29, black, and born in New York (likely an error). While in California, Moses became involved in civil rights. He was member of the financial committee for *Mirror of the Times* (1857–62), a newspaper for Blacks founded by two African-American businessmen, James Townsend and Mifflin W. Gibbs. Gibbs later moved to Victoria and was likely related to Rebecca Gibbs, Barkerville's washerwoman and poet.

Moses was a member of the Pioneer Committee, which lobbied Governor Douglas for black immigration to British Columbia. He arrived in Victoria in May 1858 on the *Commodore*. He was one of two men organizing the move of several hundred black families. Reverend Edward Cridge records in May 1858 that Moses had "lost his wife and children." The quote suggests he and Rebecca may have had a second child, and the timeline suggests they may have contracted some illness on the voyage. Just months later, on December 13, 1858, he married Sarah Jane Douglas, a black immigrant from America.

In 1861 Lady Franklin and her niece Sophia Cracroft were sailing around the world looking for Lady Franklin's husband,

Sir John Franklin, who was lost in the Arctic. Arriving at Victoria Sophia stayed at a small hotel about which she noted, "It is kept by a coloured man and his wife—the former, strange to say was very nearly going out with my dear Uncle—only his wife at last refused to let him go."

Sophia's uncle was, of course, Sir John Franklin, and she is referring to his voyage of 1845, 13 years previous, when Moses was in Liverpool or London. Moses would have sailed into a frozen Arctic death with Franklin, had his wife at the time, Rebecca, not convinced him to stay. Sophia goes on to say:

> They are very respectable people. He is a hair cutter & has a shop—the naval people especially patronise him (Mr Moses) & his wife [Sarah] has the reputation of being a first rate cook.
>
> Considering Moses' newly found naval background it now makes sense why they patronised him, and why he might have sailed with Sir Franklin. He was a long time sailor.
>
> They are probably one generation if not farther from being pure Negro, & Mr. Moses calls himself an Englishman, which he is politically & therefore justly. She is a queer being, wears [a] long sweeping gown without crinoline—moves slowly & has a sort of stately way (in intention at least) which is very amusing. Sometimes she ties a coloured handkerchief round her head like the American Negroes (she is from Baltimore). The language of both is very good.

One year later, on September 23, 1862 the *Colonist* ran the following item:

> Attempted Suicide—Mrs. Moses, the wife of Wellington Delaney Moses, the colored barber, suffering from a violent attack of the green-eyed lobster, plunged into the water of James Bay at the foot of the bathhouse stairs, last night; but repenting of her rashness after undergoing

immersion, screamed loudly for help, and was drawn to dry land by passersby. After she had got safely out she endevored [sic] to throw herself into the water again, but was seized by a policeman and escorted to the Barracks. The woman alleges as a reason for her conduct that her husband has eloped with another woman.

Moses, in fact, had not eloped. His wife Sarah was delusional. While in Victoria, Moses operated the Pioneer Shaving Saloon and Bath House. It is not clear when Moses packed up his renowned "Hair Invigorator," a supposed cure for baldness, and left for Barkerville on his own. He was shaving faces and cutting hair in Barkerville in the spring of 1865, though it appears he came to Victoria for the winters in the early years. On December 23, 1869, Moses got a letter from Sarah saying she had gone to England. In spite of previous back-and-forth correspondence between the two of them, he never mentioned her again and no longer made winter trips to Victoria.

In Barkerville he ran a series of barbershops, or "Fashion Saloons," which carried a selection of ribbons, silks, combs and other fine articles. Moses kept a diary of Barkerville life, paying as much attention to the new women in town as he paid to his accounts. His incomplete journals, while difficult to read because of his phonetic spelling and absence of punctuation, are a wealth of information on the stage arrivals, births, deaths and gossip of the town, as this book frequently indicates.

Moses's main claim to fame in the Cariboo is his testimony in the case of James Barry, who was charged with the murder of Charles Morgan Blessing near Pinegrove House in 1866. Moses was travelling with Barry and Blessing but went ahead when they reached Bloody Edward's House at Pinegrove. Later, when Blessing did not show up in Barkerville with Barry, Moses questioned Barry about the disappearance. Barry replied that he had left Blessing on the road. When Blessing's body was found with a bullet in the head, Moses suspected Barry—particularly after a distinctive tie pin was found in the possession of a hurdy, who claimed that Barry had given it to her. Moses knew the tie pin had belonged to Blessing, and Barry was arrested and later convicted, mainly on basis of Moses's testimony. He was hanged at Richfield on August 27, 1867.

Moses (never called Wellington or Delaney) was often described by others as popular or well regarded, but it is not clear what that impression was based on. He was popular with the demimonde, sold liquor to Natives, was involved in fights, consorted with madams and prostitutes, and in 1878 was sentenced to one month in Richfield jail, "arrested on a false charge of [giving liquor to] Indian woman Annie Lesure and [making her] drunk."

His shop was burned in the fire of 1868 at a loss of $2,000, but by October 23 the *Sentinel* wrote, "W.D. Moses is at his old stand adjacent to Sterling and Barry's Saloon." He had a new shop built shortly before his death in 1890 [see page 202]. He is buried in Cameronton cemetery in an unmarked grave.

First Nations

The Natives of BC were an active part of the gold rush at all levels: they helped miners find gold, fought off invading miners in the Fraser Canyon and the Chilcotin, provided knowledge of the country, became packers, worked on claims and married many of the first Europeans to settle in the country.

The Native peoples of the Cariboo goldfields called themselves the Takulli, the "people who go upon the water." When Alexander Mackenzie canoed across the continent in 1792–93, 12 years before Lewis and Clark traversed the United States, he met these people and learned of the Grease Trail that led him to the western sea. Simon Fraser followed in 1808, navigating the river that was to bear his name, to the sea.

Oral histories of some bands still tell the stories of these first whites. One story, told by the Shuswap people around Soda Creek over three generations, recalls that some of the Soda Creek people were about to leave to go west into the Chilcotin when a runner came to the village with news of strange people coming down the river. It was Fraser, heading for the sea.

Mackenzie and Fraser, and the fur traders who followed, called the tribes of the upper Fraser the "Atnah" or "Carriers," named for a custom surrounding death. When a man died his body was placed on a pyre and his widow stayed near until forced away by the flames. The bones were later gathered and placed in a bark container that the widow carried on her back during waking hours for one year.

The Takulli were fishermen who followed the spawning salmon along waters of the Bowron River upstream to the chain of lakes, where they used weirs and barriers to funnel the fish into baskets. With natural fibres they fashioned dip-nets similar to those still used today by Natives on traditional, hereditary fishing rocks.

During the spring and summer months they lived in permanent or semi-permanent villages of rectangular lodges. In fall and winter, when they followed the salmon to lakes such as Bowron, they built villages of dwellings called Keekwillies— semi-subterranean circular pits covered with a conical structure of poles and earth. One such village was at the Bowron Lake outlet, a site with about 10 dwellings that unfortunately slid into the lake as a result of undermining caused by the 1964 Anchorage, Alaska, earthquake. Smaller camps were scattered along the portage trails of the chain.

When miners moved into the area in the mid-1800s there were few reports of Natives. One early miner was Neil Wilson, the "Swamp Angel" or "Swampy," a man who moved through the area's history like a fall mist rising from warm water. One gold rush myth, still perpetuated today, is that Wilson was "brought up by the Indians." In fact, he was born in Sweden in 1833 and arrived here when he was 31. He was named for his early exploration of the upper Cariboo River, then called the Swamp River. Swampy fished the lakes to augment his prospecting and mining. One ounce of gold bought one sockeye salmon or a dozen rainbow trout.

Swampy travelled through a country few others saw, and on an early trip to Bowron and Bear Lakes he reportedly met an First Nations woman who said she was the last of her tribe. The rest of her people were buried on Deadman's Island (now Pavich Island), killed by smallpox. More recent archaeological work on the island has not found any graves, only pits used for storage. However, Native fishing and hunting grounds were about to be drastically changed by the men who came to dig for gold.

South of the Quesnelle River, the Carrier territory gave way to the Shuswaps, and west of the Fraser was the stronghold of the Chilcotins. The exact boundaries are still being negotiated. When Peter Dunleavy and his party came up the Fraser and camped at the mouth of the Chilcotin in the spring, he met a Shuswap man called Tomah whose cousin Long Bacheese later led them north from Kamloops to the first gold strike on the Horsefly River. Despite the minor "wars" or skirmishes in the Fraser Canyon, Native peoples were soon working for miners as packers and labourers.

In his 1862 diary Samuel Hathaway wrote, "There are numbers of Indians all through this region . . . all along the route. They work pretty well, packing over the portages, loading wagons and boats, etc. and the squaws bring us branches of grass to sell."

Showing that First Nations people were well aware of the concept of supply and demand, George Eves reported in May 1862 that "packing is done from Forks of Quesnelle to Williams Creek principally by Indians 30¢ [per pound] but has recently gone up to 40¢, and $5 worth of grub for the trip.

The first contacts were not always welcomed or civilized. Gold Commissioner Philip H. Nind complained from Beaver Lake in the fall of 1861 that men "are in the habit of giving whiskey to their squaws and violating them." He warned that this must stop and that he would prosecute any offenders he catches.

Many miners, merchants and settlers took Native wives. William Pinchbeck Jr., whose father was an early settler near Williams Lake, south on the Cariboo Road, wrote, "There were very few women, white women, in the country in earlier days, except for an occasional one coming in with a settler husband. When a man wanted to marry he had to take an Indian or half-breed wife, but they made good wives."

The names Dunleavy, Sellars, Nason, Mason, Bowe, Rohr,

Moffat, Brown, Whitecott, English, Resendes and many more, soon spoke of mixed-race marriages. Most of these men stayed with their Native wives; others, like Joe Mason and Ithiel Nason, deserted them when white women became accessible through immigration.

The First Nations people who worked and lived along the gold creeks came from a variety of bands and areas. Some nicknames can help differentiate between indigenous people and those who travelled here, some from as far away as the US and the coast. Sarah was a Klickitat woman who likely came north with the early cattle drives; Hyda (or Haida) Annie was surely from the coast, and "Gentle Annie" sometimes went home to the "saltchuck." Scroogie, Louise and Mary Baker were known as Lillooets. Mary Ann Hallas was a well-known packer. "Joseph, a Similkameen Indian aged about 30 years," was interred at Richfield by Father McGluckin in 1867. Nellie Bouche, "married" for a time to Ithiel Nason and later to a Flynn, was a Carrier Metis from Fort St. James. And there is Nikel Palsk, whose origins are unclear, who was hanged at Richfield for the murder of miner John Morgan on the Cariboo Road.

White miners seemed to make little attempt to learn Native names, so they became know by nicknames—Haida (or Hyda) Annie, Full Moon, Lucy Bones—or just first names. (As we know, the practice of using nicknames was not confined to the First Nations residents, but was widespread among all ethnic groups.) In all over 40 First Nations people can be identified by name. Of the few written records of Natives, most appear in the newspapers or police records surrounding illegal liquor sales by whites. However, a close look at mining photos shows many Native labourers, and we know that the first Hurdy dancers hired by James Loring were Native women. The Dominion Day events had races, "Indian sports" and other events for "Siwashes," the contemporary term for First Nations people.

Barkerville diaries and newspapers refer to Natives going "to the lower country" or the "saltchuck" for winter and returning in the spring. In *The Days of Augusta*, by Jean Speare, Mary Augusta Tappage remembers Lillooets going north from a First Nation's point of view, an aural window into another time, place and culture. A couple of verses illustrate the journey:

That was a big cloud of dust way down
to the south in the spring, yes.
It was the Lillooet Indians coming north,
coming north to the goldfields
up by Barkerville.

They go north into that country to work,
to work all the time, hard,
horses and wagons, women and children,
and dogs, hiyu dogs, all going
up by Barkerville.

It was the Lillooets going by in the spring
with packing horses, packing freight, yes,
into the mines somewhere in the mountains
and into the creeks
up by Barkerville.

These excerpts are consistent with a letter from Harry Jones to Louis Lebourdais:

The Lillooet Indians were in the habit of spending the summer months in Barkerville in the [18]70s—their camping ground was on the East side of Williams Creek, opposite the hospital—the same camping [site] every year, as it was their custom to camp on the same ground when traveling up and down the road. Their favorite spot on Lighting Creek was a green patch of ground near the Victoria Shafthouse.

The story of First Nations in the goldfields and specifically on Williams Creek is still unfolding, and we can expect that within a few years their story will told by an Aboriginal interpreter on the streets of Barkerville.

The Cameron claim.
CHRISTOPHER FULTON, 1863. CITY OF VANCOUVER ARCHIVES AM54-S4-: LP 169.

Cameronton. FREDERICK DALLY, 1848.

Government buildings in Richfield.

Pack train on Main Street, Barkerville. MAJOR JAMES SKITT MATTHEWS, 1898.

Kafue Copper Company Dredge, Barkerville, 1920s.

Mucho Oro claim, Stouts Gulch.

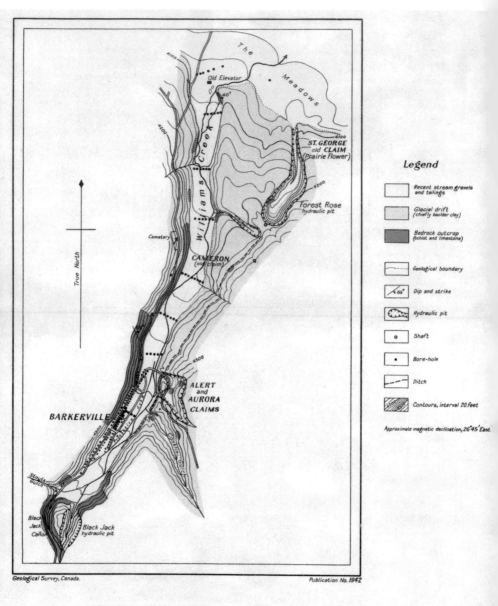

Geological Survey, Canada.

Publication No. 1942

Part of **Williams Creek,** Cariboo District, British Columbia.

Map of Williams Creek. W.A. JOHNSTON, 1921. GEOLOGICAL SURVEY OF CANADA.

John A. "Cariboo" Cameron, ca. 1870.

Judge Matthew Baillie Begbie, ca. 1870.

William Barker, 1860s.

Old timers in Barkerville (*left to right*): James Stone, John Bibby, Richard Berry, Sam A. Rogers, Alex Coutts, George Isaac and William Fitchie, 1906.

James Anderson, the bard of Barkerville.

The last of the Cariboo camels.

Portrait of Catherine Parker.

Hurdy-Gurdy girls.

8 CULTURE AND DAILY LIFE

Gold Rush Music

Barkerville was a noisy town with its cacophonous blend of mechanical and animal sounds. The creek rushed; the Cornish wheels thumped and squeaked; wagon wheels crunched in gravel; animals bellowed, neighed and barked; blacksmiths' shops echoed with the clang of metal being worked; doors slammed; men shouted; skirts rustled; and from the many saloons came the sounds of the fiddle, concertina, piano, cornet, and a variety of other brass and stringed instruments. Barkerville was making music.

When men and women left their homes for a new land, they brought a few items to remind them of a home they might never see again and that might help pass some of the lonely, weary hours. As a traveller today might throw a guitar over her shoulder or stick a harmonica in his pocket, so the gold rush men and women brought their musical instruments to the creeks.

Instruments that were popular in the 1860s and that were recorded in Barkerville were those easily carried—the fiddle, guitar, banjo, cornet, clarinet, concertina, flute, bombardon and tin whistle. As families established roots, the most popular instruments of the day—the piano, harmonium and organ—

were brought in. Many are the tales of men who packed a particular piano over some mountain trail. Parlour music was a family's most common entertainment, with an occasional outing to a church concert or the Theatre Royal.

In saloons and the theatre, popular music was played, songs such as "The Old Oaken Bucket," "Dixie Land," "Yellow Rose of Texas," "Castles in the Air," and "Maggie May," as well as the many songs of Stephen Foster that often went with a minstrel show. Poet James Anderson wrote locally themed songs, and miners brought songs from the California rush written by "Old Put," the pseudonym of John A. Stone, and tunes from Australia that told mining stories and folklore.

Then there were the songs of the homeland, the Scottish and Irish tunes and patriotic British hymns such as "Rule Britannia," "Men of Harlech," "British Grenadiers" and, at every concert, "God Save the Queen." St. Saviour's Church Institute, begun by the Reverend Reynard, quickly became a focal point for town musicians. The frequent concerts were social highlights for the town.

For a miner, an institute concert began with a hike to town and a visit to a bathhouse to remove not only the grime of a mine but also some of the aches gathered along the way. Then came dinner at the Wake-Up Jake cafe or a saloon and a leisurely stroll down the boardwalk to St. Saviour's to enjoy a "Benefit for the Town Band." Tickets were one dollar, or $1.50 for a reserved seat.

Arthur Bushby made diary notes about the music he played in Barkerville, which gives us some sense of his musical life:

> **1873, Jan 7:** Dined with Ross Hitch & Bowron at "Wake up, Jake" smoked pipe at Bowron's, played on Harmonium.
> **Jan 8:** Went down Town by appt to Band practice, amusing! My Chinaman Ah Fou just asked me if band Hyu sabe music"—could not say they did.
> **Jan 21:** . . . making progress on E flat Horn, gum bad though—played violin.

Jan 29: Band practice—and rehearsed songs &c at Dodd's Saloon where there is a piano—shake down at Hitch's after writing some verses.

Feb 8: Rehearsal—Amusing. I'm supposed to accompany no music and most of the things unknown to me—the fact of the "Judge" taking his seat at the piano is supposed to suffice!

Feb 9: Performance a great success - House crammed Gomar Johns recitation of Lady Jane really first rate. Miss F. Wilson acted very neatly reminded me somewhat of Mrs. Keeley. Sang Local Hits—encored.

Mar 1: Rehearsal in afternoon dined Lunched at Hotel Performance in evng a success I pray I sang Village B'smith & Skipper and his boy.

For many of Barkerville's residents, music and theatre were an important part of their life, whether it be in church, a saloon or at the Theatre Royal's concerts.

JAMES ANDERSON—BARKERVILLE'S POET LAUREATE

Every developing nation or region has its unofficial poet laureate. The Klondike had Robert Service; Australia had Banjo Paterson—and the Cariboo had James Anderson.

Anderson was born into a prominent family in Coupar Angus, Scotland, in about 1835. He received a good education at the Dollar Institute and in 1860 was married to Lucy Lechmere, whose landed gentry family went back to the 1200s. The following year they had a son, David. In 1863 Anderson left his family and, like so many Scots before him, crossed the ocean to seek his fortune in a new land.

Anderson's significance on Williams Creek is not because of any fortune he found as a partner in the Prairie Flower claim or the Ayrshire Lass on Lightning Creek. He is remembered for the songs and poems he wrote, published and performed. Anderson became the miners' voice. The feelings he captured are preserved in his book *Sawney's Letters*. Anderson and John McLaren published a weekly manuscript that they read aloud in coffee saloons, and the *Cariboo Sentinel* often printed his verse. He was an original member of the Cariboo Amateur Dramatic Association, where his writing and performing skills were in great demand. He often used tunes from popular songs and composed lyrics that were more relevant to the miners.

In later years Anderson wrote that "barring Sawney's letters I would have been pleased had the others rhymes been buried in the tailings of Williams Creek. They were written on the spur of the moment, and for the moment and are not worthy of reproduction." Yet decades later his rhymes such as "The Rough but Honest Miner," "Waiting for the Mail," "Dead Broke," "Hard Luck," "The Prospector's Shanty," "The Young Man from Canada," "The Dancing Girls of Cariboo," "The Bar Room Song" and many more were still remembered and repeated by Cariboo miners.

When Anderson left the Cariboo in November 1871, he took over his father's estate of Pitfar near Dollar, Clackmannanshire. After Lucy died of breast cancer in 1886, he moved to Tarvit Mill House in Fife. He remarried to his cousin Catherine van Someren in 1903 and moved to Stainforth, Yorks, England, to be near his son and grandson, both doctors. He died there on September 14, 1922. He did not take a fortune with him but left a fortune in words to be enjoyed by many generations. His last lines on leaving the Cariboo are an appropriate epitaph:

'Twas all I asked of thee,
One handful of thy plenteous golden grain,
Had'st thou but yielded, I'd have sung "Farewell!"
And home again.
But, time on time, defeat!
Ah, cold and cruel, callous Cariboo!
Have eight years' honest persevering toil
No more of you?

Once again James Anderson was speaking not only for himself but for those thousands of men and women who had asked for just one handful and left defeated.

Newspaper Pioneers

The founder of Barkerville's *Cariboo Sentinel,* George Wallace, first appeared on the British Columbia scene in 1862 as a *Toronto Globe* correspondent with the Overlanders' party. Wallace went to Victoria at the end of the trek, where he tried to start a new weekly called the *Globe.* This venture failed before a single issue was printed, so he joined the *British Colonist* staff. In spring 1863 he and Charles W. Allen launched the *Daily Evening Express,* which published from April 26, 1863, to February 12, 1865, and vigorously promoted the union of the separate colonies of British Columbia and Vancouver Island.

Wallace left his partner to run the paper and headed north to the Cariboo where on August 9, 1863, he received Free Miner Certificate #65 and became a partner in the Aurora claim. On April 5, 1865, the *Colonist* reported on Wallace's return to journalism:

> Cariboo Newspaper. The steamer *Enterprise* carried up yesterday morning a printing press, and part of the regular material for a newspaper, which is about to be established at Williams Creek, Cariboo, by Mr. George Wallace, formerly of the *Evening Express.* The name of the new journal is to be the *Cariboo Express.* The press was supplied from the Colonist office.

The press George Wallace used to publish the *Cariboo Sentinel* (the name *Express* was never used) came to Barkerville with its own history. It was originally owned by the Society for the Propagation of the Gospel of Paris and had been sent with its archaic French type to do similar service in California. In 1856 it was shipped up the coast to a Roman Catholic bishop named Demers in Victoria. It was the first press west of the Great Lakes in British North America. When the gold rush hit the colonies in 1858, the *Vancouver Island Gazette* printed on the rented Demers press. But the *Gazette* published only eight issues, and when Demers tried to found a French newspaper it lasted only two issues.

Demers sold the press to Amor De Cosmos who used it to found the *British Colonist*. And in 1863 Amor De Cosmos sold the press to George Wallace, who brought it north, in pieces, on men's backs, over the mountain trails to Barkerville.

Amor De Cosmos sold the *Victoria Colonist* for 12.5 cents, or one bit, per issue, whereas the Barkerville *Sentinel* was a costly one dollar. Still, miners eagerly awaited the *Sentinel*. The circulation was about 500, and it was later reported that the advertisements were a "mine of wealth." Wallace was content with one season's profits of $3,500, and in 1866 he sold to Alexander Allan and Warren Lambert.

Allan was not as successful as Wallace. Two years after buying the paper, he wrote a bitter letter to his mother explaining that his poor circumstances were the result of the paper.

I have for the last 2 years owned and conducted the first newspaper ever published in these extreme north western settlements . . . but it has not been a source of profit to me, on the contrary it has been a constant source of annoyance and expense and I am only too glad that I have managed to sell out of it a few weeks ago. My intention is now to resume mining by which ere the season closes I hope to realize sufficient means to enable me to pay a visit to the old sod once more . . .

Even now when I have concluded a sale of the business the sum I receive will not extricate me from the debts I owe. If I could collect all that is due to me I should be clear with the world.

Allan obviously had troubles. A letter of January 1870 bemoans his "misfortune, disappointment and lack of opportunity" and goes on to describe his continued bad luck and the recession that was affecting Barkerville. Times and work were hard. Allan was not able to stand the gaff.

After Allan, the *Cariboo Sentinel* continued under various editors, including John McLaren, for several years. The last editor-proprietor was another Overlander of '62, Robert Holloway. Holloway's wife joined him in Victoria soon after he came out. In 1864 they had a daughter and in 1869 a son. Holloway journeyed to the Cariboo in 1865 as a prospector but chose to winter more comfortably with his wife and children in Victoria. In 1868 he bought the *Cariboo Sentinel* from "Wallace and Dearburg," indicating that Wallace may have retained some interest when he sold to Allan and Lambert. Holloway had no sooner taken over than the 1868 fire destroyed the *Sentinel* office (but spared the printing press). By some accounts Holloway then moved the paper to Richfield. When the *Cariboo Sentinel* folded in 1875, Holloway moved to Victoria where he worked for the *Colonist* and later for the provincial government. He died in 1909.

George Wallace's life after the *Cariboo Sentinel* was decidedly more interesting than Holloway's. After selling out in 1866, he was elected to the Legislative Assembly and brought machinery from San Francisco to begin a newspaper in the Columbia River's Big Bend Country, site of a gold rush. The newspaper failed, but he did eventually publish the *British Columbia Tribune* at Yale for a season, leaving "in consequence of pressing business of a private nature . . . in the old country."

Wallace's next employment was a long step for a Cariboo newspaper editor. In Japan he was contracted to manage "The Great Dragon Troupe" of native acrobats and jugglers. This evidently brought him profits of over half a million dollars. A few years later he took a pair of celebrated Siamese twins (most likely Chang and Eng Bunker) on a similar tour for similar profits. Wallace then settled in London, married and had two sons. In 1881 he was back in Canada as a journalist, his wife having died a few years previous. His obituary in the *Montreal Star* on May 19, 1887, said he had died about 10 days before, "having never recovered from the shock of his wife's death." He was, according to the *Star,* "universally respected" and "left many friends."

The little Demers press that Wallace had used to found the *Cariboo Sentinel* churned out newspapers on Williams Creek and elsewhere for many years after Wallace, Allan and Holloway left

PHOTOGRAPHY

Photography, as practised by the photographers of Williams Creek such as Louie Blanc, Frederick Dally, Charles Gentile and saloon-keeper Christopher Fulton, was in its infancy in 1870. The first photograph to attract any significant public attention was the daguerreotype, a permanent image of superb detail. The medium was announced with great excitement in January 1839, but each photo was an original that depended on the viewing angle to make it a negative or positive, so they were inappropriate for hanging.

Collodion, a hard, colourless transparent film that brought in the wet-plate process, was the next major development. It took a skilled photographer to prepare the plates, expose them while the emulsion was still wet, and then return to the darkroom to develop the image. The advantages were a glass negative that would produce prints and an exposure time reduced to five seconds. Even so, portraits typically show a tense, unsmiling subject, desperately trying to hold still for several seconds.

Goldfield travellers often stopped in cities like Detroit or San Francisco to have "a likeness taken" and sent home before they disappeared for months or years into the wilderness. The photos they purchased were usually ambrotypes (which Louie Blanc advertised in his studio; see page 198), small wet-plate negatives with a dark cloth or varnish backing that caused the negative to appear positive. Also popular were the faster and cheaper tintypes. A disadvantage of both was the lack of duplicate prints, like the modern Polaroid, but tintypes were soon being exposed in special multi-lensed cameras producing enough copies for the whole family. Although most tintypes were crude, a skilled photographer could produce striking photos. Tintypists prospered as late as the 1930s in North America.

Frederick Dally was one of the most prolific and important photographers on the creek and also a dentist by trade. He was born at Southwark, London, England, on July 29, 1838, the youngest of nine children, and apprenticed with a linen and woolen draper. At age 24 he decided that British Columbia offered better prospects, so he packed up some merchandise and set up shop in Victoria. Four years later he turned to photography. His best-known images were taken from 1867–68 along the Cariboo Road and in Barkerville. He sold his photos and albums to miners, visitors and government offices such as the colonial offices in London. He charged them an average of five dollars for original prints, and just a dollar for copies. On an 1870

Barkerville. After surviving the fire of 1868 it went to Richfield for 10 years. Later the press was used in Yale and Kamloops to print the *Inland Sentinel*. The press was retired in 1887 when it went to the Sisters of St. Anne in Kamloops, who later placed it in their Victoria convent museum.

Medical Care and the Royal Cariboo Hospital

Digging Cariboo gold was hard, dangerous work, and miners suffered a variety of ailments, from fractures and heart attacks to diarrhea and syphilis. Doctors followed miners to the creeks and did their best in what was still a primitive science to alleviate suffering. However, there was no place for doctors to practise and patients to recuperate.

Miner John Morris wrote: "Sickness is very prevalent throughout the creek; a dangerous fever has broke out amongst us and carried off several of our fellows. There is no provision yet made for the indigent sick; a hospital is much required."

Barkerville and Cameronton had barely been born when a typhoid epidemic, caused in part by poor sanitation practices, raged up and down Williams Creek. In the early years of mining on Williams Creek, it was not unusual for old shafts to be used as latrines, and water to become polluted. How many were affected is unclear, but we know that at least four were diagnosed as having died of "mountain fever"—a general term that covered a variety of illnesses, including typhoid. Others likely succumbed to the disease without ever being diagnosed—not surprising in an era when doctors still attributed illness to foul winds, poor humours, bad blood and poor air.

One such doctor was Barkerville physician Dr. John Chipp. Considered well educated by the standards of the day, Chipp had earned a diploma from the British Royal College of Surgeons in 1857 and that same year earned another diploma from the Master Wardens and Assistants of the Society of the Art and Mystery of Apothecaries in London. After the typhoid outbreak he wrote a letter to the *Cariboo Sentinel* debunking the popular myth that Cariboo's climate and elevation were inherently damaging to one's health. He also had some interesting thoughts on the cause of the typhoid outbreak:

Much has been said about the climate here; that it is unhealthy in the summer and all but uninhabitable on account of the severe cold in the winter.

The chief support of the first statement is based on that of the elevation of the country, but looking at its effects on the human economy I have failed to see that a residence among these hills is as damaging to the constitution as is generally believed.

In the summer of '63, there was an endemic fever with typhoid symptoms which proved fatal to several, and although confined to Williams Creek, I believe it was not the climate but the amount of vegetable matter which, falling from the clumps of trees, let loose the poisonous miasma.

Every season sees the timber being cleared from our neighborhood, and the miner in his cabin and the merchant in his store will find this makes the climate more healthy.

As to the severity of the winter, this has been greatly exaggerated. During the past season frostbites and scurvy were entirely banished, better cabins and a better supply of vegetables have expelled those evils.

The general health of the Creek at present is good, and I have no doubt that a moderately warm season and plenty of 'dust' will keep both body and mind healthy.

Unfortunately the good doctor was not entirely correct; Cariboo men would continue to die of scurvy, frostbite and typhoid for the next 50 years. Eventually it became clear that the region's medical resources were totally overwhelmed by the demand for treatment. A public meeting in response to the typhoid epidemic held on July 22, 1863, resolved that a hospital was "imperatively demanded."

At the time, such care was not considered government responsibility, so miners sold subscriptions and held a ball to raise funds for a hospital. A week later a design and location were decided on. The location was Marysville, on the creek's east side below Cameronton. In August, Judge Begbie and Gold Commissioner O'Reilly laid the foundation, and on October 1 the "dingy, quaint-looking log cabin" institution was opened. The Williams Creek Hospital consisted of one ward, a doctor's office and a kitchen. It was several years before a bathroom was added. While several doctors had private practices on the creek, Dr. Walter Shaw Black, who had trained in London and came to the Cariboo from the Australia rushes, was appointed as hospital surgeon.

In the first nine months 32 men were admitted. By July 1, 26 had been discharged, 3 had died and 3 remained in hospital. Illness and accidents of all kinds taxed the skill of the surgeons, and some even invented treatments for ailments they had never encountered before. In 1866, Dr. Thomas Bell did some plastic surgery on a man whose nose had been bitten off in a fight. In an early example of reconstructive surgery, Bell facilitated a living graft by tying the man's arm to his head. With one end of the skin graft on the host arm and the other on the nose, he grew the man a new, if misshapen, nose.

Already the facility was in debt by a third of its budget. Hospital board chairman James Wattie, an Overlander, appealed to Governor Seymour for a bailout and $6,000 a year for future operation of the hospital. Newspaper editorials asked how the hospital could continue without government support, suggesting that Cariboo miners were heavy tax contributors and therefore should be given financial support.

But miners did not sit back and wait for government grants to roll in. They held a concert and ball to raise more funds. After much negotiation, the questioning of every expense from beef to brandy and chloroform to firewood (and in particular the costs of a doctor and steward), and several months delay, the government in Victoria agreed to a yearly grant of $6,000. In 1867 the facility was dubbed the *Royal* Cariboo Hospital, for unknown reasons. The hospital averaged 20 to 40 inpatients and as many as 300 outpatients a year, with two to three casualties per year.

The hospital experienced more than its share of troubles. It was always scrambling for funds, often in debt. Surgeons commonly had to wait months to be paid and often volunteered their services free of charge. There were charges of misappropriation of funds, incorrect billing, mismanagement, incompetence and arguments between the surgeon in charge and the board. Arguments over costs and who should pay were still rampant in 1881.

In 1891 the Marysville site was abandoned when the hospital burned down. A new hospital, also called the Royal Cariboo Hospital, was built on the old Cariboo Road above Cameronton, a site now marked with a cairn.

According to 1892 Sessional Papers:

> In consequence of the destruction by fire in June last, of the old building, a contract was let tender to McIntyre and Pinkerton, for the erection of a new Hospital building, the contract price being $2,645, and consists of two wards (capable of accommodating five patients in each), hall, kitchen, bathroom, steward's room, and surgery. . . A good cellar and outbuildings have also been put up. The total cost will somewhat exceed $3500. Although not yet completed, it has been occupied for the past month and the patients express great satisfaction at the comfort it affords.

The next year the hospital was "further improved by an additional verandah around the front of the building and the securing of sufficient terra cotta pipe for chimneys. A protection from fire is now afforded by the building of a tank on the hill with pipes leading from there to the Hospital."

This hospital served until 1925, when it closed for 10 years. In 1934 a new society formed to reopen the hospital in response to the Wells mining boom. The resurrection was short-lived. On March 29, 1936, at 4 a.m. the hospital burned to the ground. Miss Olsen, the matron, was the only occupant and escaped. This hospital was not replaced for at the same time the Cariboo Gold Quartz Hospital opened in Wells to cater to Cariboo Gold Quartz miners. The Wells hospital closed in 1967 and is now an apartment building.

Religious Life on Williams Creek

While the Methodist church and St. Saviour's Anglican church (see pages 147-50) are the only physical evidence of Christianity on the creeks, they were not the only missions in the area to target miners. In her book *Canada's Gold Rush Church*, Joan Weir details the various efforts employed by religious groups to bring the miners closer to God.

Roman Catholics arrived first; in 1861 Father Charles Grandidier held a service in Richfield and was intimidated by what he viewed as immoral and profane miners. Also in 1861, Anglican reverends Luden Brown and Christopher Knipe held services in Antler Creek. By 1862 Knipe had unofficial headquarters at Van Winkle, Reverend Sheepshanks was holding services at Antler, Reverend R.J. Dundas was visiting regularly and Bishop George Hills made several visits.

None was particularly successful; all were appalled at the rough and rowdy miners who reserved Sundays for saloon going, gambling, relaxing, drinking and fornicating. When Reverend Brown spoke out publicly against such behaviour, not a single miner showed up for his next service. Nevertheless, in 1863 Sheepshanks paid $500 for a lot in Richfield and built a small log church. Methodists Ephraim Evans and Arthur Browning did the same in Cameronton.

Weir says that as the mining community matured the

men turned more toward church life, but at the same time the missionaries were short of funds and discouraged. In 1866 and 1867 not one service was held along the creek. Then, in 1867, Welsh miners were granted a lot for the Cambrian Hall and began to hold weekly church services there. Organized religion really established itself in 1868 with the arrival of Anglican reverend James Reynard (who built St. Saviour's), Thomas Derrick at the Methodist Church, and the Roman Catholics at St. Patrick's in Richfield.

Barkerville poet and social commentator James Anderson expressed the winterer's disdain for deciduous summer transients in this March 1866 verse:

We've three toom kirks upon this creek—
Our ministers are a sae meek—
They canna live a year up here,
But gang below for warmer cheer;
But maybe this is just as weel,
When they're awa' so is the devil.

Following the Great Fire of 1868, clergy seemed to stay for longer periods of time in Barkerville. While it remained difficult to attract a congregation, three churches were soon vying, unsuccessfully, for the miners' attention. Miners worked hard and played hard, and church was not a part of either activity.

The Anglican St. Saviour's was the iconic church in Barkerville, built by Rev. Reynard, but he could get no help with construction and wrote about how the harsh winters affected his small family.

The Methodists built close behind the Anglicans and sometimes harranged the Anglican congregation. The Roman Catholics established St. Patrick's church in Richfield. Early in 1861 a service was held, though Father Charles Grandidier did not stay. Close behind the church, the Richfield cemetery—the burying ground for Catholics and Chinese—was established. While there were several Jewish men and a few Jewish women in town, no mention is made of their worship; to our knowledge there was never a synagogue.

A VISITOR'S GUIDE TO WILLIAMS CREEK

PART 3

9 INTRODUCTION

Barkerville as a Historic Site

The federal government was initially off the mark in recognizing the importance of the town of Barkerville and the Cariboo gold rush. Barkerville was not only the centre of the Cariboo goldfields, which were the catalyst for the economic and political development of British Columbia, but it was also the terminus of the great wagon road from Yale, completed in 1865. Over the next three decades the historical value of Williams Creek in general and Barkerville in particular was pointed out to the provincial government by the Cariboo Historical Society (now the Friends of Barkerville and Cariboo Historical Society) and a few remaining residents, such as Fred Ludditt.

Fred Ludditt came to Barkerville for the second rush in the 1930s and stayed until the outbreak of the Second World War. He staked a few claims in May 1945 and returned in the fall with his wife, Esther. They planned to stay one winter but remained for 18 years.

Ludditt, more than anyone else, was responsible for Barkerville's preservation. In the summer of 1947 he watched as the original Government Assay Office, a building he considered to be "of inestimable worth historically," was torn down. The same year, the John Hopp Office was demolished. This was originally Scott's Saloon, one of the few buildings to survive the fire of 1868, and it contained many precious old records. Then Tommy Blair's store went, followed by the Hudson's Bay Company store, which held years' worth of records. Chinese buildings were ripped apart and used for firewood, and souvenir hunters ransacked the town and the cemeteries.

Responding to the destruction, Ludditt formed the Barkerville Historic and Development Company in 1953. With the support of many—including pioneers such as Lottie Bowron, Minister of Trade and Industry Ralph Chetwynd, Cariboo MLA Bill Speare and Governor General Vincent Massey—the value of Barkerville was gradually recognized. When British Columbia Centennial celebrations and projects were initiated prior to 1958, the seeds of a Barkerville renaissance had been sown. The Wells-Barkerville Centennial Committee formed; Fred Ludditt published a booklet called *Gold in the Cariboo* and dozens of articles and stories about the gold rush years appeared in newspapers and magazines throughout the province.

"Suddenly," Fred Ludditt wrote, "there seemed to be too many visitors." Ludditt viewed this new interest in Barkerville as ironic, after so many years of receiving little or no support for his cause, but it was his dogged persistence that finally "struck the lead."

As BC's centennial approached, young MLA Bill Speare gave his first speech in the house. He spoke of Barkerville and Cariboo's history. Premier W.A.C. Bennett seized on Speare's dream as a 1958 Centennial focus. Barkerville was declared a provincial historic park, and stabilization and restoration began.

The first reconstructive years were not without problems, disappointments, misunderstandings and lack of sensitivity. To Ludditt's chagrin, the restoration did not proceed as he and other old timers had planned. There was little communication between Parks Branch staff and the originators of the restoration, resulting in frayed tempers and, in many cases, permanent hostility. However, as Ludditt himself said, there was "much to offset these disappointments and create for the visitor a feeling of having stepped behind the curtain of time into surroundings and sights of more than a century ago."

The purpose of the historic park, as described in the 1958 Master Plan, is to "preserve, present and manage for public benefit the historic town and representative or significant elements of historical value related to the Cariboo Gold Rush." The site, now referred to as Barkerville Historic Town, was to be developed as a museum of the 1858 to 1958 period. But since the fire of 1868 destroyed most of Barkerville, the buildings, the goods, the services and the park's other interpretive materials focus on the period of 1868 to the 1930s. Indeed, the town cannot be seen in this 1800s context alone, for it continued to live through the quiet turn-of-the-century years into the hard-rock boom years of the 1930s and beyond. As building continued, so does the interpretation of this historic town site, with some displays representing the 1890s and the 1930s.

In 2005 the management of Barkerville was turned over to the Barkerville Heritage Trust, a non-profit charity consisting of representatives from across the north-central Interior of British Columbia. Seven local governments are represented on the trust's Board of Directors: the City of Prince George, the Fraser–Fort George Regional District, the City of Quesnel, the Cariboo Regional District, the District of Wells, the City of Williams Lake and the District of 100 Mile House as well as directors at large from the Merchants of Barkerville, the Friends of Barkerville and Cariboo Goldfields Historical Society, the University of Northern British Columbia and others. In addition there are two sites within Barkerville that have National Historic Site of Canada designations—the Cariboo Wagon Road and the recently designated Chee Kung Tong building.

Barkeville Historic Town includes 150 buildings, 3 private properties, many private businesses, the oldest operating theatre in the province, 2 cemeteries, 187,000 artifacts, 60,000 photos, a resource library and archives, and as much infrastructure as a small municipality. It sits on 405 hectares of land and contains a water reservoir, treatment plant and distribution system; a sewage treatment lagoon and collection system; a dyke and drainage protection system; a fire alarm and suppression systems—as well as three campgrounds and several kilometres of road.

Many old camps and town sites have decayed beneath second-growth forests and hydraulic mining tailings. Today, Barkerville Historic Town stands as sole representative of that time: "The days of old, the days of gold."

Urban Planning in the Goldfields

Barkerville's town planning was initially dictated by gold mining. The gold lay hidden in ice-age gravels. As it was discovered and torn from the earth, miners' humble homes, tents and rude cabins sprang up on the 100-square-foot claims. When there were enough miners to need supplies, merchants arrived. As a permanent community developed, tents gave way to log buildings. Soon an entrepreneur built a mill supplying lumber for flumes, shaft houses and stores.

With a spring and summer of only four months, the towns of Williams Creek were rough wooden settlements at over 4,000 feet in elevation, crammed into a narrow mountain valley, accessed by only a trail for years. In the early years the living was virtually medieval.

Early planning was based on staked claim lines and natural terrain. Gold dictated the location of shaft houses and Cornish waterwheels, water the route of flumes. While cabins, tents, warehouses and some flumes perched on the side hills, topography confined larger buildings to the bottom of the narrow, steep-walled valley, forced into the creek channel in a rough, straggling line. Flat land was at a premium, more so then than now, for mining refuse has since raised the creek bed an estimated 30 feet.

The first surveys were by the Royal Engineers in the summer of 1863, one year after buildings first sprouted beside the creek. Sergeant William McColl, R.E., began work along Williams Creek on July 11, 1863, starting south or upstream of Richfield and continuing north to the downstream end of Cameronton.

He surveyed the creek and staked three town sites while Lance Corporal J. Turnbull, R.E., plotted the sites. Their plans show lots, building fronts, some shafts, streams, the toe of the bluff and Williams Creek meandering as far into town as the site of the Theatre Royal. Since the three towns existed before the survey, the engineers' task was to fit the random locations of existing buildings into a semblance of regular lots. The topography that had restricted building aided this plotting.

In 1863 Barkerville there were 40 buildings on 61 lots. Richfield, a few miles upstream, had 43 buildings on 76 lots, and Cameronton, a few miles downstream, had 37 buildings on 73 lots.

Where Sergeant McColl's survey was not confined by existing buildings he drew a standard lot with a 60-foot frontage and 132-foot depth. Lots were sold based on this plan. McColl's survey numbers are now referred to as "Old Survey" lots. A 1933 "New Survey," which renumbered and reallocated, is used today.

Beyond this survey, town planning was almost non-existent. The result was an absence of cross streets, a narrow, inefficient main street, a random growth of buildings and generally crowded, unsanitary conditions. Added to these problems was a creek that ran through the town, natural hillside seepage that almost gave the town the name of Springfield, and mining refuse that threatened to bury the buildings. This combination of handicaps led to a unique response. Buildings and sidewalks were supported by pilings or stilts that could be jacked up ahead of the rising tailings. It is estimated that the current level of the street is some 30 feet above the original 1863 creek level. Williams Creek itself is even higher, as evidenced by viewing the town from the creekside bulkhead.

Domestic water came from springs in the western hillside; hollowed wooden pipes fed the water into water troughs. Sewage and garbage disposal services did not exist, so all refuse went into the nearest abandoned shaft or a hole dug in the gravel. This made the creek water unfit to drink and was the cause of the 1863 typhoid epidemic.

Barkerville and Cameronton boomed and caused one reporter for the *Colonist* to remark that Barkerville was "fast becoming the largest city west of Chicago and North of San Francisco." However, as anyone who visited St. Paul, Portland, Port Townsend, Victoria or even Quesnelleforks in the same era could confirm, this popular myth had no basis in reality.

Each of the three main towns on Williams Creek had its own personality, as a writer in the October 17, 1865, *British Colonist* reported. "The three cities . . . we have on Williams Creek within a distance of two miles, three cities. But they do not know per-haps that each one of these rival cities is altogether different from the others and has a specialty of its own. For instance, we may call Richfield the city of Lawyers, Barkerville the rendezvous of Sportsmen, and Camerontown the home of Miners." Richfield was the site of the courthouse and police station, so naturally it became the centre for lawyers. "Sportsmen" refers not to athletes but to gamblers.

The town was indeed booming ahead. The May 9, 1867, the *Sentinel* reported, "Within the last few months the town has increased to double its former proportions." The writer remarked that the principal buildings of Cameronton "have been removed to Barkerville." New buildings were going up, and the count for spring of 1867 was: 12 saloons, 10 stores, 3 shoemakers, 3 restau-rants, 3 lodging houses, 2 banks, 2 drugstores, 2 watchmakers, 2 breweries, 2 tin shops, 2 blacksmiths, 2 carpenter shops, an express office, a post office, a printing office, a public library, a paint shop, a clothing store, a butcher's stall, a public stable and a scattering of unidentified structures—for a total of 63 mercan-tile buildings. Not one building site was left unoccupied. Amateur photographer Christopher Fulton, for example, had moved his building from Cameronton and was reconstructing it to suit the times; it had a frontage of 103 feet and was described as one of the most attractive resorts in town.

And here is one of the main differences between the historical and the restored Barkerville. The historical town was definitely a mercantile town. As stage driver John Hamilton said, "It was not a residential town; excepting for thirty or more Chinese shacks at the upper end, it was principally reserved for the transaction of business and the pursuit of pleasure. The miners lived in Richfield and Camerontown . . . and on outlying creeks and gulches." Of all the buildings the *Sentinel* listed in 1867 not one was a residence. When the newspaper reported on the fire losses in September 1868, it listed only 5 of the 90 buildings lost as dwellings; 15 were saloons.

The so-called Great Fire of 1868 was the second dramatic tipping point in the story of Barkerville, the first being the arrival of the Cariboo Wagon Road in 1865. The fire levelled the rough-and-tumble town into a clean slate ready for redevelopment.

In the summer of 1868 the crowded, unplanned town gave more cautious citizens cause for alarm. There was an embryonic fire company, but the tightly packed buildings left no fire lanes in a town where land was "too valuable to waste." Fires were not uncommon. In 1864 the *Colonist* reported that a massive fire had swept "through the timber near Barkerville and extended to the lower town."

According to stage driver John Hamilton, "fire was inevitable; buildings were crowded shoulder to shoulder, stovepipes shoved thru flimsy roofs at crazy angles . . . [There was] not even a barrel of water" accessible to most buildings, and there was no such thing as fire insurance. The summer of 1868 was long, hot and dry. The town was a tinder pile. Fire was on the mind of photographer Frederick Dally as he sat and watched a spectacular display of the aurora borealis on the night of September 15:

> Whilst viewing this grand spectacle my attention was drawn to the town . . . where dancing and revelry was going on, by the number of stove-pipes very close together coming through the wooden roofs of the buildings at every height and in every direction that were sending forth myriads of sparks. Numbers of

them were constantly alighting on the roofs where they would remain many seconds before going out and from the dryness of the season I came to the conclusion that unless we shortly had rain or snow to cover the roofs . . . the town was doomed.

When I mentioned the probability of a fire to the businessmen of the place they answered me . . . that the wood the town was built of was different to other wood and that it would not burn . . . so they remained passive in their fancied security and had nothing done to guard against so dire a calamity.

The morning was bright and clear and the sluice boxes bore traces of a hard frost as the icicles were two or three yards in length by several feet in depth looking very beautiful. The business of the day commenced. A young man, Patterson . . . showed me over his large and well-built premises containing a large stock of goods . . . all paid for.

September 16 was windy. Sam Drake was working the dump box of the Wake-Up Jake claim when he heard a woman scream. "I looked up," he said, "to see smoke pouring through the roof of the dance hall. I called to the men, who came running."

John Hamilton was bringing Barnard's stage into town and "saw the fire as I rounded the top of the mountain. Barnard's office and stable were in the stricken town. I whipped up my four-horse team to be in at the death. Down the mountain side we flew, my passengers hanging on by their toenails and the wind parting their whiskers."

Frederick Dally gives a chilling account of the scene and provides one explanation of the fire's origin:

I heard several [people] running on the plank sidewalk and heard one exclaim, 'Good God, what is up!' I ran instantly to see the cause of the alarm and to my astonishment beheld a column of smoke rising from the roof of the saloon adjoining the steward's house. I saw the fire had a firm hold and as there was no water to be had I felt certain that the town would be destroyed, so I collected as much of my stock of goods as possible together, and hastened with them to the middle of the creek.

The fire originated in a small room adjoining Barry & Adlers Saloon . . . and in no less than two minutes the whole saloon was in flames which quickly set the opposite business, the Bank of British North America, in flames, so the fire travelled at the same time up and down the sides of the street, as fast against the fire as before it. Although my building was nearly fifty yards away from where the fire originated in less than twenty minutes it, together with the whole of the lower part of the town was a sheet of fire, hissing, crackling and roaring furiously.

There was in a store not far from my place fifty kegs of blasting powder and had that not been removed at the commencement of the fire, and put down a dry shaft, most likely not a soul would have been left alive. Blankets and bedding were sent at least 200 feet high when a number of coal oil tins (5 gallons) exploded. The top of one of the tins was sent five miles and dropped at the sawmill on Grouse Creek.

Every person was thinking of his own property and using desperate efforts to save it, and some not placing it sufficiently far out of reach of the element had all consumed, and others had taken it so far that during the time they were away trying to save more property Chinamen and others were stealing from them as fast as they could carry it away.

The town was divided by the "Barker" flume crossing it at a height of about 50 feet, and as it was carrying all the water that was near, it kept the fire at bay for a short time from the upper part of the town, but the hot wind soon drove those that were standing on it away. The fire then quickly caught the other half of the buildings, also the forest on the mountain ridge at the back. As the sun set behind the mountain . . . the cold frosty wind came sweeping down the canyon blowing without sympathy on the houseless and distressed sufferers . . . Household furniture of every description was piled along the side of the creek, and the people were preparing to make themselves as comfortable . . . as circumstances would allow.

In the early morning as I passed down the creek I saw strong men rise from their hard beds on the cold stones. At a quarter to three p.m. the fire had commenced; at half past four p.m. the whole town was in flames, and at 10 o'clock the next morning the signs of rebuilding had commenced and lumber was fast arriving from the sawmill and selling at $125.00 per one thousand feet. Before the fire it sold for $80.00. The number of houses destroyed was one hundred and sixteen. After the fire I found I had the key of my house in my pocket.

The fire was caused by a miner trying to kiss one of the girls that was ironing, and knocking against the stove displaced the pipe that went through the canvas ceiling, and through the roof, which at once took fire. This information I got from an eye witness who never made it generally known thinking that it might result in a lynching.

That is one version of how the fire began. In 1936 Joe House said "that Billy Hodgkinson was trying to kiss one of the dancing girls who was curling her hair by a lamp and in the scuffle the lamp was turned over and set the place on fire." John Hamilton believed House's version of events.

Jeanette House, however, heard that "John Goodson the Baker was over to Grouse Creek and had a batch of bread ready to bake on his return. He was a bit late and started a big fire in the Cook stove.

The sparks fell on the house the Dancing girls stayed in and set the roof afire. It was a hot day . . . the hottest day in September."

When the fire abated, one building, Scott's Saloon, was left standing near the upper end of town. It was close to the Barker flume and water had been dumped on it to quench the flame. Most of Chinatown also survived. At the lower end, McInne's Saloon and a couple of warehouses survived. The rest was gone.

The losses were staggering. Strouss' Store lost $100,000; the Hudson's Bay Company, $65,000; the Barkerville Brewery, $4,000; Kwong Lee Store, $40,000; F. Castagnette Store, $33,000; Cohen & Hoffman Store, $32,000; Lecuyer & Brun Hotel, $20,000; the British North America Bank, $10,000; and the Masonic lodge, $4,000. In all, the losses totalled over half a million dollars.

More tragic were the losses of small businesses and individuals who saw their hopes, hard work and savings disappear in a matter of two hours. A few packed what little was left of their belongings and turned their backs on the town. Those who stayed began immediately, as Dally indicated, to build a new and better-planned town. However, the fire and the resulting debt was the beginning of the economic decline of Barkerville—the beginning of the end.

In the immediate aftermath, Gold Commissioner Chartres Brew ordered some changes to the layout of the town. The main street was widened, allowance was made for cross streets and buildings were built a uniform three feet off the ground, a move that helped even out the sidewalks.

By September 22, 1868, less than a week after the fire, 20 buildings were up, with many more under construction, their completion delayed only by a shortage of carpenters and tools. By spring the town was rebuilt, and by the time BC entered Confederation in 1871 Barkerville was a mature community serving several thousand people.

THE WILLIAMS CREEK FIRE BRIGADE

The Great Fire of 1868 instilled a desire in Barkervillians for increased protection. On October 13 of that year, less than a month after the fire laid waste to the once-thriving town, a meeting was held to discuss how the citizens of Barkerville could be better prepared for a similar event in the future. Out of this discussion grew the Williams Creek Fire Brigade, with Isaac Oppenheimer as the first captain. Within two weeks of the formation of the brigade, $1,638 had been donated, hooks and ladders were made by locals, buffalo hide hoses were ordered from San Francisco and the name WCFB was adopted. The only thing that was not decided was the location of the brigade headquarters and whether it would use a pump engine or cisterns and hydrants.

On November 28 a meeting accepted the idea and plan of British civil engineer and constable Edward Howman: the WCFB would join forces and funds with the Cariboo Amateur Dramatic Association, and rather than occupying two separate buildings, the organizations would share one. The Barker Company would move their flume, and a 30-by-40-foot two-storey building would go up, with the theatre on the top and the brigade on the lower floor. It was built under the direction of Howman and a building committee made up of Hill, Wark and Jones for WCFB and McNerhanie, Mann and Bruce for CADA.

By December 12, 1868, the building was under construction, and it was reported that it would be in use by Christmas, ready for the first firemen's ball to support "our red shirts" (a tradition that continues to this day). However, it was not until the spring, after months of discussion, that they decided to use cisterns on the hill fed by the Morning Star ditch. The two tanks were 18 by 12 by 10 feet, holding 13,000 gallons with 400 feet of iron pipe. When the system was tested in July 1869, "the Brigade threw a stream high enough to cover any house in town." In their weekly drills brigade members sprayed the roofs of the town with water, their practice sessions serving to allay the danger of sparks and the nuisance of dust. Poet James Anderson did not agree with this decision, writing "[This] grieves me very much indeed, and makes me rather cross. We are to have tanks on the hill and trust to luck for water." The final crowning touch for the fire brigade hall would not come until 1871 when the 263-pound fire bell arrived from San Fransisco and was hoisted to the belfry.

The brigade's popularity as a social organization was such that members paid fees to belong and in return had the privilege and honour of parading through town in their attractive scarlet-and-black military-like uniforms on public holidays. James Anderson's "I Belong to the Fire Brigade," to the tune of "Riding on a Railroad Car" not only illustrates the brigade's popularity, but also describes the uniform: "My shirt of wool, in scarlet dyed, and pants and belt agree—with helmet hat and badge on that, of the WCFB."

Another fire precaution was the idea of storekeeper W.W. Dodd, who in April 1871 ran a narrow wooden walkway along the peak of his store roof, accessible by a ladder and stationed with water barrels. The barrels remained full, compliments of the heavy rainfall, and were used to douse sparks from a chimney or nearby fire landing on the highly flammable spruce-shake roofs. Fire marshals also recommended sweeping the roofs of ignitable litter and a night watchman in the dry season.

Because of the precautions and the relative care taken in rebuilding the town, Barkerville was never to know the destruction of another great fire. Despite the careful planning some owners were reluctant to conform and slow to make their buildings a standard height. Others neglected their buildings altogether, only to find them half buried when they returned from a winter in the south. The regulations soon fell into disuse and irregularities returned. The brigade, however, survived for many years. Fire marshals inspected chimneys; the cisterns and pipelines were kept in repair. We know that the brigade lasted until at least the end of October 1911, when the last notes in the WCFB minutes book were recorded, but the organization likely dissolved soon after.

The Decline of Barkerville

In the early 1920s, according to the *Cariboo Observer,* John Hopp took an option on all the buildings of Barkerville, allowing the owners the price of the buildings for the sites and giving them permission to move to a more suitable site about a mile below the town, to the north. The intent was to construct a dredge that would move up the creek, or south, from the meadows and scour the creek to bedrock, extracting all the gold that had been missed by early miners.

In May 1923 the *Observer* reported that "the moving of the

town is now a live subject" and that "there are a number of old buildings being torn down on Main street, and in the place of these historic old landmarks are being erected castles in the air." Although the possibility kept surfacing in *Observer* reports, the proposed dredging never took place, but many structural changes did. In 1933 Louis Lebourdias reported:

> Across the street from the Masonic Hall in Barkerville, Stead & Bunderson are putting up a combination restaurant and cabaret. The walls as yet cannot be seen for snow shoveled out to make room for its green log foundation, but long before spring comes they will be ready.
>
> Albert Boyd of Quesnel has acquired a building next to Bibby Bros. old tin shop in which he will conduct a plumbing and tinsmith shop and garage. And in addition there will soon be a modern barbershop, butcher shop and up-to-date drugstore. Three beer licenses are being applied for.

And so Barkerville's facade kept changing. As buildings burned down, new ones went up. When a cabin in Chinatown suited a purpose elsewhere, it was moved. Cabins and shacks from Barkerville went to New Barkerville or Wells or Stanley. The process continues today, as is evident on the streets of this old and new gold rush town.

10 A WALKING TOUR OF WILLIAMS CREEK

AS BARKERVILLE APPROACHED 1870s maturity, it was a town planned and built in response to disaster, epidemic, inconvenience and unimagined wealth. The town's life, though, did not stop. It suffered periodic ups and downs as fortunes in gold fluctuated. As a mature town it was alive in the 1930s when hard-rock mines developed in Wells, and though its fortunes were declining there were still folks living here when it became a historic site in 1958. It was a town unique in Canada, likely in North America, and today stands as an example of ingenuity and determination, of laborious debt and death, and of hard-earned, short-lived wealth.

As you walk the town remember that it is built around and over mining claims. It is undermined; shafts, drifts and tunnels are lagged with thousands of board feet of timber. Men died in these drifts. Some are still buried here. Remember them as you walk on this hallowed ground.

The walking tour of Barkerville begins at the visitor reception building and leads you along Barkerville's Valley of the Flags

opposite: This map uses a now defunct numbering system, but gives a good idea of the size and layout of the town. COURTESY OF BARKERVILLE HISTORIC TOWN

BARKERVILLE

HISTORIC TOWN

1 Administration Building, Archives and Library
4 Visitors' Reception Centre, Admissions, Security, Washrooms
5 Eldorado Gold Panning & Souvenirs ◆
6 Tregillus Family Buildings (a-g)
7 Wesleyan Methodist Church
9 Frank J. McMahon's Confectionery ◆
10 Blair House
11 Miners' Boarding House
12 St. Saviour's Anglican Church (privately owned) ✤

13 Williams Creek Schoolhouse ✤
14 King House Bed & Breakfast ◆
15 Bibby's Tin Shop
16 William Bowron House
17 John Bowron House
18 Wendle House ✤
19 McIntyre House
20 Cameron & Ames Blacksmith Shop ✤
21 Provincial Government Office & Cariboo Literary Institute's Library
22 Wilford Thomson House
23 J.H. Todd General Store
24 Barnard's Express Office (stagecoach tickets & rides) ◆

25 Wake Up Jake Restaurant & Coffee Saloon ◆
26 Goldfield Bakery ◆
27 W.D. Moses's Barber Shop
28 Barkerville Post Office (full postal services) ◆
29 Dr. Hugh Watt's Office & Residence
30 J.P. Taylor Drugstore
31 Nicol Hotel Museum ✤
33 St. George Hotel Bed & Breakfast ◆
34 Dr. Jones's Dentist Office
35 Masonic Hall Cariboo Lodge #4 (privately owned) ◆
36 Louis A. Blanc Photographic Gallery ◆
37 Joe Denny's Saloon
38 Louis Wylde, Shoemaker

39 House Hotel Coffee Saloon ◆
40 Pioneer Clothing ◆
41 Government Assay Office; J.O. Travaillot, Surveyor; Joseph Parks, Barrister & Solicitor
42 Carriage Shed #2
43 McPherson's Watchmaker's Shop ◆
44 Kelly Saloon
45 Kelly General Store
46 Mason & Daly General Store
47 C. Strouss & Co. General Merchants ◆
48 Barkerville Hotel ◆
49 Carriage Shed #1
50 Theatre Royal & Williams Creek Fire Brigade ◆
51 Williams Creek Fire Brigade Hose Tower
52 Van Volkenburgh Cabin
53 Sandy McArthur's Blacksmith Shop
54 Cariboo Sentinel Print Shop
55 Giddings Cabin

56 Giddings Shed
57 The Clearing (special events)
58 Dr. Callanan's
59 Kerr's Phoenix Brewery, Washrooms, Lai Soy Lum ◆
60 Kwong Lee Wing Kee Butcher Shop
61 Tsang Quon Residence
62 Marie's Sporting House
63 Lung Duck Tong Restaurant ◆
64 W. Hill, Painter
66 Kibbee House
67 Halverson House Mining Museum ✤
68 Tai Ping Fong (Peace Room)
69 Chee Kung Tong (Chinese Freemasons)
70 Wa Lee Store
71 Yan War Store
7-b Torstenson House
72 Lee Chong Co. Store Chinese Museum ✤
73 Min Yee Tong
73b Mok Wo Cabin
74 Kwong Sang Wing Chinese Store

75 Lee Chung Laundry
76 Sing Kee Herbalist
77 Houser House
78 Fink Garage
79 Chinese Miners' Cabin
80 Ruston Engine
81 Waterous Sawmill
82 Eagle Claim Cabins
83 Cornish Water Wheel & Flume ✤
84 Stamp Mill
85 Sheepskin Co. Shaft
86 Sheepskin Co. Cabin
87 Wong Dan's Cabin
88 Trapper Dan's Cabin
89 Anderson Cabin
90 Beamish Cabin
91 Myatovic House
92 Ah Cow's Cabin
93 Hibernia Co. Claim Building
94 Theatre Royal Storage
95 Lowhee Mining Co. Cabin
96 Lowhee Mining Co. Barn
97 Butterfield Barn
98 Barkerville Hotel Ice House
99 McKinnon Barn
100 McKinnon House

101 Kelly Woodshed
102 McKinnon Warehouse #1
103 McKinnon Warehouse #2
105 Blair Barn
106 Michael Claim Cabin
107 Barwise House
108 Barkerville Power & Light Co. Power House (1/2 of original)
109 Kelly House Bed & Breakfast ◆
110 Turner Warehouse
111 W. Baker Stables
112 Mundorf Stables
113 McIntyre Cabin
114 Goldfields Garage
115 Holt & Burgess Cabinetmakers
116 Chicken House
117 Barkerville Power & Light Co. Power House (1/2 of original)
118 Morford House (privately owned)
119 McLeod Cabin
120 Tregillus Cabin
122 Smoking Room
125 Kelly Workshop
126 Canadian Co. Cabin & Tunnel
127 Gunn Claim Hydraulic Mining Pit
128 Richfield Courthouse ✤
129 Wells-Barkerville Cemetery

◆ Operating Business
✤ Walk-in / Interpreted Exhibit
T Outhouse Toilet
S Smoking Area

PUBLIC WASHROOMS: Visitors' Reception Centre (#4), Kerr's Phoenix Brewery (#59) and outhouses (see map for locations). T

SERVICES FOR THE DISABLED: Wheelchairs are available from the Visitors' Reception Centre. Most buildings are accessible via ramps.

Toll Free Phone 1-888-994-3332   Phone 250-994-3332   Fax 250-994-3435
www.barkerville.ca   barkerville@barkerville.ca
Barkerville Historic Town, Box 19, Barkerville, BC V0K 1B0 CANADA

128 Richfield 1.6 km

129 Wells-Barkerville Cemetery 800 m (access from end of parking lot)

TOWN ENTRANCE

(no access through gate)

Emergency Evacuation Route

North

Williams Creek

to the buildings and the stories of people who inhabited the town. The tour begins at the north end of town, moves up the west side, down the east side, then up the back street and over to the bulkhead. This puts you back at the south end ready for a walk to Richfield and a visit with Judge Begbie.

Avoid the tendency to rush. Visit more than once, early in the morning or late in the evening when the town is quiet, when the old residents, Billy Barker, Fanny Bendixen, John Cameron, the Chinese merchants and all the others can best be felt. It is a time of magic.

Please note that Barkerville buildings have recently been renumbered. The new numbers are on small metal tags posted on each building, and they correspond to the numbers indicated below. Unfortunately they are not necessarily in numerical order, but chronological due to later additions or construction. Please also note that lot numbers are not the same as building numbers.

Barkerville Visitor Reception Centre (4)

The reception centre should be a visitor's first stop. Displays and audiovisual presentations provide a gold rush overview and put Barkerville in its historical perspective. Once you leave this building, you will find that the displays focus on 1870, when Barkerville was a mature town but when gold fever had died and many merchants were moving.

The curatorial and administrative offices for the site are in the building on the left of the reception centre, outside the main town.

The El Dorado Shaft House (5)

This modern-day concession fills the needs of 21st century Barkerville visitors just as the general merchants filled miners' needs in the 1800s. Visitors can buy souvenirs, books on the area, or gold. More importantly they can also learn the skill of gold panning in the sluice boxes provided under the tutelage of Canada's top gold panners. The building replicates the size and shape of shaft houses common on the creek. In the 1930s it was a livery stable for Crawford Feed and Grain.

The gold pan was the prospector's basic tool. He used it not only for testing creek gravels, but also as a frying pan, a dinner plate, a porridge bowl and an oven for bannock. In testing gravel it was used in a simple fashion, based on two principles: first, that a shaking or rocking motion causes gold to settle to the bottom; and second, that water action washes away lighter gravels leaving gold—five times heavier than rock—in the bottom of the pan. These principles served not only the prospector's pan, but also the miners' sluices and rockers.

Tregillus Family Buildings (6, A-G)

The Tregillus family owned these seven buildings until 1998, when Mildred Tregillus donated the building to Barkerville and the Province of BC. The main house is reported to have been moved here from Reduction Road in 1905. It is unclear whether the outbuildings were built after that time, as the need required, or if they are older buildings moved in.

The buildings now reflect the life of the Tregillus family through period and interpretive displays. They include the main house, four cabins, a garage, and a blacksmith shop and office.

Displays include the home, a collection of photos from a world tour, the office and the blacksmith shop. Some of the buildings are not open to visitors.

Fred Tregillus came in 1886 after mining in other parts of BC and actively mined in the Lightning Creek area. In 1905 he married Mary House, daughter of Charles and Margaret House of the House Hotel. He continued mining in the area for many years. Mary Tregillus died in 1947, Fred in August 1962, just short of his 100th birthday.

Security/Service Building (8)

Hub King had this prefab building erected where the present-day King House stands, a little to the south. It was then moved near the Eldorado, then to this spot in the 1960s and significantly altered in appearance.

McMahon's Confectionary (9)

Frank McMahon operated the Red Front Cigar Store in the Masonic Hall building in the 1930s and in the 1940s had a confectionary in the building that is now the bakery. The building has been moved from in front of the Eldorado.

Wesleyan Methodist Church (7)

Wesleyan minister Thomas Derrick arrived on October 7, 1868, as the townsfolk began to rebuild after the fire. Within two weeks the church foundation had been laid. In a month it opened. Parishioners presented Reverend Derrick with a parsonage in October 1869, after his house washed away in a spring flood. The parsonage was moved to a safer location in 1874 and added to a house formerly occupied by Andrew Weldon, an Overlander of '62. In February 1914 the manse was leaning with a heavy load of snow, so it was pulled down. The church was torn down in the early 1900s. This building is a 1966 reconstruction based on photographs, with the addition of a belfry. The interior is sparsely furnished, as it would have been in the 1870s.

Reverend Thomas Derrick was a native of Cornwall, England, and had been a local preacher there for several years before coming to Canada in 1857. Leaving his Canada West circuits, he came to British Columbia, where he was a minister in the Cariboo, Nanaimo, Victoria and New Westminster. Derrick had superior social qualities and was remarkably at ease with strangers. These attributes combined with his excellent voice, fluent speaking style and remarkable memory, made him well suited for his work. His British Columbia travels hastened his failing health and in late 1879 he resigned to winter in California. On March 30, 1880, he headed east by railway. According to his obituary, a little east of Sacramento on the Central Pacific Railway, "God took him." He is buried in Sacramento, California.

Joseph Hall, born 1843 in Ontario, was the next minister, followed by Christopher Thompson and William Sexsmith, who ministered here from 1877 to 1882. Sexsmith came here from Maple Bay on Vancouver Island. He married on September 11, 1879, while stationed here and brought his wife to the creek. His diary is a window to the daily life and death of Barkerville and Stanley.

Tommy Blair House (10)

This house, now used for storage, was built for merchant Tommy Blair in 1933. Blair's outfitting store was farther up the street. The house is closed to visitors.

Miner's Boarding House/Catlett House (11)

This mid-1890s building was the home of Charles Catlett during the 1930s. According to Bill Hong, Catlett worked in the Royal Cariboo Hospital until the early 1920s; he also worked on the Waverly Hydraulic Mine and for the fisheries department at Bowron Lake. Catlett had a girlfriend who left him to marry a rival. A couple of years later Catlett disappeared. His clothing was found on the banks of the Fraser some time later.

The house is furnished as Mrs. Parker's boarding house for miners. In fact, boarding houses were quite different, though a home such as this might have rented out a room to one or two miners. However, during Victorian times it was unusual for widowed or single women to rent rooms in their homes to men.

St. Saviour's Anglican Church (12)

In Barkerville's early days, before 1885 and the relocation of the Cariboo Road through Devil's Canyon, St. Saviour's was the focal point of the bustling main street. Miners arrived from Richfield to the south, and St. Saviour's stood as a beacon at road's end. It dominates early photos. When the road was relocated, the town's orientation changed. Chinatown was now at the end of town rather than the entrance, and St. Saviour's stood as a roadblock, not a focal point.

Reverend James Reynard acquired the lot for St. Saviour's Church in the spring of 1869 and began work in November. Before the 1868 fire he had held services in a saloon. On November 21, 1869, the *Sentinel* described the church: "The new church building promises to be an elegant structure. It is being built from designs by the Rev. J. Reynard, which are being carried out by Messrs. Bruce and Mann. The style is early English. The church will consist of a nave, 30 by 20 feet and apsidal chancel 16 feet by 12 feet . . . a school room and vestry complete the building."

The man behind the church, Reverend Reynard, was 36 years old when he brought his wife and children to Barkerville in 1868. He had left his home in Hull, Yorkshire, two years previous and travelled to Vancouver Island as Indian missionary at Victoria and later the principal of the Indian mission. He was ordained when he volunteered to move to Barkerville. Reynard felt that "the church of England stands or falls in this effort."

There were many difficulties in building the church. Unlike the builders of the Methodist church, Reynard received little help or encouragement from the miners. He was simply too rigid and strict for the community. More popular were a series of Church Institute concerts he began—concerts still carried on today.

It was a hard life. In 1870 Reynard wrote:

We were poor, my lord, and the cold made life all the harder. We were camped at nights round the fire in the most sheltered part of the house, the little ones crying from the cold . . .

A bottle of port wine froze under my wife's pillow the day the baby was born, although the bedstead touched the stove in which the fire was maintained . . .

Hoarfrost covered the windows half an inch thick; nailheads were like English daisies; the boards cracked like pistol shots, and the knots flew out with great noise.

If the decrease of income be not made up my wife and children will have to leave before next winter. I cannot allow them to face another such time of hardship.

Within a few years Reynard's health was broken by the harsh climate, and in 1871 he moved to the coast. He died on June 11, 1875, while serving as rector of St. Stephen's church in Saanich.

St. Saviour's itself went through several incarnations.

St. Saviour's Anglican Church.

Originally it was bare wood, but some time later it was painted white, according to photographs. Then in the 1920s it fell into disrepair and was the subject of restoration of the foundation and the belfry in 1930 at a cost of $1,000, raised through subscriptions.

The architectural style of the Barkerville church is referred to as Gothic Revival, with the woodwork meant to suggest the stone Gothic churches of Europe. The siding is board and batten, commonly used in quick construction with green lumber. Green lumber would shrink and open cracks in the siding, which the covering batten shielded and lent a solid appearance in a country where most buildings were temporary. The decorative work and furnishings were crafted by Barkerville cabinetmaker John Endt. The church was formally opened on September 18, 1870.

All the woodwork in St. Saviour's is original, as are the stove and most of the plain glass windows. Reynard ordered the bishop's chair from England. Baroness Angela Burdett Coutts, a wealthy Englishwoman who was a friend of Bishop Hills, the first bishop of British Columbia, donated the organ in 1885. The front porch was constructed in 1933, and the stained glass window was added in 1949 to honour the 80th anniversary of the church. In 1970 the Masonic lodge donated an electric air pump for the organ to replace the original leaking bellows. Until 1900 oil lamps were used for light, then gas lamps until 1934 when electric lights were installed. The church is owned and operated by the Diocese of Cariboo of the Anglican Church of Canada.

The Cariboo Wagon Road
Branching off the town's main street and curving along the west hillside perimeter of the parking lot and picnic grounds is an original stretch of the Cariboo Wagon Road—the road that connected Barkerville with the Royal Cariboo Hospital, the cemetery, Cameronton, Marysville and lower Williams Creek. Now closed to traffic, the road makes a fine walk for those wanting to visit the hospital site or the cemetery. Another entrance to this road is off the north end of the parking lot, next to the Shamrock mine dump and below the cairn marking the end of the Cariboo Wagon Road. The cairn was erected by the Historic Sites and Monument Board of Canada in 1928 and unveiled on August 10, 1929, with over 1,000 visitors in attendance.

The road's location explains the orientation of the northernmost buildings in Barkerville, such as the Methodist Church, for they were built facing the main street—the Cariboo Road. The present lower road was pushed through during a wet spring, when the hillside route was impassable. Since this road became more frequently used than the old Cariboo Road from the south, it shifted the town's entrance.

Barkerville View Trail
As the creek valley became crowded, miners built cabins and even established claims on the hillsides. Early photos show that these

buildings were accessed via a trail that ran along the hillside, which at times was clear-cut. While this trail tended to shift over time, it offered a backdoor view of the town. Street interpreter Kevin Brown and I relocated this trail in the late 1980s; it was reopened by the Friends of Barkerville and Cariboo Goldfields Historical Society. Now maintained by Barkerville staff it travels along the hillside to the upper part of Chinatown and is reached just a short distance north along the Cariboo Road from St. Saviour's church. It offers a good view of the wildfire fuel management clearing designed to help protect the town from wildfires.

Cariboo Hospital

A few hundred feet north on the Cariboo Road is the site of the second Royal Cariboo Hospital. The history of the hospital and medical care is found on pages 121-24.

Dr. R.W.W. Carrall

A provincial "Stop Of Interest" sign near the Royal Cariboo Hospital site gives a brief biography of Barkerville's Dr. R.W.W. Carrall:

> Of Ontario Loyalist stock, Carrall settled at Williams Creek in 1867, practising medicine and encouraging the depressed mining industry. He became the Cariboo representative on the colonial Legislative Council in 1868. On the 1870 Confederation delegation to Ottawa, he was the Canadian government's greatest ally. When British Columbia joined Canada in 1871, he was appointed one of the new province's first senators.

Cameronton Cemetery

One kilometre along the Cariboo Road, past the site of the Royal Cariboo Hospital and the 1930s Shamrock mine, is the Cameronton Cemetery. A list of burials is at the site.

Barkerville Jail

Where is the jail? It is a common question of visitors—not surprising considering there is no sign or monument commemorating where it once stood. In the early years, the jail was located in Richfield, which remained the centre of administration and government long after Barkerville matured. In 1869 the local grand jury recommended that a "lock-up" for disorderly characters be built in Barkerville. Presumably it burned down in the Great Fire, as a couple of weeks before the fire it was mentioned as "the standing monument of civilization, the jail."

The next year County Court Judge Chartres Brew had bought a "gaol" building for $186, at this end of town, near St. Saviour's church. In 1875 the *Cariboo Sentinel* described it as "a small but comfortable log building, one story, well mudded without, with double door and lined inside with planed lumber . . . two cells with the usual grating for the admission of air. No mattresses provided."

In 1924 it was reported that the Richfield jail was being dismantled and that it had been 14 years since anyone had been housed in the Barkerville jail.

The Valley of the Flags

On a windy day long ago, flags of almost every nation in the world fluttered and cracked on spruce poles hoisted high above the muddy main street of Barkerville. Each resident announced his nationality and patriotism with a banner. The flags of the United States, Wales, Scotland, England, France, Prussia, Canada and other countries gaily waved. Although at one time a few hopefuls called it Broadway, most residents thought of it and newspapers wrote of it romantically as the Valley of the Flags.

On February 24, 1872, the *British Colonist* reported Kenneth MacLeod, who attracted much attention one day in the Valley of the Flags:

To K. M. [Kenneth MacLeod], a Scotch Canadian, is due the honor of climbing Wells Fargo's flagstaff, reeving the halliards and lowering the flag which was reduced to ribbons by the wind of Thursday. McLeod had "climbers" attached to his feet. He was only up 20 minutes, and appeared almost as much at home clinging to the tapering pole, which swayed to and fro with the wind and his weight, as if he were on terra firma. He regained the earth and received the plaudits of a large number of persons. The brave fellow received $12 from Mr. Garesele' and a collection of $5 from the crowd.

MAIN STREET—THE WEST SIDE

Doody House/ Williams Creek Schoolhouse (13)

The first mention of a teacher for Barkerville's growing population of children was in 1867, well after the town's hectic first years. Government representative H.M. Ball wrote Victoria that parents were willing to pay two dollars per week to hire Mrs. Galloway as schoolmistress. The location was not recorded, but we know that the site bounced around town, from Stouts Gulch to the Masonic Hall and back down to this end of town. William Bowron, son of John and Emily, remembers it moving here after Stouts Gulch. The Stouts location was abandoned and the building silted up to the extent that William and his pals had to squeeze through the top of the door to get inside to smoke illicit cigarettes.

Originally this lot had a bathhouse and laundry operated by Chong Lee. He sold to Mrs. E.M. Roddick. Norman Scott and Red Swicker constructed this building in 1933 for James and Violet Doody. It was restored in 1977 to represent the schoolhouse, but in 2012 it was decided to gradually bring the building back to represent the home of the Doodys.

James Doody came to Barkerville in 1931 to work for Cariboo Gold Quartz. He later worked at the Shamrock Mine, just west of the present Barkerville parking lot. On March 4, 1933, he married postmistress Violet Roddick, whose mother was the organist at St. Saviour's. The Doodys had one son who

The Doodys in 1991. COURTESY OF LEIF GRANDELL

died at age five. They left here in the 1950s and moved to Ten Mile Lake near Quesnel. They generously gave the whole of Ten Mile Lake to the province for a provincial park. James Doody was one of those "old timers" who was not happy with the treatment of his town when it became a park and unfortunately his archives rest in private hands.

William Bowron House (16)

After the fire this lot was the site of the Holt and Burgess Carpenter shop.

Willie Bowron was born in Barkerville in 1872, the son of John and Emily Bowron. In 1898 he built this house, directly across the street from his parents, while working for various mining companies. Willie was a drinker, the black sheep of the family. A local sporting girl covered his debts, and when he moved to Bella Coola as a telegraph operator she followed. They married and became respectable citizens.

The Willie Bowron house, like the Wendle house next door, represents a later period in Barkerville's development. During the first two decades there were few separate dwellings. Merchants lived behind or above their stores. The town was crowded, and there was no room for "unproductive" buildings in its core. Not until the late 1890s did this type of house come on the scene.

Wendle House (18)

The Wendle House was built in the 1890s by or for blacksmith Alexander "Sandy" McArthur. McArthur, a Scot, spent nearly 50 years in Cariboo as a miner and smithy. He left in 1888 and died in Victoria on May 1, 1916, aged 81. (See McArthur's blacksmith shop next to the Theatre Royal.)

After changing hands several times, it was purchased by Joe Wendle and Beech LaSalle from the Fry family in 1904. When Wendle brought his wife Betty to Barkerville in about 1910, he bought out LaSalle's share.

Joe Wendle came from the US. He worked for several mining companies while developing prospects such as the Guyet, La Fontaine, Cunningham Creek claims and, with Beech LaSalle and John Bowron, the successful Hard-Up claim on Grouse Creek.

Wendle and his wife established Bowron Lake lodge and guiding business, which operated until 1935. The Wendles also recognized the recreational potential of two small lakes (Bonner and Wendle) just north of Barkerville and eventually had them declared part of a park. To honour the couple's forethought, the Wendle name is preserved in Wendle Lake Provincial Park, and Betty Wendle Creek in Bowron Lake Provincial Park. In 1958, shortly before his death, Joe Wendle was presented a Certificate of Merit by the lieutenant-governor and the premier of BC for his contributions to the Barkerville community.

This house had a porch at one time, likely added by the Wendles. The upstairs door is a feature of many buildings from this period. It provided access for large pieces of furniture and may also have been a fire escape. In the back was a garden tended by Betty Wendle.

Cameron and Ames Blacksmith Shop (20)

William Birnie Cameron, an owner of this shop, was born in February 1839 in Lottingstone, Rathen, Aberdeenshire, Scotland. As a child he came with his parents to settle in Quebec, where he apprenticed to a blacksmith. He served four years at $25 a year, plus board and lodging. When word of gold in Cariboo reached him, 23-year-old Cameron joined the Overlanders of '62. He financed the trip by borrowing $100. He received $90, 10 percent being deducted as advance interest.

When Cameron reached Cariboo, he worked on the Cariboo road. His first money was sent east to repay the loan and pay off the mortgage on his father's farm. He went into business with James Amm (also known as Ames) in 1869 as "Farriers and General Blacksmiths." Cameron lived behind the shop in a small room with a bunk, stove and stool. He paid $25 a week for board at a place where one was expected to "walk in and eat as quickly as possible and leave room for someone else."

Cameron's story gives a view of the social life and structure of a gold rush town. In 1875 Samuel Greer sued him for "debauching his wife." Greer and his wife both came from Canada West via California. They had been running a saloon on Jack of Clubs Creek, but Greer went south to farm at Chilliwack in 1872. Some folks thought he had abandoned his wife, but when he came back and found "Cameron lying on my bed" he shouted he would "murder you the first chance I get."

Wellington Delaney Moses testified that he had seen Mrs. Greer "leaving Cameron's house at all hours between 10 at night and 5 in the morning." However, Greer could not convince his peers that he was the wronged party and that Cameron "had made a whore of my wife." The jury found for Cameron.

Irish Sam Greer moved to his Chilliwack farm, then to land near the growing city of Vancouver where he battled the CPR, which took his waterfront land. Greer got two years in the penitentiary for obstruction and his beach was named Kitsilano, not Greer's.

For the greater part of the 1870s, blacksmithing involved

shoeing express horses and making tools for the mining trade. Iron was packed in 500 miles; shoes and nails were made by hand. Local charcoal burners, such as Greenbury Harris, produced charcoal.

Amm left in 1872, but Cameron carried on pounding an anvil until October 1875, when he sold the business to C.P. O'Neill and returned east for a family visit. There he met and married Elizabeth Margaret Gardiner, a school teacher, settled near Dewittville, Quebec, and raised a family of three boys and five girls. He died in Huntingdon, Quebec, on January 28, 1919.

American blacksmith Charles Patrick O'Neill opened shop in 1875. In 1878, at age 40, he married 16-year-old Mary Ann Veasey. They raised three children, Martha (also know as Mattie) Washington, William (or Wiggs), John and Catherine. Charles O'Neill died on December 8, 1887. His daughter Martha says he "was shoeing one of Barnard's fiery stage horses when he was kicked clear across the shop and fell against a pointed stick and died that night. A December 10 inquest into O'Neill's death, however, makes no mention of an accident, except to say he had been injured a year previously. He died that night of inflammation of the bowels.

This was originally the site of Grunbaum Brothers store, built after the fire. Cameron and Ames was just to the north. Grunbaum's was replaced with this garage, now displaying a wheelwright and blacksmithing shop.

F.J. Barnard's Express (24)

Francis J. Barnard started his express company in 1861 by carrying letters to the gold creeks on foot. Within a few years he was operating the longest stagecoach run in North America, Yale to Barkerville. The building was begun in May 1869, according to Moses's diary. By August the company's name was being lettered and the workers had moved in. Ten years later it was rented to the San Francisco Quartz Mining Company.

During stagecoach days, which ended about 1914, the express office was the hub of the town's activity. Stages brought in long-awaited mail, friends, children from school, visitors, new dancehall girls, merchant and madams. Light freight and goods kept the town alive, and it all passed through these doors. Heavier, bulky freight came via wagons or bull teams. The boardwalk was piled high with goods, the walls plastered with bills and schedules, the air filled with stories and rumours of the towns and people down the line.

The original Barnard's office was next door where the bakery stands. This structure was built in 1968, based on 1869 photographs, and once again serves as a stagecoach office.

Goldfields Bakery (26)

The mouth-watering aroma of freshly baked sourdough bread, scones and bannock coming from the Goldfields Bakery often greets early-morning Barkerville visitors. This building was constructed in 1933 as the Red Front Cigar Store and Buckley's Drug Store—thus the two front doors—with living quarters upstairs. In 1969 the building was renovated to house the bakery, based on a bakery operated here in the 1930s by Louis Hayd.

The Post Office (28)

The Barkerville Post Office, now operating during summer months, is a 1964 reconstruction based on photographs of an 1869 building on this site that housed the Bank of British North America. By 1879 the building was used as a postal and telegraph office. It burned down on May 18, 1946. It is considered to be the eighth-oldest continually operating post office in the province. The tall doors are a matter of style, designed to let light in, rather than a response to tall miners or deep snows, as has been suggested by some.

The first postage stamps were issued in 1861, from British Columbia and Vancouver Island. They bore a profile of Queen Victoria on a pink background and were printed in two pence and halfpenny values. Decimal currency came into use in 1862, so two new stamps of five- and ten-cent values were introduced in 1865.

Early gold rush communication was limited to word of mouth and mail. The importance of the mail cannot be overestimated. Letters from the east often took months, during which time people died, children were born and mortgages foreclosed. There is the story, for instance, of the miner who after several years of labour sent his wife a letter and the fare west, asking her and their small child to join him. She left, but by the time she arrived her husband had died in a mill accident. True to the code of the day, his friends made sure she and the child were cared for.

Other examples of the importance and peculiarity of 1800s mail service are the personal letters of Robert Harkness. Harkness was an Overlander, a storekeeper with a wife and three children (one of just two weeks) when he headed west. Travellers heading into the wilderness of the west wrote at every opportunity as they approached the frontier, always hoping for that one last letter from home. In Detroit Harkness wrote:

> I was sure the one I wrote from Toronto had got home and that I should have an answer here this morning, at the latest. The first thing I did when I got up this morning was to strike a beeline for the post-office and when I found nothing I was awfully disappointed. I am more homesick than ever I was in my life before but if I had a letter from you it would half cure me.

Prairie travellers often had to rely on someone eastbound to carry mail and forward it at the next town. One method, called "making up a mail," involved tying letters in a waterproof packet and leaving them in a conspicuous place at a campsite or along the trail, with a request that travellers bound in the opposite direction should carry and pass on the mail. This was, to say the least, unreliable. At one point on his way west Harkness wrote, "It is almost three months since your last letter to me was written & what may not have occurred since that? How sincerely I pray that you may all be well."

When travellers reached the "civilization" of the goldfields or the coastal towns, there were still frustrations, for mail could be obtained only at the end of daylong lineups. Unemployed miners would sell their places in line to the more affluent. But the wait or the payment to avoid a wait might still be in vain.

Robert Harkness reached Williams Creek in 1863 and wrote a series of melancholy letters to his wife, Sabrina, always mentioning how he missed her and their children, how he hoped to be home soon, how he always thought of her and what life was like on the creek. In June 1863 he wrote:

> I suppose you will be longing to hear from me before this reaches you but I have not been able to write to you sooner . . . Provisions are high here. Pack animals can come no farther than Van Winkle . . . everything coming here from there has to be carried on men's backs for which they get 25 cents a pound. I did a little of it but it is very severe labor . . . You must pardon my writing on such a dirty sheet of paper but it cost me a quarter & I was too stingy to throw it away because it got soiled. It will cost me another quarter for an envelope & two dollars to send the letter to New Westminster . . . I had hoped that the express that came in here yesterday would have brought me a letter but it didn't.

A year later, Harkness wrote from New Westminster:

> I got a letter from you the other day dated March 1863 & addressed "Bob Harkness" so it was about two years in reaching me. The Postmaster had the impudence to tell me he was burning up some old newspapers & found that little letter in one. Well, even if he does steal some of my papers you must still continue sending as a newspaper is the next best thing to a letter.

Robert Harkness stayed in Cariboo for four years, and like many miners he returned home no wealthier than when he left. A telegraph line that offered a new means of communication was run into town in 1867, but reports in the newspapers mention that it was often out of commission because of downed lines.

J.P. Taylor's Drugstore (30)

In 1866 James Taylor opened Barkerville's first drugstore, with a wide variety of drugs and patent medicines, newspapers and cigars. This store burned down in the 1868 fire, but as the ashes cooled, Taylor and David Lewis were rebuilding. Taylor operated his drugstore on one side, and Lewis operated a barbershop, dentist office and bathhouse on the other. Wellington Moses worked for Lewis for a while. Lewis advertised he was "prepared to fill teeth with gold, silver or tin foil, set teeth on pivots, repair plates and extract teeth."

In May 1873 the *Cariboo Sentinel* noted that "David Lewis, an old and good colored citizen, died Tuesday at his Barkerville residence. Barber for a number of years. Native of Columbus Ohio. Age 60." Lewis had died of tuberculosis.

The building's subsequent history is unknown. Reconstruction is based on similar buildings.

Barkerville Brewery

The empty lot between the drugstore and the Masonic Hall once held a series of buildings. The first was the Barkerville Brewery and the Brewery Hotel, built before the fire and rebuilt afterwards. The hotel was a large building with 14 rooms. The brewery's Triple X Ale won several prizes in the 1870 fairs. Its quality may have been the result of natural spring water drawn from the hill behind. In the late 1870s owner Nicolas Cunio, an Italian who came to the creek in the early 1860s, sold the brewery for about $3,000 and then a couple of years later brought it back for $1,000. It appears he was one of the few people who could make it work. The building burned down in the 1880s.

The empty lots also held a Chinese store, later Fanny Bendixen's boarding house and, in the late 1880s, an outdoor ice-skating rink with a snowshed roof and walls of banked snow that was illuminated at night by torch lights.

Schoolhouse

This building was constructed in 2012–13 to represent a school that was built around 1900 and burned down in 1947. The school of Barkerville moved around town like a migrant miner. At one time it was between Richfield and Barkerville at Stouts Gulch, then it was in the Masonic Hall, then down near St. Saviour's.

This building will be used to house not only the Barkerville school programs but also as a conference and study centre.

Masonic Hall Lodge #4 (35)

As soon as men arrived on Williams Creek, Masonic brethren began meeting in the coffee houses and reading rooms of Barkerville and Cameronton. When the *Cariboo Sentinel* began, the editor encouraged "the brethren on the creeks" to be sure to celebrate St. John's day, a date important to Masons. By October 1866 there were regular weekly meetings, and two months later Jonathan Nutt took papers to Victoria from the 14 Cariboo Masons asking for endorsement as a lodge. He returned in April 1867 with a dispensation for Cariboo Lodge No. 469. As many men were from the California goldfields, they adopted the "California rituals" of masonry.

The inaugural meeting was held on June 24, 1868, with a feast of St. John in the evening. That afternoon the 27 members climbed the hill to the new cabin of Jonathan Nutt and had their photograph taken, resplendent in aprons and sashes.

When "The Most Worshipful Grand Lodge of Ancient, Free and Accepted Masons of British Columbia" was formed in 1871, the lodge was given the designation No. 4 BCR. By this time the membership was about 50, though it declined with the fortunes of Barkerville. This was the most important social club on the creek with many members and great influence.

Soon after becoming official, and immediately after the fire of 1868, the Masons arranged with "Messrs. Bruce and Mann to build a commodious hall over the new building they are erecting on the lot formerly occupied [before the fire] by the Occidental Hotel."

In February 1869 the *Sentinel* reported, "The Bank of BC will be removed to Bruce and Mann's new building on March 10th, the upper story of which is now occupied by Cariboo Lodge #469 F&AM as their lodge room." The meeting room was kept secret by a Silent Tyler, a staircase that was pulled up to the ceiling after the brethren were gathered. This Bruce and Mann building burned down in the early hours of December 29, 1937 (not 1935 as some site reports indicate). The lower floor was the tobacco store of Frank McMahon, the Red Front Cigar Store, and next door was a billiards hall. A faulty stovepipe was the suspected cause of the fire. Frank Mahon rushed out but went back in. The door slammed shut and latched behind him, trapping him inside until he escaped through a window. The fire was only barely kept from other buildings by the work of the volunteer fire brigade, the Chinese residents' Chinese water pumps and other residents throwing snowballs and melted snow. Twice the Nicol Hotel and Stead's Cafe across the street caught fire, but the loss was held to the Masonic Hall and a billiards hall next door. A vacant lot protected the schoolhouse. The next year a new hall was constructed, and in 1967 a facade resembling the original 1869 building was added. The lodge is the property of the Masonic Order.

Joe Denny's Saloon (37)

The saloons of Barkerville ranged from large, noisy dancehalls to small, friendly rooms like Joe Denny's. The original building on which this reconstruction is based was a tailor shop operated by Colin McCallum, an Overlander of '62. McCallum rebuilt after the fire and then sold to Perrett and Harding in 1870, who operated the unlikely combination of a tailor shop and saloon.

Joe Denny was on the creek by 1863. Although active in all facets of the community, he was best known as captain of the fire brigade. He operated this saloon from May 1879 until his death at age 60 in September 1891. He is buried in the Cameronton Cemetery. The glass doors of this reconstruction are from the Grotto Saloon in Victoria.

The House Hotel (39)

The original House Hotel building was constructed in 1869 as a general store for Angelo Pendola, an Italian merchant. In the 1870s it became home for the Mechanics Institute, later the library and then the telegraph office. In 1884 it was purchased by Charlie and Margaret House for use as a hotel. The hotel reconstruction now represents a saloon and serves food and drink. It flies an early American flag as an indication of Charlie House's strong American patriotism.

Charlie House of Syracuse, New York, arrived in Williams Creek in the late 1860s and worked a claim on Conklin Gulch, and later on Jack of Clubs Creek. House was popular, handsome, witty, respected and liked by both miners and their families. He was also known as a sport and sometime professional gambler. When John and Jeanette Houser returned to the creeks in 1875, they brought with them Mrs. Houser's younger sister Margaret. Margaret Ceise and Charlie House were married the next summer.

In 1885 the Houses established the House Hotel, soon to be a favourite stopping place for miners who appreciated the homey atmosphere. The House Hotel was more of a boarding house, with people taking rooms for long periods. After Charlie died in 1913 Margaret continued to run the hotel until 1939. Charlie and Margaret had two children, Joe and Wesley Charles. The Houses are buried in the Barkerville Cemetery.

McPherson's Watchmaker's Shop (43)

This replica building depicts what the newspaper described as "a handsome little building" erected by watchmaker Alexander D. McPherson in November 1868, immediately after the fire. For two years it housed the Bank of British North America, until June 1869 when McPherson moved his business here. It was short lived. In June 1870 McPherson contracted "mountain fever," or typhoid, and died at the French Hospital in Victoria. He was 50, a native of Quebec.

The original building was then used as a boot and shoe store by C.A. Noltmeyer and later a house for the Nordburg brothers, Daniel and Thomas. In 1879 Moses noted that "Madam Coulon was moving from the lower end of town to W. Nordburg's house, next to Walker."

Dan was described by Will Bowron as a "queer character" who liked his drink—"more of recluse." He was hired as chief mourner for Chinese funerals, "making the most mournful sounds and weeping copiously." It earned him five dollars and a skinful of booze.

Thomas died in Barkerville of typhoid in 1881, and Daniel moved to ranch at Alexandria.

This building was first built as a ticket booth in the late 1980s.

Mason and Daly General Store and C. Strouss Merchants (46 and 47)

These two buildings have undergone many changes. The one on the right was originally the Hudson's Bay Company Store, built in 1868 by Messrs. Bruce and Mann. It had an office and bedroom attached and a fire and frost-proof stone warehouse between the two buildings. The warehouse disappeared from photos in the 1880s, when the store was moved. The warehouse was relocated behind the buildings, where its foundations can still be seen from the Barkerville View Trail.

The Strouss store was built in 1868 and had lean-to living quarters. It was sold to Charles Oppenheimer in 1871, a year later to Felix Neufelder. In 1880 the HBC bought the store. In 1885 Mason and Daly took over both buildings. The buildings were in good shape in the 1940s. However, volunteer fire departments could earn $100 for equipment by burning down potential fire hazards. The 1968 stores were torched to earn the Wells Fire Department $200. The present buildings are a reconstruction based on photographs.

Prior to their Mason and Daly store, Joe Mason and John Daly operated the Antelope Restaurant and saloon. Mason had an interest in the lucrative Heron claim, brought in cattle and operated a dairy farm in Pleasant Valley, three miles north. The dairy buildings can still be seen a short distance east on the 3100 Road.

Joe Mason was another who had a First Nations wife. Moses notes in his diary:

1876, Jan 19: Joe Mason cluch Marry [*sic*] Ann was safely delive[r]ed of Girl child at Victoria.
1878, May 11: J[oe] Mason left with Marry Ann & 2 children, Joe for Clinton, Marry & Children [for] Victoria.

In 1882 he married Ada Jane Bruce and settled in Barkerville. They had five children. Joe died in 1890 and is buried in the Cameronton Cemetery.

Hudson's Bay Company

The Hudson's Bay Company, formerly on the Strouss and Mason and Daly site, was one of the first wholesalers and retailers to begin business in Barkerville. Like all merchants, they lost their store in 1868 but rebuilt on this location, operating until 1885.

The Outward Correspondence for 1869–85 from manager John M. Wark is a wealth of information about the town and the business climate immediately after the devastating fire. Wark mentions goods being brought by packers and freighters such as Hamilton and Red-Headed Davis, who was apparently unreliable. He documents details about mining claims and general notes. In 1869 for instance, the ditch running along the west hillside gave way and flooded the HBC warehouse and the Strouss and Grunbaum cellars next door. Wark rebuilt at a cost of $400 and added iron doors.

The year 1869 did not start well for Barkerville. Wark mentions a forest fire that was raging around the town, but notes the fire brigade managed to save the Stouts Gulch slaughterhouse. Fire wardens kept everyone apprised of the danger. After the 1868 losses it was a frightening prospect.

"Business dull," he writes and notes that already, just months after the fire of 1868, merchants J.H. Todd, Wolff and

Greenbaum are all reducing the cost of goods and selling out. Wark's board of management writes to him in September noting the large outstanding debt the store is carrying. Wark replies that it is "utterly impossible to do a cash business here now." He has strong opposition from the closing out of merchants and miners are delaying purchases waiting for the first freight to come in, so he has to offer credit. Plus, "it must be kept in mind that less than a year ago the entire community was rendered penniless" from the fire and have not yet recovered financially. They are tough times.

By the end of the summer Wark addresses the request from Reverend Reynard for a donation for St. Saviour's, but notes, "that if our population continues falling off at the rate it has been . . . Mr. Reynard will have a good deal of difficulty drawing a congregation."

In his next letter, dated September 25, 1869, C. Strouss is selling out, "including premises." Wark writes: "I do not think the present state of the country would justify an investment in such property."

The Peace River mines and Omineca were coming on line and miners were abandoning the Williams Creek area, looking for that next rush. Even poet James Anderson headed north, leaving his favourite Ayrshire Lass in search of new fortune. Others like John Sanders returned home to England, promising to pay their HBC debt when they reach Victoria.

Wark and the retreating merchants and miners make it clear that following the 1868 fire, Barkerville began its decline. Some merchants left immediately after the fire, even the next day. While others stayed and rebuilt, they did so on credit or with savings. As miners left for the Omineca or skedaddled south without paying debt, revenues dropped and merchants such as Strouss, Todd, Wolff and Greenbaum could no longer "stand the gaff," nor could they offer miners "jawbone" or credit. Those merchants who were savvy businessmen knew it was time to move on.

From 1868 to 1870 many stores closed. Then in 1871 a rush of merchants began, such as the Parkers, Florence Wilson and

Fanny Bendixen, heading for Lightning Creek. Barkerville was in a depression from which it would never recover. The mining boom days were over.

As Canadian singer Hank Snow would later reflect:

Oh! the gold rush is over so honey bye-bye
Stake out your claim now on some other guy
I've wined you and dined you till my money is gone
But the gold rush is over and the bum's rush is on.

Carriage Shed (49)

This carriage shed is storage of a variety of wagons; from buckboards to ore wagons and belly dump wagons, all necessary vehicles in a mining town. A loft is storage for old harness and tack. The corregated roof was replaced in 2013. There are plans for the wagons and carriages to be displayed and interpreted on another site within the town as funds and time permit.

Van Volkenburgh Cabin (52)

Originally called the Nason House for the family that lived here in the 1930s, this building is an example of Cariboo add-on architecture. It was thought this was an early 1900s dwelling until a one-room log cabin was discovered beneath the walls. The cabin, since dated to about 1870, was built by or for Benjamin van Volkenburgh, butcher and cattle dealer. He married Anne Cameron, a divorcee with three children, in April 1869. It is thought they lived here until 1874. In 1880 T. Harding took it over. Later Senator S.A. Rogers owned the house. When Rogers died, Floyd deWitt Reed, an American trapper and guide in the Bowron country, moved in.

Then in 1933 it was reported in the *Vancouver Province* that "E.J. Avison, practicing barrister here for the past twenty-three years, has acquired the residence of the late Floyd Reed, opposite the Theatre Royal and will shortly open an office." Avison sold to Oliver Nason.

This succession is typical of Barkerville buildings. The log cabin became a bungalow with a bay window. It has been returned to its 1870s facade with 1890 and 1910 additions on the back.

Cariboo Sentinel Print Shop (54)
The first *Cariboo Sentinel* came off the press on June 17, 1865, in "Barkerville, Williams Creek, British Columbia," a four-page weekly paper, edited and owned by George Wallace and sold for one dollar a copy.

Under various owners the *Cariboo Sentinel* was printed until 1875. Copies of all editions exist today, a valuable record for a decade of Barkerville's life. After the fire of 1868 the *Sentinel* moved to the Louie Blanc Photo Studio building at this location. The building was torn down before 1900. As no photographs or descriptions exist, this 1967 construction is based on speculation. The office houses a print shop using period presses.

Dr. Callanan's (58)
This house was built in the 1890s for Dr. Callanan, an Irish physician at the Royal Cariboo Hospital, and restored in 1965. This log building is covered on three sides with drop siding to lend a more finished appearance. After the fire this was the site of P. Manetta's Miner's Provision Store. A couple of years later Andrew Jeffray and renamed it the Miners Saloon, then T. Walker had a store here and finally Edward and Nell Dowsett lived here at the time Barkerville was restored.

Dr. Michael Callanan was born in Clonakilty, Cork, Ireland, on March 29, 1849. He came to Canada and practised on Vancouver Island and Quesnellemouth before moving to Barkerville with his wife, Hannah, in 1898. From 1909 to 1916 Callanan was the Conservative representative for Cariboo in the legislative assembly. He died in New Westminster in 1922.

Kerr Brewery (59)
Little information exists about the James H. Kerr and Son Phoenix Brewery except that it appears in a September 1869

photograph and was mentioned in the July issue of the *Cariboo Sentinel*. Kerr brewed Columbia Pale Ale and Porter, not the usual lager. Perhaps the competition with Cunio's Barkerville Brewery down the road was too stiff, for in 1871 he closed and offered the building for sale or rent. He moved to Quesnellemouth where he and Dan Duhig opened a brewery and saloon in what is now the Cariboo Hotel. He died on April 30, 1878.

The name Phoenix and the image of a creature rising from its own ashes were popular with businesses that rebuilt after the fire. The 1980 reconstruction houses toilets and a rest area.

CHINATOWN

There is a school of thought that says Chinese miners and merchants were kept out of Barkerville or the Cariboo and that they were not allowed to own claims or mine. This is false. Mortgage records and mining records show that property and claims were freely exchanged, even in the early years of mining. A database of Cariboo mining licences compiled by the Friends of Barkerville and Cariboo Historical Society shows that in 1861 alone 123 Chinese were issued licences. Up until 1868 over 800 had licences. Both I.P. Diller and William Dietz sold Fraser River mining claims to the Chinese, and throughout BC they were issued mining claims, water rights and property deeds. The main complaint against the Chinese was that they would work for lower wages and work ground given up by Caucasian miners at a profit. This is not to suggest there was not discrimination, but discrimination took many forms and affected all cultures. Compared to other mining areas in Idaho, Nevada and California, BC was a tolerant, harmonious blending of cultures.

Kwong Lee Wing Kee Butcher Shop (60)
This building was originally a lean-to attached to the Kwong Lee Butcher Shop that stood on the north side of this building, in the space now taken by the brewery.

Kwong Lee Wing Kee Company (Tsang Quan) Manager's Residence (61)

This residence for the manager of a large Chinese company was built in 1901 by Tsang How Quan and is all that remains of the company buildings. The story has it that the manager ordered a large fence built around the dwelling, a Chinese custom to protect his wife from prying eyes. The company the manager controlled—Kwong Lee Company, predecessor to the Kwong Lee Wing Kee Company—was one of the largest and most complex businesses in Barkerville. The company was established in Victoria and New Westminster as early as February 1860 and followed the gold rush north. By 1864 they operated a branch at Quesnellemouth and an advertisement in the *Sentinel's* first edition of June 6, 1865, suggests an established Cariboo firm. They were large dealers in opium, which was legal until 1908.

The Kwong Lee Company's Barkerville store was open by June 1866 on property that Celine Armand sold to two brothers, Loo Chuck Fan and Loo Choo Fan, principal partners in the company. The sale involved land plus "a dwelling house, a small building attached to said premises, tenements and appurtenances."

As a retail and wholesale general merchandiser, the Kwong Lee Company advertised "a Large Stock of Groceries, Provisions, Rice, Tea, Sugar, Cigars, Tobacco, Opium, Clothing, Boots and Shoes, Hardware and Mining Tools which are offered for sale at Reasonable Rates." The store operated in connection with firms in San Francisco, Guangzhou and Hong Kong. By 1868 there were branches in Yale, Lillooet, Quesnelleforks, Quesnelle and Barkerville. It could be said that the Kwong Lee Company ran the first chain store in British Columbia.

In the 1868, fire all buildings and stock were destroyed. The loss was appraised at $40,000, the third-largest of any individual or company in Barkerville. The company immediately rebuilt and began to branch out, buying more land, investing in the Cariboo Gold Quartz venture and, by the 1880s, acting as a bank for residents.

Like the rest of Barkerville, the Kwong Lee holdings

dwindled in the 1880s. By 1885 a receiver had been appointed for the troubled company, and in 1888 Gee Wing was indicated as the assignee or purchaser of the Kwong Lee Estate. His firm was known as the Kwong Lee Wing Kee Company and operated until after 1900. The manager's residence represents the once prosperous Chinese firm and the residence of a Chinese businessman who enjoyed a far more affluent lifestyle than the common Chinese miner.

Chinese Interpretive Cabin/W.W. Hill, Paint Shop (64)
Although now used as the centre of Chinese interpretation, this building is still known as the W.W. Hill Paint shop. Hill had property a little to the north. Known as "a good reliable man" to locals, he was a set painter with the Cariboo Amateur Dramatic Association, a member of the Williams Creek Fire Brigade and an active Mason. He died at Cottonwood on October 23, 1869 while on his way out for a rest.

The Wah Lee and Kwong Lee wood yards once occupied the empty lots between lots 14 and 15.

Garage (65)
This garage is thought to date to the 1930s. It is not open to the public. The Lee Chong Company Restaurant once occupied this lot.

Kibbee House and Original New England Bakery (66)
In Barkerville's later years, the distinct boundaries of Chinatown faded, and many homes for non-Chinese were found in Chinatown. Kibbee House is an example. The house is named for the Kibbee family who lived here in 1918 and who figure in the history of the Bowron Lake country, where Frank Kibbee was a guide and lodge owner. The house illustrates that Barkerville's research and story continues to evolve.

The original building was constructed about 1869 and was located down the street between Louie Blanc's photo studio, which may have been part of the building, and Dr. Jones's office, as Fick's

New England Bakery and Coffee Saloon. It was thought that Kibbee moved the building here in 1917, when a few windows and some rear rooms were added. However, the *Cariboo Observer* reports in July 1920, "F. Kibbee intends erecting a dwelling on Main Street, above Dr. Callanan's," so it was likely moved that summer.

Beneath the exterior siding is the original work, still in good shape, and beneath the interior wallboard lies the old wallpaper. Some of the additions to the home have been removed. The house was restored in 2011 and contains a display about BC Parks, recognizing Kibbee's long association with Bowron Lake.

Water Lines

Overhead water lines are an example of early waterworks. Small-diameter trees were cut down and laboriously sawn in half, then hollowed out and bound together to form a pipe. The hillside above the town has many springs, and it was then, as now, a good source of domestic water. Springs were especially important because the creek was usually a muddy stream where men and machinery sloshed around and fouled the waters.

Wah Lee Store (70)

This display represents a typical Chinese general store catering to both Asians and Caucasians. On the shelves are rice, samsui (rice wine) in small jugs with a tiny neck, porcelain dishes, Chinese baskets and opium, which was popular with both Chinese and Caucasians. The small fiddle-shaped wooden cases hanging on the wall contain a portable gold scale of brass and ivory.

The Chinese man who ran this store was established in Barkerville soon after the first miner had dirty clothes to wash. In a pre-fire photograph we see Wa Lee Washing and Ironing at the north end of the street, one of several Chinese businesses located in the main section of town.

By all accounts, Wah Lee was accepted in the white community. Wiggs O'Neill remarked in 1880 that "when there would be a big do or party everyone would be there, even to Moses the colored barber and Wah Lee, the big Tyee Chinaman merchant."

Wah Lee may not have been the proper name of the man. Chinese often named their businesses after a favourite phrase or a line of poetry. Wah Lee, for instance, might translate as "Peace and Harmony" or "Righteousness and Goodness." The proprietor then became known by his business's name.

Whatever his name, when fire destroyed Wah Lee's original building, he built a small wash house, which he operated until 1875. At that time he followed many Barkerville merchants and moved to Lightning Creek in response to the new activity. By the time he returned in 1882, his business had changed; Wah Lee's was no longer simply a washhouse. He had taken partners and obtained licences for liquor, retail goods and opium—all more profitable than laundry. Eventually a larger store was built on the lot next door, near the wood lot. Each month a partner would drive pigs from Quesnellemouth to Barkerville, where they were slaughtered and delivered to the surrounding mining camps.

When Wah Lee left Barkerville in 1907, his two stores were taken over by a group of five Chinese known as the Sing Kee Company. Both buildings were destroyed by fire in 1914. This building was moved from Wells in 1973 and restored to resemble Wah Lee's store.

Yan War Store (71)

This display reflects a store of the 1870s, with open bins of food of interest to Chinese and Caucasians. During building restorations many interesting artifacts were found. At the Yan War Store, newspapers dating to 1873 were found beneath upstairs floorboards, indicating that it is one of Barkerville's oldest structures. Evidence suggests the lower floor was built sometime before 1873 and the upper storey added around 1874. During reconstruction five layers of floorboards were uncovered, each one showing a different wear pattern and suggesting a different use. The main floor walls show signs of extensive shelving, indicating that the earliest occupants used it as a store. At the turn of the century it was known as the Yan War Store.

Garage

This simple structure shows how mining town buildings changed use and how difficult it is to ascertain when and why buildings were erected. A Sam Toy came to Barkerville about 1909 and worked as a partner in the Lun Wo Company. He lived in a building on this lot. Another report says that Tan You Company occupied the cabin at one point. As the building now resembles a garage, it is difficult to know if this is the original structure lived in by Sam Toy, having been made more utilitarian, or whether the original was torn down and replaced with this garage.

Torstensen Cabin

This cabin was one of several built in the 1930s "squatting" area that is now the Barkerville parking lot. These cabins were hastily moved to New Barkerville on Reduction Road when the town became a provincial park. Einar Torstensen was living in it at that time and moved with the cabin about 1959. It was later owned by Lorna Robb, then Gary and Lana Fox, who donated it to Barkerville in 2010. It is undecided how this building will be used in Barkerville in the future.

Min Yee Tong (73)

Chinese tongs have, for the most part, been misunderstood by Western society. They are seen as secret criminal associations, like the Mafia. Although some were, tongs generally were fraternal associations based on clan, surname or locality. The word tong (or t'ang) translated literally means "hall," as in a meeting hall. The tongs or fraternities played a major role in North American Chinese communities, particularly a mining camp, where men were cut off from friends and family. The tongs served as boarding houses, hospitals, old-age homes, gambling halls and community centres. In a broader context, they served as political organizations dedicated to protecting Chinese rights and preserving Chinese language and culture.

One aspect of Chinese culture was gambling, represented on the rear wall of this tong house by the White Dove lottery.

This was a version of the numbers racket involving 88 numbers. Draws were made several times a day. Chinese "runners" circulated up and down the boardwalks and back streets of Barkerville collecting bets and then later distributed winnings. Profits helped keep the tong operating. In some gambling houses, walls were painted white because it was the colour of the spirit world and therefore unlucky for the gamblers and profitable for the house.

The posters are originals discovered under wallpaper during restoration. Also posted are the rules of mahjong, another gambling game depicted here. Fantan was played with beads and a bowl and involved guessing whether an even or odd number would come up. Fantan beads are found in the floor cracks and the foundations of many Chinese buildings.

According to the Min Yee Tong, they have owned the tong house since before 1894. The weathering of the siding, the square nails and the wear patterns throughout indicate that the tong house may date to the time of the Great Fire or before.

Mok Wo Cabin

This log cabin has moved around Barkerville. Its origins are unclear but it may have come from Chinatown. It was moved near the present-day administration building by 1960, where it was used by the waterwheel operators and called the Aurora Claim Cabin. The Aurora claim was downstream near Cameronton. The cabin was then moved next to the Masonic Hall around 1997, and to this location in 2010. Logs were added to the foundation, and a porch was added. It now represents one the houses in Chinatown based on a 1933 photo. The building may become a Chinese business.

Kwong Sang Wing Store (74)

The Kwong Sang Wing Company constructed this building in the late 1890s according to most accounts—although archaeological work done in 1980 indicates the site may have been occupied much earlier. Restoration work involved complete dismantling and rebuilding, replacing rotted logs and rebuilding the porch and lean-to.

The main floor was a general store and the upper floor a residence for proprietor Eng Fong, his wife and four children. The family returned to China in 1915, but the store continued to operate for many years. The Kwong Sang Wing Company was an important business in turn-of-the-century Barkerville and owned several lots and buildings.

The building is now an operating Chinese general store.

Terrace Gardens

Chinese miners no sooner started mining the bars of the Fraser, Thompson and Quesnelle Rivers than they used what little extra time they had to plant gardens. All along the rivers they rented or squatted on garden plots, often bordering mining claims, where they grew vegetables and fruit to supplement their diet. If they had extra they sold it. As the land was steep and water precious, they used a terrace system as they had in Kwang Tung province. Considerable research has been done on similar sites in Idaho, and it is known that there are many similar Chinese gardens in BC.

On the hillside above and behind the empty lots south of the Kwong Sang Wing Store is the rockwork of terrace gardens the Chinese built along Williams Creek. Though the growing season at this elevation is short, the terraces served to trap warm air and delay frosts on chilly nights. There is no record and no sign of what was grown here, but the crops grown in Idaho varied from root crops to rhubarb, strawberries and grapes. In the *Sentinel* there is mention of the Chinese taking over the fresh vegetable market, so these gardens, or similar ones, must have been successful. Recent archaeological work has found the remains of a couple of buildings and some water catchments.

Local miners appear to have used these hillsides as well. A photograph from the turn of the century shows Robert Heath tending raised beds on a hillside strikingly similar to this one. He has surrounded the plots with fencing, presumably to keep out vegetable predators.

Robert Heath in the terrace gardens.

Diller Corridor
This end of town is referred to as the Diller Corridor for the Diller claim, a short distance north and east

The Bulkhead
The bulkhead, or creek-side dam, seen here on the east side of the street, which was built in 1872 to contain the creek, keeps it much farther away today than it did in 1872. At that time the road was squeezed against the hillside, as seen in early photos. One of the main purposes of the bulkhead was to keep tailings or gravel, rather than water, out of the town. A complete description is on pages 213-18.

This is the beginning of the Last Mile walk to Richfield Courthouse, two kilometres south, described later in this book (see pages 236-37).

MAIN STREET — THE EAST SIDE

The walking tour now goes down the east side of Main Street to St. Saviour's church.

Chinese Miners' Cabin (79)
This late-1880s cabin depicts the living arrangements of Chinese miners. Meals were often eaten at the tong house, so the stove would only have been used for heating. The blankets are a Chinese design and the poster typical of those seen in Chinese buildings. The cabin has been substantially restored.

Mrs. Houser's House (77)
Jeanette Houser (née Ceise) came from Germany to Barkerville in 1867, probably as a hurdy-gurdy girl. She left town after the Great Fire, possibly to return to Germany but ended up in San Francisco in 1870, where she married John Houser, a Barkerville miner who was wintering in California. She may have met Houser on the creeks years before.

In 1871 the Houser family, now including young son, William, came to Barkerville but stayed only a year before returning to San Francisco. In 1875 the Housers were drawn back to Barkerville again, this time accompanied by three children and Houser's sister Margaret. Margaret later married Charlie House of the House Hotel.

During their years in Barkerville, John Houser worked at his claims—the San Juan was one—and he and Jeanette took an active part in community life. Of particular interest to them was the Dramatic Society. John was an accomplished musician and a popular violinist, in demand for dances and parties along the creek. He taught each child to play an instrument and soon had a Houser orchestra.

As the boys grew they joined the Houser claim crew. A cave-in collapsed on 19-year-old Billy Houser, forcing amputation of one leg. John Houser died in the spring of 1900, but the boys kept prospecting and digging. One claim was the Ketch Mine, a hydraulic operation opened in 1921 by Billy Houser and John MacDougall, where in 1937 a 16-ounce nugget surfaced.

Jeanette Houser outlived her husband by many years. She stayed in Barkerville and greeted visitors with stories of the old days. Not all visitors were polite. Some insisted on taking photographs, barged through her home and sometimes almost took possession of it. In later years Jeanette Houser considered this location "out of the town centre." She once remarked that she "had to go down-town to the stores once a month" but hadn't got to it yet that month. In 1933 this grand old lady of Barkerville was found dead on the floor of her home by her nephew Joe House.

This display depicts the residence as it was when Jeanette Houser lived here. The house's age is unknown, but during restoration in 1980 and 1983, newspapers dating from 1897 were found pasted on the wall. The House family continues to maintain the garden and yard.

Barker Company Shaft (75C)

On August 17, 1862, the men of the Barker claim bottomed out at 52 feet—44 feet lower than the average shaft near Richfield. It was the richest claim on the creek, and gold literally poured into buckets.

The Barker Company had eight partners, each with a claim of 100 feet—so the entire claim ran 800 feet down the creek from this point to the vicinity of the Theatre Royal, where a second shaft, the actual discovery shaft, was sunk. Although it was more usual to start at a claim's lower end and work upstream, thereby having less drainage trouble, the Barker Company men knew where the lead, the gold vein, was on other claims and did not want to drift or tunnel too far away. They decided to deal with water here and follow the lead downstream.

Over a period of several years, the Barker Company claim took out $600,000 in gold. In the 1860s a full one-eighth share was valued at between $10,000 and $20,000. Barker's story is told on pages 61-65.

Shafts and tunnels such as those of the Barker Company undermined the streets and buildings of Barkerville, and their frequent collapse caused more than a few problems. In 1871 a Barker Company shaft collapsed beneath P. Manetta's Miners' Provision Store, now the location of the *Cariboo Sentinel* office.

Sing Kee Herbalist (76)

The Chinese medicine practised by Sing Kee traces its origins and development through thousands of years. It is based on the healing powers of herbs, minerals and animal products. Those who practised this medicine were known as herbalists, though herbs played only a small part in the practitioner's knowledge and cures. Herbalists were found in most Chinese communities in gold rush British Columbia.

Sing Kee, a partnership, purchased imported medicines for this shop from China, by way of Victoria and San Francisco, and gathered native plants such as chamomile and sage. They may also have grown some herbs in the terraced gardens across the road, but as the strength of the medicines was attributed to the region where they grew, it is more likely they came from China.

At one time the building was owned by the Kwong Sang Wing Company and later by the Lee Chong Company. This cabin, an example of crude log dovetailing, houses the shop of herbalist Sing Kee as it would have appeared in 1870. The building's origin is questionable. In appearance, the Sing Kee Store and the Gee Quon House belong to the immediate post-fire era, but they do not show up in early photos. It is thought this building dates from 1868.

Lee Chung Laundry (75)

This residence was built between 1885 and 1900 and now shows what a Chinese laundry might have looked like. Lee Chung operated a laundry in Barkerville around 1899.

Lee Chong's Store (Museum) (72)

This two-storey 1930s building was a general store operated by

Bill Hong, a resident of the 1900s whose company was known as the Lee Chong Company. It is another good example of Cariboo add-on architecture; Hong kept extending the building backward to solve his storage problems. In recent years the rear additions have been torn down as they were deemed unsalvageable.

The building is now a Chinese museum, showing the China that emigrants left behind. There are many Chinese artifacts and furniture pieces. Upstairs the rooms show where the Hong family lived.

(There is an entrance to Barkerville's back street at this point, described later on page 205.)

Chih Kung T'ang (69)

The Chih Kung T'ang, or Chee Kung Tong, earlier known as the Hung Shun T'ang, was a North American expression of the Triad Society, an association that traces its origins far back into Chinese history. In 1644 a series of peasant uprisings led to the overthrow of the Ming dynasty of the Chinese Empire. "Triads" or secret societies were formed to restore the dynasty's power. The name *Triad* is based on the myth of three knights who founded the order, and their motto was "Overthrow darkness, restore the light," a thinly veiled reference to the light of the Ming dynasty. One name the Triad Society was known by translates as the "Patriotic Rising Society."

The T'ang came to North America during the California gold rush then travelled north with the Chinese who sought gold in British Columbia. This Barkerville lodge, established by Skenkui Huang in 1863, was Canada's first. As well as secretly supporting the Chinese government's overthrow, it offered social, cultural and political contact for over 1,000 Cariboo Chinese who were strangers in a strange land, in much the same way as the Welsh Cambrian Society or the Freemasons did for Caucasian miners. The T'ang went a step further. According to Dr. David Lai, "it controlled the socio-economic activities of most miners not only in Barkerville but also in other parts of the Cariboo." As well as being a fraternal and political society, it acted as a welfare organization and a court for settling disputes amongst members. It wielded a powerful influence over all Chinese residents.

In 1882–83 the Hung Shun T'ang, under master Nuanta Chen, changed their name to the Chih Kung T'ang. The next masters were Wofeng Ho, 1888–90; Wong Hung, Dea Wai Suey and Chong Quin, 1890–1917; and Dea Song, 1917–50.

When Sun Yat-sen rose to power in 1912 following the revolution of 1911 that overthrew the Manchu dynasty, it was with the financial support of the Chih Kung T'angs throughout China and North America. With the T'ang's raison d'être gone, a change in name was in order, so it became the Chih Kung Party. In 1946 the Hung Leaque Congress decided to change all their societies to "The Chinese Freemasons Party." As the Barkerville T'ang was declining, there is no evidence that they followed suit.

The Chih Kung T'ang had three buildings, this general hostel and gathering place, a hospital such as the cabin next door and a meeting hall down the street near the Lung Duck Tong, with various levels of rooms and altars for use by members of different status in the organization.

The roof and porch have undergone some restoration in recent years. In 1992 the building was moved off its foundation to allow for a 1993 archaeological dig. It is thought the building was constructed in three phases: the main portion is frame dating to 1870s, the kitchen is log from about 1881, and the northern addition dates to 1905. The interior now shows how the tong house might have appeared when it was in use.

The red sign above the door reads: "The Branch of Chinese the Hung League Chih Kung Party," reflecting the 1945 name change. The two blue posters contain classical couplets. The characters on the left translate as, "Outside nine mountains lie beautifully verdant." The characters on the right say, "Inside the temple three gods are solemnly seated." The three gods would be Lao Tzu, Buddha and Confucius.

This significant building was designated a National Historic Site in 2008.

Tai Ping Fong (68)

The Tai Ping Fong or Peace Room was an old-age home and hospice, a place where Chinese people could spend their final days in comfort. It was often the intention of the Chinese in the Cariboo as elsewhere to return to their homeland when they earned enough money to ensure a comfortable life but, as with Caucasian miners, this goal often eluded them. Poverty, sickness or age might make the final pilgrimage impossible. In these cases, it was up to the Chinese community, usually the tongs, to become responsible for those stranded in a foreign land.

Dannhauer/Halverson House (Mining Museum) (67)

Vince and Gunner Halverson constructed this house in 1939 in three weeks. They used timbers from a building at Slough Creek Mine and roofing made from flattened hydraulic pipes. Originally this area was part of Chinatown, and there may have been a building here as early as 1870. It is now the "Gold in Cariboo" mining display.

Lung Duck Tong Restaurant (63)

The Lung Duck Tong was another Chinese fraternal organization. This 1970s reconstruction is more freely interpreted as a teahouse or restaurant. A tearoom was a common feature of community life in southern China. Men could come here and spend a few hours in conversation with friends while being offered a snack or lunch, Dim Sum, small dough-wrapped delicacies stuffed with seafood, meat, mushrooms, chestnuts or any number of other tasty morsels. This building is now an operating restaurant where visitors can sample similar food.

It is thought the building dates to around 1904, when it was owned and operated by the Lung Duck Tong fraternal organization.

Marie's Sporting House (62)

This "sporting house," or brothel, dates to the 1830s. In the 1870s a Chinese man named Ah Mow ran a brothel near this spot as early as 1866. Among other things Ah Mow was a pimp, an occupation that led to his death.

In the summer of 1871 he "turned out" John Baker, alias Jean Boulanger, from his "Chinese house of prostitution." A short time later Ah Mow was murdered in front of this house and Baker was charged. He was acquitted, moving the judge to remark that "he was sorry he could not conscientiously agree with the verdict. He then told the prisoner he was discharged, that he had escaped by the skin of his teeth, and he hoped that he would take care never to be brought up on a similar charge."

The site was a butcher shop of Dominique Ercole, a Lightning Creek miner turned butcher who had been a partner with Billy Barker on the Fraser River. He filed for bankruptcy in July 1875.

This building was constructed in 1933. On the Barkerville fire insurance map of 1934 it is described as a "sporting house." A 1930s miner visiting Barkerville pointed out the house and said, "See that place? That was a sporting house. Cold Ass Mary ran it. She didn't do none of that stuff though. She had five, six girls who worked for her." Smiling he added, "Ya, Cold Ass Mary."

Mary, or Marie, was Marie Roth, born Marie Poffenroth, likely in Canada. At age 22 she went to Hyder, BC, and under the alias Marie Smith, housewife, rented the Ocean View Hotel for the sum of $75 per month. The agreement was terminated in May 1932. In the winter of 1934 she showed up in Barkerville, buying this building on lot 65.

By all accounts she was well liked. More than a few former Barkervillians fondly remember her establishment. Obviously aware of her delicate standing in the community, she donated to worthy causes.

Marie stayed until about the end of the Second World War. In 1944, '45 and '46 she still owned the property, but was in arrears with taxes. Previously it has been thought she moved to Comox, BC, in 1946, but in 1949 she was still in Barkerville, and from there she went directly to jail, sentenced to six months for "inflicting bodily harm on Mrs. Violet McLeod of Wells and an additional three months on a charge of keeping liquor for sale."

At this point her trail grows cold. But memory lingers on with old timers who pause here and smile.

Several other women ran similar businesses here and in Wells in the new rush of the 1930s, including a black woman by the name of Snowball, and two Wellsian ladies who went by the names Zip and Zoom.

Barkerville buildings continue to give up their secrets. A few years back curator Bill Quackenbush was rearranging displays in here and, noticing a cut in the linoleum floor, lifted it up. Sure enough, it was a trap door and in the small compartment were two old bottles of Scotch Whiskey and a collection of mouldy letters. Underneath the hall linoleum was a wad of US bills totalling $70, with serial numbers from the 1930s.

Giddings Cabin and Shed (55 and 56)

This cabin represents a typical 1800s miner's cabin. The ownership records illustrate how buildings passed from resident to resident. Eugene Giddings told a survey that Henry Wilcox owned the cabin in 1899; he sold to Robert Jones, who sold to Samuel A. Rogers, who sold to Alfred J. Harper, and from him to Thomas Nicol, who sold to Giddings.

Sandy McArthur's Blacksmith Shop (53)

P. McIntee opened this blacksmith shop in November 1869. Exactly one year later he advertised a set of second-hand blacksmith tools for sale. Alexander "Sandy" McArthur bought the tools and used the same shop.

See also the Wendle House, which was built for McArthur, on page 155.

Barker Company Claim

The Barker claim ran from the end of Chinatown downstream to this point. Just a few feet in front of Sandy McArthur's shop was the site of the August 17, 1862, discovery shaft that started the rush to the lower creek.

The *Mining Record,* in June 1896, reported that, "the old shaft descending to the gravel which Barker and his associates so profitably worked, still opens into the ground near the black-smith shop and is pointed out to the curious." Unfortunately, it has been filled in and no monument marks the most historic spot on the creek.

At this point the Barker Company flume crossed the street, bringing water from the hillside to the workings. It aided in stopping the 1868 fire and in saving Scott's Saloon, which stood next to approximately where the lane and 1930s hose tower is today.

Theatre Royal and Williams Creek Fire Brigade (50)

Folks like John Bowron, Joseph Hough, Florence Wilson and Mrs. S.P. Parker formed the Cariboo Amateur Dramatic Association in 1865. The first performances were held in the Parlour Saloon, which the association soon purchased and renamed Theatre Royal. It was destroyed in the 1868 fire, but in the best theatrical tradition, the show went on as actors and performers arranged to share a new two-storey building with the newly formed Williams Creek Fire Brigade. The theatre was located on the second floor and the fire hall on street level, a unique frontier solution.

The idea came from Edward Davison Howman, an unsung, unrecognized but pivotal character on Williams Creek. Howman was born in Hockering, Norfolk, England, July 1836, the son of Reverend Edward John Howman and Margaret Davison. He became a civil engineer. In 1868 he was 31 years old, an imposing man of 6 foot 3 three. He had farmed near Victoria and preempted land near Deep Creek in 1863 and only just arrived in Barkerville the summer of the fire. When he left in 1869 the CADA said, "It is impossible to repay your labour of love in designing and superintending the building of our little architectural gem—the Barkerville Theatre Royal." Howman returned to England to farm in Norfolk. He died in April 1906.

All went well for a few years, but Barkerville's buildings had unusual problems—they all needed to be jacked up ahead of the rising creek-borne gravel. This was not done with the fire hall/theatre, and by 1876 it was half-buried. When the lower floor

The Theatre Royal in 1870. CITY OF VANCOUVER ARCHIVES, AM54-S4-: OUT P418

The Theatre Royal in the 1930s.

could no longer be used, Joe St. Laurent came along and sawed the building off at ground level, jacked up the top half, cut a new doorway and built stairs to the old second floor, as in the present facade.

When Judge Eli Harrison was here in the late 1870s, he remarked that there was a lawsuit about who owned the building. As half the building was under tailings the question was who owned what remained, the Williams Creek Fire Brigade or the Cariboo Amateur Dramatic Association.

This truncated building was used until 1937 when, ironically, it was condemned by the fire marshall and torn down. A new community hall was soon built and during the early years of Barkerville restoration, a new front section was added to resemble the original theatre/fire hall.

While this story of sawing and burying buildings may seem a little far-fetched, confirmation was provided a few years ago. A pit was excavated to one side of the present theatre. At a depth of 10 feet, the old foundations were struck and, immediately below, a thick layer of black ash from the 1868 fire.

Extensive research indicates that the Theatre Royal is not a patent theatre (that is granted a licence or Letters Patent by the king or queen to use the name and present legitimate plays), as most of the many Theatre Royals scattered around the globe are. Likely the name was evoked to remind the mainly British folks involved of their home theatres.

The Theatre Royal began offering shows to the public on a daily basis in 1962 under the direction of Werner Aellen. Today's Theatre Royal continues the tradition of presenting a variety of entertainment for visitors who find an hour in the theatre a Barkerville highlight.

The tower beside the theatre is a hose-drying tower from the 1930s and contains some old fire fighting equipment.

Phoenix Saloon
The space between the Theatre Royal and the Barkerville Hotel was the site of Florence Wilson's Phoenix Saloon. Wilson was

a mainstay of the CADA. She arrived in BC on the brideship *Tynemouth* in 1862, had a store in Victoria, then opened a saloon and began the first library in Barkerville. Long thought to be a single woman, she was in fact living with blacksmith Samuel Tomkins, who had his shop next to the assay office. Like many gold rush personalities she came with a past. Sir Hector Langevin visited in 1871 and noted that she was, "connected as a servant with the family of the Emperor of Russia as governess"—a mystery that is unsolved. Wilson disappeared from BC without a word in 1874. Recent records indicate she may have returned to England and died in London in the early 1900s.

Barkerville Hotel (48)

The building now known as the Barkerville Hotel is the most architecturally significant building in town. Its uniqueness comes from the Victorian gingerbread ornamentation and the cantilevered balcony that extends from the building front without the support of posts. The hotel was constructed by Johnny Knott. He began in 1869, but financial difficulties delayed completion. Strangely, there are few recorded references to the hotel's construction, aside from one oblique mention in the *Sentinel* to "Knott's new building." The building served several proprietors: it was a butcher shop for C. Beak, then a saloon, then a boarding house run by Mrs. Tracey followed by Mrs. Funk, and later it was the Brown Hotel, renamed the Barkerville Hotel in 1890.

According to the Brown family records, Catherine Brown-Fraser, widow of H.N. Brown who ran the Richfield Hotel, bought this hotel in 1899. Her daughter Catherine (Katie) and son Alfred inherited the hotel and then sold it in 1913 to brother-in-law William Kelly, who died in 1917. His widow, Lottie Brown/Kelly, remarried to Malcolm McKinnon and was owner from 1920–33. Malcolm died in 1943, Lottie in 1956.

The upstairs of the hotel has display rooms as they might have been set up for guests. One is a display of James Anderson and his music, the author of Sawney's letter and Barkerville's poet laureate, though he had his own cabin and did not live here.

Builder Johnny Knott was one of the busiest carpenters in Barkerville. He was born in England in 1820 and was in Barkerville by 1863. Knott mined on Antler Creek, kept a hotel, and was a boxer and a runner. Knott was responsible for much of the building in Barkerville, including the quartz reduction mill on Reduction Road, and many of the headboards in the cemetery.

Kelly's General Store (45)

Kelly's General Store was built immediately after the 1868 fire and is possibly the oldest building in Barkerville. It represents just 1 of 20 general stores in Barkerville during peak years.

In January 1868 William Adamson sold a pre-fire building to Mary Sheldon. Her occupation is not mentioned, but she is known as a prostitute and saloonkeeper, giving credence to the theory that the original building may have been a brothel. In January 1872 Mary Sheldon sold this building and all the furniture to Annie Millar, a prostitute. On February 10, 1872, George Sargison, of Barnard's Express noted in his diary at Yale that he met "Annie Miller, German, one of the Demimonde, dressed in male attire, left in mail canoe for New West. She can thus walk easier. This [male attire] is no uncommon thing with women here."

Andrew Kelly bought it in 1879, and on Saturday, May 31, Moses noted, "Mr. A. Kelly commence to raise his house."

It is surprising that the building still stands, for it was built hurriedly, with 40-inch stud centres, making a weak frame. Snow from the roof of the Barkerville Hotel has several times crashed onto the general store, breaking rafters and necessitating repairs. Floor and wall wear patterns documented during restoration and research in 1983 showed that it has served several functions. Under the multi-layered floor, for example, many 1869–74 post office receipts were found. Also uncovered were various newspapers including the *Globe, Toronto Leader, Cariboo Sentinel, British Columbian, Christian Guardian, Scientific American, Manchester Times, Punch, Victoria Weekly Standard, Harper's Weekly* and the *Ottawa Citizen*—an indication of the occupants' reading preferences.

During the early years of restoration some of the goods left in the building were used for supplies. In 1973 actor Doug Cameron was sent to the Kelly Store to find an item. He noticed a bright colour behind the wallpaper and gently tore a piece off, finding part of a poster behind. Soon, a wealth of rare theatre posters was discovered. Although they were severely damaged by paint, glue and wallpaper, and often retrieved in tiny shreds, years later the park conservation staff painstakingly pieced them together and restored their former gloss and lustre.

The posters are usually displayed in the Barkerville Hotel or town information centre.

Kelly's Saloon (44)

This small reconstructed building set back from the street is an addition that Andrew Kelly made to the Hotel de France, later the Cariboo Hotel. Julia Picot bought the Hotel de France from Lecuyer and Brun by October 1869. Kelly purchased the hotel in 1871 and added this saloon. Although the 1868 fire was the last major Barkerville fire, many buildings burned down over subsequent years. Fire destroyed this hotel in 1949, though the addition was saved.

ANDREW AND ELIZABETH KELLY

Andrew Kelly, born in 1835 in Glasgow, Scotland, apprenticed as a baker before leaving his home for the gold rush in Ballarat, Australia, at the age of 16. In 1861 he went to California and then to Cariboo, arriving on Antler Creek in 1862. In the late fall of that year, he crossed Bald Mountain to the new strikes on Williams Creek.

He planned to dig for gold but saw a greater opportunity in his old trade as baker, filling the stomachs of hungry miners. By 1863 he not only had a bakeshop, but also an establishment called the Wake-Up Jake Bakeshop, Coffee Saloon, and Lunch House. As bread and bannock came from his ovens, gold came from his claim. Although not rich, he was soon well established.

Kelly, now a successful businessman, married Elizabeth Hastie, a coal miner's daughter from Patna, Ayrshire, Scotland, in Victoria in March 1866 and brought her to the goldfields. As Mrs. Kelly later remembered:

The only difficulty I experienced on that long walk, which was really my honeymoon trip, was during the last 12 miles. We struck a snowstorm and my high heels sunk away down, and hoops would keep bobbing up to my shoulders. The latter being such a nuisance that I asked my husband to let the six miners who were sharing the trail with us go ahead a bit. Then I took off my crinoline, and after folding it carried it on my arm. The Scotch plaid which was my mother's parting gift when I left home for California four years previously kept me warm.

The Kellys continued operating the Wake-Up Jake for a few months before selling it to Robert Patterson and John G. Goodson in order to follow the Grouse Creek rush that came on the heels of the Heron claim success. They built a boarding house and bakery, which opened on July 22, 1869. Again Kelly operated an adjoining mining claim.

When Grouse Creek waned, the Kellys moved back to Barkerville and in 1871 bought the Kelly Hotel. Mary Hastie, Mrs. Kelly's sister, came to Barkerville and married John Munroe. Andrew's sister also immigrated and married Thomas Fletcher, who ran a second-hand store in town.

The Kellys had eight children, but like so many other families in the 1800s, they suffered great loss, burying two of their children in the Barkerville cemetery. Mrs. Kelly recalled, "I had eight children, and I knitted every stocking they wore. I made their clothes. My husband kept a hotel and restaurant . . . and I did all the washing and housekeeping."

John Kelly died in 1875 at age six of scalet fever. Sadness once again met the family on April 3, 1904, with the murder of Andrew and Elizabeth's son James A. Kelly. The 33-year-old blacksmith died of a blow to the head after being bludgeoned by a First Nations couple in a Barkerville cabin. The *British Colonist* reported that on the morning of April 1, Kelly was found in the cabin of "Indian Saul and his wife." He had been badly beaten and died 60 hours later. The two Natives were arrested in Stanley by Constable Walker, and a coroner's jury charged them with murder. Nothing further was reported and the story of what he was doing at their cabin was generally hushed up.

Mrs. Kelly was also nurse and midwife to the men and women of the creek. In 30 years the Kellys never left Barkerville. Then in the early 1900s they bought a home and retired to Victoria. When Andrew died on August 1, 1923, Elizabeth's chestnut hair went white. "I had dark hair until that time," she later told Genevieve Lipsett-Skinner. Elizabeth died on January 9, 1927.

Street Bridges and Boardwalks

One of two street bridges crossed here so that the better-dressed businessmen and ladies would not have to walk through the mud, water and manure of the busy street. William Bowron recalled watching the frequent horse races from their vantage point.

When Judge Eli Harrison came to Williams Creek in the late 1870s, he remarked on the state of the town. Cameronton was gone, he wrote, and Richfield had only the courthouse and a log house the magistrate had lived in. In Barkerville itself he remarked on the boardwalks that they were all at different levels due to buildings being raised. "To get to the opposite sides of the street, I had to go up and down steps to get to and from bridges crossing the street. This is due to the tailings accumulating, and people from time to times raising their buildings to be above the tailings, and each one raises his building as high as suits his fancy or his purse."

Harrison continues, in reference to Moses's barbershop a few doors down the street:

> Noticing what appeared to be a barber's pole sticking out of the ground I remarked it to a resident, who replied "so it is."
> "But where is the barber shop?" I asked
> "Oh the barber's shop is buried beneath the tailings— so is the rest of the pole."

We have always known that bridges existed in Barkerville, but their exact location was unclear until 2010 when a four-by-four-inch glass plate photograph showing a bridge across the main street of Barkerville appeared on an online auction. Afraid it would go to a collector outside Barkerville, I outbid all comers. The goal now was to see what the photograph could tell us about the bridge and the town. The discovery shows how the story of Barkerville continues to unfold.

There is no photographer's name on the slide, but in the upper left corner a label reads: "Painted by Newton & Co. 3 Fleet

A newly discovered photo from 1883 showing one the two street bridges in Barkerville.

Street, London." Newton & Company was a well-established firm producing cameras, magic lanterns and globes with an extensive catalogue of lantern slides and films. They were associated with Louis Daguerre, a founder of photography. This indicates the Barkerville Bridge slide has some interesting provenance and a connection with the earliest days of photography through Daguerre and his daguerreotype and may be a slide that was in a Newton catalogue. (The UK collector bought the slide as one of a group of 3,400 glass slides in an estate sale in middle England.) The unknown photographer, perhaps an early stock photograph shooter, set up his or her camera at the corner of the Theatre Royal and the Barkerville Hotel and took the photograph looking north or downstream toward St. Saviour's church, which can just be seen at the end of the street under the bridge. In the bottom right corner a careful look with a magnifying glass shows the words: "Street in Barker-ville [sic] 83." So the date is narrowed down to the spring (if it is a flood time) of 1883.

Other than the bridge itself, the first remarkable feature is the height of the boardwalks. Periodic flooding meant stores and homes had to be built on pilings or stilts and periodically jacked up above the rising street level. Boardwalks accessed the raised buildings, and kept pedestrians out of the muck and manure of the street. Today's restored Barkerville has boardwalks just above street level, more like what was seen in the 1860s and '70s. In this photograph we see the boardwalks are approximately 10 feet above street level, judging from the steps and the height of the men. The bridge itself is high enough to allow a stagecoach to pass underneath.

The bridge runs from Kelly's General Store on the right, next to the Barkerville Hotel, across to the old Hudson's Bay Company store, now called Mason and Daly. At the bottom of the stairs on the right are a number of large stones. It is unlikely that these stones would have been left here for any length of time, and the street is littered with large rocks. We know from present-day examples that the weight of even a single stagecoach going up and down the street soon grinds any errant stone to dust. The photo was likely taken immediately after one of the frequent spring floods, and in fact that may be why the photo was taken.

Several more features become evident on close inspection. The bridge is accompanied by a water line braced with two long struts. Another water line, which used to carry water from fresh hillside springs to businesses, can be seen farther down the street. St. Saviour's white paint is weathered down to just a border under the eaves, indicating the "white phase" of the church must have been before 1883. To the right of St. Saviour's, the shaft house of the Davis claim can be seen on the eastern bank of Williams Creek. Farther down the street the boardwalks are lower.

With some photo enhancements we can read a sign under the left side of the bridge: "A. Pendola." Angelo Pendola was a Barkerville merchant. On the right side of the street we can see a sign with the word "Hotel" and something indecipherable, perhaps related to the quality or meals, in the location of present-day Nicol Hotel. The second water line and a flagpole can be seen to the left of the sign near a wagon or stairway. The photo also shows the remarkable height of flagpoles along this Valley of the Flags.

Three men stand in front of what was the Hudson's Bay Company store. The men are unidentified, and facial features are not discernible. It would seem likely they are associated with the HBC. The man in middle bears a resemblance in posture and clothing to Richard (Blue Dick) Berry.

So here a single photograph has opened up a new window to the 1880s streetscape of Barkerville. Similar images will likely continue to emerge from dusty attics and locked trunks.

Government Assay Office (41)

The Government Assay Office of the early 1870s housed a variety of offices and private residences. Dennis Cain built it in early 1869, and the plans by W. Bennett incorporated the Greek Revival theme, the wooden pillars reflecting the stability of European stone buildings. The private residences on the sides were occupied by Joe Mason, in the north wing, and Thomas Pattullo, in the south wing, when the building went up in flames in January 1875.

The government assayer who worked here tested the purity of placer gold and ore and melted gold into bricks for shipment south. The government promoted the search for gold ore, the miner's mother lode, and opened this office to help the search. At the time it was unsuccessful, but in the 1930s the hard-rock ore was finally found.

This 1965 reconstruction is based on photographs and houses displays of an assayer, a barrister and a land surveyor.

Pioneer Clothing/Sin Hap's Laundry (40)

The predominantly male population of the mines created a need for services usually provided by women. The two most obvious were washing and cooking. The Chinese quickly stepped in to do the first and, to a certain degree, the second. The Chinese entered the laundry business in the California gold rush when they found miners willing to pay a few cents for this service. Sin Hap operated a "washing house" at this site before the fire, then rebuilt and operated for two years before selling out and moving on. The building later became Samuel Tompkins's blacksmith shop.

In the 1930s Robert Palmer built a bootleg liquor outlet and brothel here that became the Last Chance Cafe of the '50s. The building was torn down several years ago and replaced by this structure designed to show Sin Hap's original laundry. It is now used as a costume rental outlet for the photo studio and called Pioneer Clothing.

Louis Wylde Shoemaker's Shop (38)

Louis Wylde (or Wilde) had a shoe store in pre-fire Barkerville and rebuilt immediately after the fire. He purchased this lot on June 26, 1871, from August Franke, late of Barkerville, "now of Seattle, Washington." The parcel was described as being, "between the New England Bakery and the house formerly occupied as a Chinese wash house but now in the occupation of Samuel Tompkins . . . having a frontage of 10 feet be it more or less . . . for $75.00." Later in 1871 Wylde sold to Annie Muller. The original building was eventually torn down.

Wylde's Prussian patriotism was clearly demonstrated on Dominion Day. The Cariboo Sentinel reported: "On L. Wilde's window the colors of the new German Empire, with portraits of the Prussian commanders of the late war." One can imagine the arguments between Louis Wylde and Louie Blanc (a Frenchman), as the Franco-Prussian War was raging in Europe at this time.

This building was hauled from Richfield in the 1930s. The construction is interesting, for there are no studs. The walls were simply a rough box covered with siding, lifted into position and tacked together.

L.A. Blanc Photo Studio (36)

Louie Blanc's Photographic Gallery was located where the *Cariboo Sentinel* office is today, but this late 1800s building provided a convenient location for the concession offering photographs and clothing suitable for 1870 visitors. Once again, restoration work showed this building was older than expected; it may be the second half of the New England Bakery and Coffee Saloon, the Kibbee House on lot 14B being the first half. This structure was definitely built before 1880 and at one time served as the Barkerville post office. In the 1930s the Barton family lived here.

In 1980 Jim Massier, a restoration worker, found some cloth chinking between the logs of the building, a common practice to keep out drafts. When the strips were removed the material proved to be strips torn from a hand-stitched 8-by-12-foot banner of the Williams Creek Fire Brigade. The banner has white letters on a red background and is now in the Barkerville Archives.

Louie Blanc came to Victoria from Olympia, Washington Territory, and set himself up in business as a jeweler and later as a photographer in about 1860. In 1867 he packed his cameras and headed north to Richfield. In May 1868 he moved to Barkerville, where for five years he exposed his camera to Barkerville's people, mines and streets. His newspaper ads read: "Cartes de Visite, Ambrotypes, Milanotypes, Portraits in Leather, White Silk, Linen or Cotton. Views of Houses, Claims, etc. Single or Stereoscopic. Jewellery Work."

Unfortunately, few of Blanc's plates have been found. In September 1872 Blanc left Barkerville and disappeared, perhaps to Europe. His stock was auctioned, and there is no record of his returning. Somewhere, in an attic, a basement or an old darkroom, his negatives and prints may await discovery—an historian's dream—providing a greater understanding of early Barkerville life. Alternatively, Blanc's glass plates may have been scraped for silver recovery from the emulsion and the glass plates used for window glass, both common practices.

Dr. Jones, Dentist (34)

Dr. William Allen Jones, a 42-year-old African-American man, came here in 1875 and opened this dentist's office. He lived here with his younger brother, Elias T. Jones, both of whom had been educated at Oberlin College in Ohio. Their father had bought his freedom in North Carolina and tried to establish a school for black children, but the school was burned out three separate times by racist whites. They then moved to Oberlin where four sons graduated from college. Three came to British Columbia in the black immigration of 1858. John Jones taught on Salt Spring Island. Elias eventually went back to the USA, but William stayed here in Barkerville, where no licence was required to practise dentistry until 1886. Jones applied quickly under the new act.

Moses records that W.A. Jones opened his dental practice in "Brick top house" on Friday, December 1, 1876. Moses's notes also indicate that Bricktop was Hattie Belmont, a young prostitute in town, who in February had attempted suicide. This would place Dr. Jones's first office across the street, near Joe Denny's saloon.

The shop is a reconstruction of William Rennie's shoe store. He opened for business six days after the 1868 fire and sold out in 1872.

St. George's Saloon/Bed and Breakfast (33)
This building was constructed in 1898 by the Johnson brothers of Quesnelle on the site of Julia Picot's residence. Picot was born in France and may have been another of the Ingots, explained in the section on women. St. George's, owned by Fanny Bendixen was on the lot next door. During the 1930s when Tommy Nicol ran the establishment, it was known as the Nicol Hotel.

The St. George's has seen major upgrades and reconstruction in the last decade, adding insulation and services to bring the building on line as a top-notch bed and breakfast.

Madame Fanny Bendixen's Saloon/Nicol Hotel (Museum) (31)
Originally built across the street by the Kwong Lee Company, this building saw service as a residence and then as a butcher shop, until occupied by Madam Bendixen from 1880 to 1898. About the time of Bendixen's death in 1898, a second floor was added, and then in 1915 the Sing Kee Company moved the building up the street into Chinatown. Several years later the

building was moved again, to this location, as an annex for the Nicol Hotel.

Part of the story of the move appeared in the *Cariboo Observer* on May 30, 1925:

> Within two days [of arriving in town in 1923, Fred Harper] had men tearing down the old Bucket of Blood . . . The old billiard table, the first shipped into the interior of BC and packed over the trail in 1862, was moved to the basement of the Masonic Temple. Another gang was put at work tearing down the old Hotel de Boyce, [Jim Boyce's hotel] years ago the sanctum of world politics, profanity and bad whiskey. A third gang is placing skids under the Shamrock Hotel, at one time the domicile of Madam B. Dixon [sic], and the birthplace of many a romance when Madam was young and attractive. The latter building is to be moved to the site of the Bucket of Blood and remodeled into a modern hotel and run as an annex to the White House, and the Hotel de Boyce will be rebuilt as a kitchen behind.

The building's main floor has a display of firearms and clothing, and upstairs shows an unrestored room and some of the work that takes place behind the scenes.

Dr. Watts Office and Residence (29)

This building was moved here from the parking lot area and was restored to resemble a doctor's home and office. The side door, around the back to the right, shows the kitchen and dining area, housed in a log addition.

Dr. Hugh Watt was the grandson of James Watt, the inventor of the steam engine, and was born in Fergus, Ontario. He came to Barkerville in 1885 as a surgeon for the Royal Cariboo Hospital but only stayed three years before moving to Fort Steele in BC's Kootenay country.

W.D. Moses Barbershop (27)

Wellington Delaney Moses moved around town with his barbering but had settled here by the time of the fire, when his shop at this location was valued at $2,000. On October 23 the *Sentinel* announced that "W.D. Moses is at his old stand adjacent to Sterling and Barry's Saloon."

Moses had this new shop built shortly before his death in 1890. His life his described on pages 104-8.

Wake-Up Jake Restaurant (25)

This building is a reconstruction based on 1871 photographs. The Wake-Up Jake is an operating restaurant offering meals and service in Victorian style, though more subdued and orderly than that of an 1870s mining town cafe.

The Wake-Up Jake was named for Irish miner, Jake Franklin, who had a Williams Creek claim by that name and who would come into Andrew Kelly's Bakery and Coffee Saloon, order his fill of home cooking and then fall asleep at the table before he could be served. "Wake up, Jake," Mrs. Kelly would have to say. "Wake up." And so the lunch house was named, according to Mrs. Kelly.

However, by 1862 the term "Wake-Up Jake" or Jacob, was the title or name of a wake-up holler, a race horse, a piano forte, a popular song, mining claims in California and Nevada and, according to Mark Twain, a rather horrible emetic he was given by a doctor in Virginia City, Nevada. Jake Franklin was indeed called Wake-Up Jake but his nickname likely came from the common term rather than falling asleep at the Kellys'.

The Kellys ran the restaurant until they moved to Grouse Creek, when Patterson and Goodson, who rebuilt after the fire, purchased it and later sold to John G. Goodson. In 1873 it was converted into a saloon. Goodson left Barkerville in the 1880s for a trip to Germany and later settled in San Francisco. Jake Franklin, who had reportedly shot a man in the California goldfields, drowned in the Skeena River in the spring of 1871 on his way to the Omineca rush.

J.H. Todd Store (23)

Jacob Hunter Todd arrived from Brampton, Canada West, in 1862. He opened a general store at the height of the rush, rebuilt after the fire of 1868, and operated until 1869, when he went to the coast and began J.II. Todd and Sons Ltd., a large cannery business. In May 1869 HBC manager John Wark writes to his superiors that "three of our merchants, Todd & Co., Wolff and Greenbaum are closing out and selling goods for about cost."

The building was reconstructed here in 1968, though it was originally on the lot to the north.

Wilf Thompson's House (22)

This building was constructed in the 1890s; during its first 30 years various residents occupied it. In 1931, Wilfred Thompson, who arrived in 1921, purchased the building.

In 1972 he told a reporter that when he arrived in 1921 the town had "150 people—half of them white and half Chinese." Thompson was an active, enthusiastic prospector until shortly before his death in 1979. His demise left the town without a year-round resident for the first time since its founding in 1862. The cabin has been left as Thompson furnished it.

Earlier this was the site of the Wake-Up Jake.

Library and Gold Commissioner's Office (21)

This building, formerly owned by lumber merchant I.B. Nason, houses two important Barkerville institutions: the Gold Commissioner's Office and the Cariboo Literary Institute.

The first Gold Commissioner's office was established at Richfield in the small complex of government buildings. The commissioner was responsible for recording claims, granting licences and settling disputes in his court. It was recorded in 1896 that "for the greater convenience of the public, a house in Barkerville has been purchased and fitted up, into which the Government Office has just been removed."

The Cariboo Literary Institute was formed in 1864 by a group of individuals who felt the need for a Williams Creek library.

Their first library was at Cameronton, under librarian Florence Wilson. It was moved to Barkerville in 1867, where John Bowron was librarian for many years. Although many of the 500 volumes were lost in the Great Fire, the library was re-established in the same building as the post office. Some of the original books are in the Barkerville archives.

McIntyre's House (19)
In many old photographs the store of watchmaker W. Davison is prominent. It was located on this lot until after the turn of the century. This house was built in 1912 after the postmaster bought the lots from John Bowron in 1906.

Duncan McIntyre was a carpenter in the area who married postmaster James Stone's widow Mary (formerly Mockel) on December 6, 1917. Mary had come to Barkerville with her mother in 1880 when she was just 13, and died on December 26, 1926. Duncan died on February 8, 1941.

John Bowron House (17)
When the 1868 fire destroyed the library and post office, John Bowron, an Overlander of '62, used his own money to build a replacement. For years he tried to have the government reimburse him, or at least pay rent. Officials declined, using the argument that as Bowron was postmaster, he had simply insured his own employment by having a suitable building constructed. After several years John Bowron, tired of bureaucratic delays, altered the building for use as his residence. This reconstruction is based on various photographs, including interior shots from the Bowron family album.

J. Bibby's Tin Shop (15)
Adams and Pearcy rebuilt their tin shop here after the fire and sold to John Bibby in 1871. Bibby built a log storage shed in 1890, which is used as today's tin shop. The storage shed was originally on this location but was moved back when the Kelly family built here in the 1930s. During early restoration efforts, the tin shop

storage building was moved forward, and the Kelly House was moved to the back street.

Bibby came from Canada West in 1871 with his brother James and used hand-powered machinery to fabricate everything from tin cups and gold pans to hydraulic pipe and monitors. He also sold stoves and hardware and may have made the building's fireproof tin roof. John died in Barkerville in 1917 at age 82, and James, who remained a miner, died in 1922, aged 77.

Hub King's House/King's Bed and Breakfast (14)

This was a residence and law office for Hubert King, a lawyer responsible for the passage of the Barkerville Titles Investigation Act, an act that finally straightened out confusion over land ownership. The investigation has proven invaluable to town site plotting and research, since landowners had to trace the history of ownership back as far as they could in order to prove their claim. King, a proponent of the scheme, was also the lawyer for many of the landholders.

This house was built here in 1933 by Joe Wendle and rented to King.

THE BACK STREET

Leaving the main street the walking tour now proceeds south again, up the back street on the east side of town. Building descriptions alternate from side to side. The back street did not exist as such during the first two decades of Barkerville. This area behind the main street was the factory, the working area, the busiest area of town, alive with the movement of men and machinery, brimming with activity, a cacophony of commerce and mining. As the bulkhead pushed the creek against the east side of the valley, the town could expand, and this back street became the area for warehouses, lumber storage and shipping.

McLeod Cabin (119)

Kenneth McLeod, born in Stornoway, Isle of Lewis, Scotland, in 1840, joined the Hudson's Bay Company in 1860 and worked his way west to Quesnelle, where he quit in 1867. In 1869, however, he was still doing some work for the HBC for wages. He and his partner Neil Wilson, the Swamp Angel decided that rather than dig for gold, they would set up a fishery on Bear Lake, now Bowron Lake. Miners were anxious to feed on something other than the usual beans, bacon and beef and lined up to buy salmon and trout.

"Fish! Fish! McLeod and Co. have established a fishing station at Bear Lake and are prepared to supply . . . at thirty-seven and a half cents per pound," they advertised in the *Sentinel* in October 1868. But they also trapped and kept prospecting the Bear River country.

Early historian Alvin Johnson described McLeod as a small, wiry but dominate man, and Wilson as a big Swede. While the partners had a station at the lake, they would have bought supplies in Barkerville. McLeod had a large house and acreage at the head of Bowron Lake. He was a trapper in the Bowron area for many years. Records do not indicate when McLeod built or bought this cabin, but he was living here before 1900 and sold to F.C. McCarthy about 1911. He died in the Kamloops Old Men's Home on February 3, 1911, shortly after leaving Barkerville.

This area, between the McLeod cabin, the King House and Bibby's, was likely the site of W.F. McCarthy's home and outbuilding that burned down in 1922. The *Observer* reports, "the McCarthy home and outbuildings, as well as an adjoining building owned and occupied by J. Bibby, burned to the ground on November 10, 1922, despite the entire population turning out to fight the fire." At one point it was feared the entire west side of the street would go up in flames, but a shift in the wind kept flames from spreading.

The Ludditt/Morford House (118)

Harold Garden, a surveyor who retired here in the late 1950s, built this house in the 1930s. He left it to Fred Ludditt, an important Barkerville citizen who settled in the 1930s and helped preserve the town. Garden stipulated when he left the house to Ludditt that it not be sold to the government, an indication of the hard feelings that developed when the provincial government took over the town.

Ludditt's house is one of three private properties in town, the others being St. Saviour's Church and the Masonic Hall. In 1983 Ludditt sold the house to private individuals working in Barkerville while he was in retirement in the Okanagan.

Walsh Claim Cabin/ Chicken House (116)

Little is known about this cabin, except that Charles Catlett once occupied it in the 1930s. The cabin and outbuilding are pre-1900s. For more on Catlett, see page 147.

Holt and Burgess Cabinet Shop (115)

Woodworkers of the gold rush era were classified in terms of the work they performed. Carpenters like Johnny Knott did the heavy, rough work, constructing buildings and mining equipment; joiners hung doors and windows and finished the carpenter's project; cabinetmakers did the finest woodwork, cupboards, cabinets and furniture, using tools such as the molding planes and treadle jigsaw seen in this working display. Wood was bent with the steam box seen on the porch.

The Holt and Burgess of early Barkerville were actually builders and carpenters, not cabinetmakers, and their office was near the Bowron House. For the purpose of this display, they have been depicted as cabinetmakers. The building was is a 1930 residence built for Russell McDougall, a placer miner.

The Holt and Burgess wagon seen in front of the shop is a light delivery wagon from the 1890s.

Goldfield Garage (114)

A 1930s mining company used this post-1900 garage.

Mundorf's Stable (112)

Livery stables were the truck stops and gas stations of the gold rush. For teamsters, travellers and residents alike, the stable was essential for providing food and shelter to the horses, mules and oxen used for transportation.

Jacob Mundorf had a livery and restaurant business in pre-fire Barkerville. In 1867 he converted his livery stable into the Crystal Palace Saloon, and when the hurdies came to town, they moved in. In fact, Mundorf married Katrina or Catherine, a hurdy-gurdy girl, likely the woman referred to by James Anderson in his hurdies poem, "The Dancing Girls of Cariboo": "There was Kate and Mary, blithe and airy."

After the fire the Mundorfs moved south to 20 Mile House, north of Cache Creek. Katrina later divorced Jacob on the grounds of cruelty. Jacob died in 1902 and Katrina in 1904.

The barn is thought to have been built in about 1900.

Outbuildings

Scattered on both sides of the back street are a variety of outbuildings from the 1900–30 period, formerly used as icehouses, warehouses or residences. They are put to a similar use today and are found on Lots 44, 46, 48, 51B, 52B, 57F and 106. As the town site develops, the buildings are the subject of research and will be used as the sites of further displays and interpretation.

W. Baker's Stable (111)

Like the Mundorf Stable, this building was constructed around the turn of the century. Joe Wendle used it for storage in the 1930s.

Baker was freighter in Cariboo in the 1870s. He had a stable in Barkerville and a ranch near Quesnel.

The Davis claim, wheel and flume, Barkerville. FREDERICK DALLY, 1867.

Pre-fire Barkerville. FREDERICK DALLY, 1868.

Barkerville the morning after the great fire. FREDERICK DALLY, 1868.

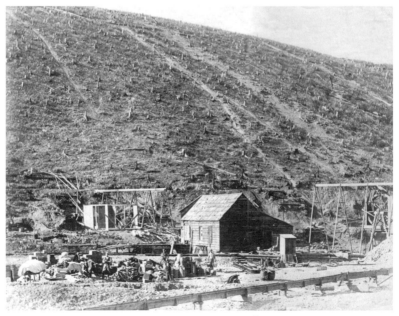

The only house left standing in Barkerville after the fire, 1868.

Barkerville today, viewed from hillside.

Barkerville at dusk.

Interior of Tregillus House.

McMahon's Confectionary.

Wesleyan Methodist Church.

Cameronton Cemetery.

Cameron and Ames Blacksmith Shop.

House Hotel.

Chee Kung Tong.

Government Assay Office.

St. George's Bed and Breakfast.

Kelly House—Bed and Breakfast (109)

This 1930s house belonged to the Kelly family, of Kelly's Store and Hotel, and stood on the main street, where J. Bibby's Tin Shop is located. It was moved here in 1967 as part of the plan to return the main street to an 1870s appearance and is now a bed and breakfast.

Barwise House (107)

This house was built on the main street, after Barkerville became a bedroom community in the 1930s. It was moved to this location around 1968. Alice Barwise lived in this home while she was postmistress, and her daughter Doreen Townsend lived here until after Barkerville became a park. It is not open to the public.

Michael Claim Cabin (106)

This cabin depicts a miner's cabin such as would have been found on many claims, including the Michael claim. R. Michael and W. Michael were in partnership with A.D. Osborn in a claim below the canyon as early as August 1862. This claim later became known as the Canadian claim, not to be confused with the Canadian claim on Grouse Creek, which precipitated a disagreement known as the Grouse Creek War, though it was the scene of a dispute with the bordering Barker Company claim. There is no evidence they used this cabin, which first appeared here in 1961. The Canadian claim was farther downstream next to the Cameron claim.

Maintainence Yard (east)

This fenced area of new buildings is used for maintenance of the town site.

McKinnon Barn (103)

This building shows on a 1930s map. It is used for storage.

Butterfield Barn (97)

There is not a lot known about this building except that a large barn appears in 1930s photos of this lot and that it was sold by Alexander Butterfield to Catherine Fraser in 1899. It may or may not have been a barn at that time.

It was formerly the machine shop for Barkerville, which has moved to the fenced compound. It is being restored for archival storage.

Lowhee Mining Company Barn (96)

This large building was owned by the Lowhee Mining Company, though its use is unknown. It later became the carpentry shop for Barkerville. It is now being renovated as climate-controlled archival storage.

Barkerville Hotel Ice House (west) (98)

On the 1934 insurance map this is called an icehouse. Ice was cut on local lakes and used to cool meat and vegetables.

Lowhee Tool Shed—Mining Cabin (east) (95)

This log building, with its unusual north-south alignment, dates from pre-1885, indicated by the cut nails used in construction. Compare the weathering on these logs with those of a later period and note the squared, dovetailed corners. It underwent restoration in 2012.

John Hopp of the Cariboo Goldfields Ltd. purchased the property by 1896 and used it as a residence for his foreman. His office was in the old Scott's Saloon. Hopp turned this building over to the Lowhee Mining Company in 1929.

Hibernia Company Claim (east) (93)

Records indicate this pre-1900 building was used as a blacksmith shop or warehouse. The Hibernia Company had a claim in this area. It was unique in that a woman, Margaret Cusheon, is recorded as a partner. Often women's mining involvement was transacted and disguised through male agents, perhaps because of long-seated superstitions about women being bad luck around any mine. Cusheon was on the creeks by 1862, in company with her mother Mary Ann Webster and a sister.

Sandy McArthur's/Ah Cow's Cabin (west) (92)
This building dates from a pre-1885 period, indicated by cut nails and the gable's board and batten construction. Parts of the exterior have been fire-charred, but it is not known whether this is from the 1868 fire.

Now interpreted as the residence of blacksmith McArthur, it was once the home of Ah Cow, who had a 1870s Barkerville trading business and a claim at Nelson Creek. In 1910 he sold this building to W.W. Kelly.

Myatovic Cabin (west) (91)
The story of buildings and residents is still unfolding in Barkerville. For years this cabin was listed as "post-1900—origin unknown"; but in 1983, 80-year-old Nick Myatovic visited Barkerville to show his nephew from what was then Yugoslavia where he had worked as a young man. Myatovic came to Canada in 1926. In 1983 he identified this cabin to me as the one he had built in 1932.

The building has since been completely rebuilt and is now used as a Chinese school.

Anderson Cabin (east) (89)
Ah Quan sold this cabin in 1920 to Marius Anderson, who lived here until 1934. It had a front porch, which has been removed.

Beamish Cabin (east) (90)
Iner Beamish built a cabin here in the 1930s, but it is not clear if this is his original cabin or whether it was moved in later.

Sheepskin Mining Company Office and Shaft (86)
This display illustrates a rather prestigious early mining setup. Most claims had few frills. Furnishings are typical, however crude, often handmade by miners. The chair is called a Cariboo

Tipster, a style developed from American Civil War sentry chairs. The balance is such that if one slumps forward, in sleep or drunken stupour, the chair ignominiously tips the sitter on the floor. The bucket wheelbarrow was used in the Slough Creek claim in the 1930s to haul gravel from the drift. The cabin was moved from Stanley in 1960. Beside the cabin is a shaft, at one time 60 feet deep, which used a two-man windlass to hoist buckets of gravel-bearing gold, the men hoped, to the surface.

The men who operated this 1870s claim were members of the Sheepskin Mining Company. The Company's claims adjoined the Barker Company's eight claims on the east side. In Gold Commissioner John Bowron's 1896 report, the Sheepskin Claim is said to have earned a total of $150,000. Unlike many companies, the Sheepskin relied on its owners to work the claim; the Barker Company, for instance, hired others to do the digging. The name Sheepskin likely comes from the practice of using a sheepskin to trap fine gold. The gold-filled skin was then burned or washed to remove the gold.

Wong Dan's Chinese Miner's Cabin (west) (87)
"China Diggings" producing only "China Wages." That is how Caucasian miners referred to claims they considered worthless but which Chinese miners meticulously worked to show a profit. To the scorn of white miners, they would work for four dollars a day, half the usual rate, share a cabin with four others, and work the claims passed over by those looking for higher pay. Grubstake earned, they could then go into mining for themselves, methodically reworking old claims. This pre-1900 cabin of unknown origin has a display depicting a typical Chinese miner's cabin. Wong Dan lived in this cabin around the turn of the 19th century.

Trapper Dan's Cabin (west) (88)
Chan Lung Fong, known as Trapper Dan, came from the Kootenay District in 1921 and operated a trap line near Summit Creek, 10 miles north of Barkerville. His story is similar to other

Chinese who lived along the creek. He sent money home to a girl in China, hoping this would enable her to join him. Blocked by head taxes and an immigration policy against women, she died before their dream could be realized. Dan died in this cabin in 1957.

The cabin may have been built shortly after the Great Fire, as both cut and wire nails were used. Trapper Dan's cabin was one of the first displays in Barkerville Historic Park. Although his name is attached to the cabin, a succession of Chinese miners used it over the last 100 years.

The empty lots between the Sheepskin Mining Company cabin and the Lee Chong store have at different times been used as vegetable gardens and for various buildings. The back street joins the main street here. For the purposes of the walking tour, you should now move toward Williams Creek and the bulkhead.

Waterous Sawmill

This sawmill dates to about 1868, though when it arrived Cariboo is unknown. The last owner was Joe Wendle, who used it on his Bowron Lake property. The mill was restored in 2009 and is operational, though not currently used for display.

Ruston Engine - 80

This engine was used to power the Cariboo Gold Quartz Company's power plant in the 1930s and was restored by volunteer Jim Hawke.

THE BULKHEAD-CREEKSIDE AREA

Canadian Claim and Gunn Hydraulic Pit

The small mining operation across the creek is based on photos of the Point claim on Lightning Creek and shows a typical setup for a cabin and shaft. The name comes from the Canadian claim, downstream several hundred yards, next to the Cameron claim, not to be confused with the Canadian claim of Grouse Creek, the centre of a court case.

The wingdam and hydraulic pipe and monitor show how a small hydraulic operation functioned. The hydraulic mining phase was generally a period two decades after the first placer miners. It was a method used from the late 1800s to the 1930s but now banned because of the destruction it causes to streams and streamside environments.

Hydraulic mining needed great volumes of water, so mountain lakes were tapped and creeks dammed around Barkerville. Examples of this activity are Groundhog, Ella and Pinkerton Lakes to the west. Long ditches streamed the water to flumes, and the flumes led to the pipe that decreased in diameter, building pressure so that the water roared out of the nozzle to erode and wash huge pits up to a mile long, a quarter-mile wide and several hundred feet deep. The gravel and water then flowed through a series of sluices with riffles that gradually separated the heavier gold from the gravel, which was washed downstream. The two-mile-long Lowhee pit at the summit of Stouts Gulch is an example. It was operations such as this that caused the streets of Barkerville to fill with tailings.

Several pits along Williams Creek are examples of test pits made in the early days of hydraulic mining when miners sewed canvas pipe together over the winter and attached it to a primitive nozzle with only 40 pounds of pressure. Low pressure meant miners had to work close to the face, where undercut banks sometimes fell and buried the nozzleman. At the Lowhee and several other places, old rusting sections of the pipes are mute monuments to man's impact on the land.

The Friends of Barkerville and Cariboo Goldfields Historical Society built this display with the assistance of various work programs, donations of materials, volunteers and grants. A trail leads to the top of the pit and a headgate, offering a good view of Barkerville.

Heavy Equipment
Near the Cornish wheel and flume are a Keystone drill, stamp mill and several other pieces of mining equipment, some

restored, some not. Nearby is a four-stamp mill, powered by water or steam, used for crushing ore found in exposed veins. The mill was rebuilt by Iner Torstenson and came from either the old reduction works on Reduction Road or the Cariboo Hudson mine in Cunningham Pass. Primitive mills such as this are still operational in parts of Africa and South America.

Cornish Waterwheel and Flume (83)

The extensive flume and large waterwheel are typical of the many overshot waterwheels that were working on Williams Creek during the gold mining period. They are essentially a water-powered engine, used to move water and lift gravel out of the deep shafts and drifts. They may also be used to drive any kind of machinery such as stamp mills, sawmill or drills. In Scotland, for instance, they were used for woolen mills.

Water was rushed to the wheel by flumes and ditches tapping springs, a creek or a lake. The water turned the wheel and then splashed into the sluice box where it separated gold from dirt, washing away the lighter gravel and leaving heavy gold trapped behind the box's riffles. It was an indispensable engine for miners but took skill and money to construct, restricting its use to companies of men who joined claims and resources to mine the deeply buried ore.

The technology is not Cornish but rather dates back to ancient Greece and Rome. In some countries the wheels were built underground and used in series to power pumps and lift water out of deep mines. At the Rio Tinto mine in Spain there was a series of 16 wheels and pumps to dewater a mine, and in Austria a 30-foot underground wheel did the same. In Wales a subterranean wheel was found on a Roman gold mine. The Islamic world adapted the Greek wheel in the seventh century for use in canals. The Chinese also perfected use of waterwheels for a variety of uses but their development began with horizontal wheels.

The term Cornish was adopted because it was used by Cornish tin miners and brought to California by these miners. However, in California the undershot wheel, where water was forced onto the bottom of the wheel, saw extensive use. During the creek's heyday dozens of these wheels were working the creek, with many an argument ending in court over water rights and the disposal of tailings.

This display and the interpretation is one of the most popular, interesting and educational on the site.

Eagle Claim Cabins (82)
These two cabins have moved around Barkerville for the last 60 years, sometimes together, sometimes not. In 1865 the Eagle Company was described as being "opposite Barkerville," yet it does not appear on the earliest maps of claims on Williams Creek in 1862. The Eagle Company was staked by J. McLaughlin and David Edwards on September 19, 1862, and situated next to the Michael and the Sheepskin Companies. Eagle had a variety of owners and was not a major claim. Gold Commissioner Bowron estimated its output at only $10,000. Put in a historical context, today's miners are trespassing, as the original Eagle claims were on the creek's east side, though Williams Creek has been known to wander from one side of the valley to the other.

The Bulkhead—Floods and Gravel
Spring freshets or high water following a heavy rain sent Williams Creek water and the accompanying tailings washing down Barkerville streets, adding as much as two feet a year to the street's level, making it necessary to constantly raise buildings. The Hudson's Bay Company recorded in 1871 that they had to raise their store 18 feet. In late May 1879 Moses noted, "clear water runing strong through the Street men all still imployed raising houses [sic]."

Vince Halvorsen, who lived here in the 1930s, estimates there are 40 feet of tailings under the Visitor's Centre. Archaeological investigations in 2011, during a major infrastructure upgrade, did indeed find buildings buried under the main street.

The laborious task of raising buildings was still necessary even after the construction of a bulkhead or wing dam at the top end of the town in 1872 by Thomas Spence. At its wildest, the capricious creek still tore down the street.

One such flood occurred on the evening of Saturday, June 11, 1911. The *Cariboo Observer* reported that citizens "were aroused by the tumbling of timbers, and within an instant Williams Creek, which is at this season of the year a river of mud and gravel, came rolling down the main street . . . carrying wood piles, sidewalks and all kinds of loose material, while a number of children were rescued just in time to prevent being carried away."

Residents were pleading with the government for help with flood control, and this led to the proposal to move Barkerville to a safer location, as it was felt the creek would continue to rise. At that time the main street was reported as being approximately 20 feet above its original elevation. The town was not moved, and the creek continues to rise. Today's bulkhead keeps the creek farther away than in 1872. At that time the road was squeezed against the hillside, as seen in early photos.

The bulkhead has only been moderately successful in keeping Williams Creek and tailings out of the town and requires constant maintenance. Every few years spring floods or landslides deposit debris, raising the streambed until now the creek is considerably higher than the town site. A 2009 flood washed out a Williams Creek bridge and the Bowron Lake road, and in the spring of 2012 a slide and flooding again brought the creek came within a foot of breaching the bulkhead.

The creek flooding was not the only natural event that could endanger creek bottom residents. On May 17, 1866, the *Cariboo Sentinel* reported on a landslide that came down near Barkerville the previous afternoon:

> The denizens of Barkerville were startled at hearing a very unusual noise similar to what might have been produced by the caving of a steep bank, a general rush was made for the street, it was observed that a large portion of the earth on the Western hill side behind town was on the move carrying everything before it, until it was obstructed by

the Hibernia Co.'s shaft house; had it taken a course a little to the left it would have undoubtedly carried away Messrs. Floyd and Co.'s store, as it was water and mud forced an entrance through the back door and swept right through it into the street destroying a great deal of goods. Messrs. Floyd and Co.'s loss will amount to $500.

The Bedrock Drain Company

Williams Creek miners were working in an ancient creek bed 40 feet deep and filled with gravel, water and gold. To get the gold, gravel had to be removed by a shaft sunk to bedrock, an operation frustrated by the ever-present water. Cemetery grave markers attest to the danger. Two men died in this drain; Alex Stobo and John R. Edwards both drowned in separate accidents when the drift walls gave way.

One method of keeping claims free of water was the Cornish waterwheel and companion pump, but it was expensive and subject to frequent mechanical problems.

It was proposed that a drain be built along the creek at bedrock depth. A company was formed, and miners bought subscriptions to finance the operation. In 1863 a tunnel and open flume were begun almost 1,800 feet below Cameronton, the tunnel moving southward up the creek. It measured 36 by 51 inches, timbered on the sides and top to keep out gravel. By April 1864 almost 1,300 feet of the drain were complete. Miners decided to extend it another 300 feet to a point just below the mouth of Stouts Gulch on the Foster-Campbell Claim. The completed drain cost $120,000, the equivalent of close to two million dollars today. The costs were somewhat offset by cleanups that collected gold from the drain floor, which was made of blocks of wood.

Over the last century all traces of the drain disappeared, but in the fall of 1979 the Ballarat claim at the north end of town began to rework the creek's gravel. During excavation, the old Bed Rock Drain was unearthed, intact and still draining water from the claims of Williams Creek.

11 OTHER AREAS NEAR BARKERVILLE HISTORIC PARK

BARKERVILLE HISTORIC PARK extends beyond the confines of the town. Upstream is Richfield, and beyond the courthouse trails lead to the headwaters of Williams Creek, Groundhog Lake (the site of an early roadhouse) and Mount Agnes. For the more adventurous a trail follows the old Cariboo Road to Stanley on Lightning Creek. Several maps are available showing these and other trails.

Cameronton

> But the lion of the Creek seems to be the Cameron claim; their success and prospects are fabulous . . . They now employ over 60 and in a few days they will employ over 150 men. . . . The Cameron Claim has got down with their upper shaft and struck it richer than any yet. They now have it from end to end of their claim. . . . no use talking of ounces; they are getting it in pans full.
> —*Cariboo Sentinel*, August 5, 1863

William Barker may have been first, but there is little doubt that John Angus "Cariboo" Cameron's claim was one of the richest. The town's namesake and major shareholder had a sense of drama. As a town grew around his shaft house, he had a huge flag made at a cost of $500, 18 by 30 feet, and flew it at the top of a 70-foot flagpole. On July 18, 1863, a celebration was planned, and Judge Begbie called on to dedicate and name this new town. He asked Mrs. Richard Cameron [not related to Cariboo Cameron], who had been here over a year, to help him raise the flag and named the town "Cameron Town." Cameron then hosted some 500 to 600 people to a party. The newspaper observed that he could well afford it.

Cameronton rivalled Barkerville for size and influence during its first few years but gradually receded in favour of the upstream settlement. Several Cameronton buildings were moved upstream as the town declined. Nothing remains today except the cemetery high on the western hill accessed by Reduction Road.

Lower Williams Creek
Below Barkerville were the towns of Cameronton, Marysville and several large mining operations. Although these towns are now mostly gone, the creek shows signs of the work carried on here with old trestle foundations exposed in the eroding creek banks. Nearby is the old hydraulic pit of the Prairie Flower and Forest Rose claims.

Ballarat Claim, Grant Number 35F
Downstream of Cameronton is the Ballarat mine, a large gravel hole in the creekbed. It has been the site of a mine for over 150 years. It was named for a gold strike in Australia and is one of the oldest continuously worked claims on the creek. The "F" designation indicates that the claim operates under a crown grant from Queen Victoria and has mineral rights to the centre of the earth. This was once the site of a large dragline dredge that worked the creek's deep gravel deposits. Another dredge still rests beneath the water of Antler Creek at Whiskey Flats, a few miles east on the 3100 Forest Service Road. The Kafue dredge operated from 1924 to the 1950s and the ponds and tailings piles make for an interesting afternoon.

Please note that trespassing on mineral claims, though legal, is considered poor manners, foolish and sometimes risky. Panning for gold on someone else's claim is downright dangerous.

The Meadows, Kurtz and Lane Claims

The area below and around the Ballarat mine were once known as the Meadows. Early miners knew that this was not the old course of Williams Creek, which cut to the east, but they still felt that somewhere deep below they would find gold. And they might, but water always proved the deciding problem.

Similarly the Kurtz and Lane claim succeeded in leasing a large portion of the meadows from the airport down to One Mile or Downie Pass Road. Americans John Kurtz (a former California vigilante) and Charles C. Lane had major investors such as George Hearst, who purchased steam pumps and heavy equipment. They sunk a shaft 125 feet into the fen but came up with no gold. One of their ditches can still be seen just east of One Mile bridge, and a patch in the highway shows where the shaft gave way a couple of decades ago.

Downie Pass Road

In 1858 Major William Downie, a 39-year-old Scot, came to British Columbia from California (where Downieville is named after him). He explored coastal regions for Governor Douglas and in 1859 made one of the most notable exploring expeditions in BC history, up the Skeena and Babine rivers to Babine Lake, then to Stuart Lake and down the Nechako and Fraser rivers to the goldfields—an impractical route but a magnificent journey of discovery.

Downie and his wife, Adeline, mined on Grouse and Williams Creek, where he profited, but he lost it all trying to reach gold in the soft ground of this creek delta. From Cariboo, Downie went to the Columbia River Big Bend gold rush, where a creek is named for him.

The Downie Creek Road, also known as One Mile Road, is a seven-kilometre loop through a pleasant low pass with many signs of old placer workings. It reaches Eight Mile Lake and the Big Valley Road at kilometre 5.2, where a right turn will bring you to the Bowron Lake Road. Another right completes the loop to the Wells-Barkerville Road. It is now blocked and used as a cycling or hiking trail.

The area immediately across the creek was the site of two brothels in the 1930s. One madam moved her operation from Stanley and housed her girls in tents while the house was built. Some of the workers were accused of not always accepting cash in payment from "Zip and Zoom."

Strommville

The collection of cabins between One Mile and Wells was an early rival to Wells and was named for Harry Stromme. In 1934 Louis Lebourdais wrote of its "new and modern Antler Hotel and string of neat-built dwellings above the roadway." The area became noted for its gambling dens and houses of ill repute.

The swamp or fen fed by Williams Creek is the headwaters of the Willow River. When Wells was at its height of activity, a racetrack was located on the flats near Moose Island. This is still clearly visible from Cow Mountain or on aerial photographs. The mountains to the north are the Two Sisters.

In the late 1860s Williams Creek flats were the site of four "milk ranches" with 80 cows, producing "the whole of the lacteal fluid" consumed in the area. Milk sold at one dollar per gallon. One of the dairymen who operated here for many years was Samuel Rogers.

Mosquito Creek—Centerville

The Mosquito Creek and Red Gulch collection of mines such as the Minnehaha and Hocking claims prompted a small town or collection of buildings to blossom around the shafts and drifts. Poet James Anderson once said, "Red Gulch eased me of my cash," referring to a poor investment.

The claims were first mentioned in the 1866 *Cariboo Sentinel*. On October 4, 1867, 80 people gathered at Babbitt's and voted that the new town should be named Centreville. The next issue of *Sentinel* in noted that "Centreville is rapidly being built up and is expected before spring to be a lively little town."

There was the Centreville store run by John B. Lovell, from Buckinghamshire, who was "fond of booze," we are told. Samuel Walker and Isaacs had a saloon and restaurant; C.H. Babbitt had a general store, Jeffree a grocery store, Van Volkenburgh a butcher shop and Janet (Scotch Jennie) Allen had the Pioneer Hotel.

A trail was pushed through from Cameronton in 1868 and it gradually became a passable road. Perhaps because of its distance from Richfield and the lack of a town constable or a strong Masonic influence, the town seems to have been rough. There was a fight resulting in manslaughter, several mine thefts and prostitution.

The town appears to have only lasted a few years. It was later the site of Mosquito Creek hard-rock mine.

Wells Town Site

Wells is the product of a 1930s gold rush. Before the town was built here, the hill was the site of George Clarke's Stopping House, built in 1901–2. It was a magnificent house with porches and 11 bedrooms, and was decorated with the gingerbread trim typical of Victorian homes. It was sometimes referred to as the Sawmill House, as Clarke had built a mill here in partnership with millright Archibald McIntyre. McIntyre had staked out a large pre-emption claim here in 1896. The machinery is now in Barkerville.

For years before and after Barkerville's glory, every prospector hoped to find the elusive mother lode of gold that had for centuries fed the creeks with nuggets and the rivers with flour gold. Greenhorns expected to find gold on the top of a mountain; the more skeptical believed Cariboo gold had been dropped by retreating glaciers and that no mother lode existed. When Richard Willoughby found gold on Lowhee Creek in 1861, he noticed pieces of quartz still attached but paid little attention. John Bowron, however, thought this had some significance and as placer gold was exhausted, he convinced the government to support the search for quartz gold by opening an assay office in Barkerville. After several years with few results, it closed.

In the 1920s Fred Wells came to Barkerville, a veteran of the Kootenay mines, with a theory that the quartz-bearing nuggets indicated a buried ore body. To the Department of Mines, he was "an opinionated prospector, devoid of geological knowledge."

There were those who backed Wells, however, including Dr. W.B. Burnett, a Vancouver physician, who with O.H. Solibakke of Seattle and several other investors formed the Cariboo Gold Quartz Company. In 1930 Fred Wells found his mother lode and proved the doubters and the Department of Mines wrong.

The result was the immediate construction of a new town, Wells, laid out in 1933 and designed to be a progressive community. The company chose miners for their mining skills and their interest in art, music or sport. The company built a large community hall with a dance floor and gym, a racetrack and a baseball park. The result was that Wells was more than just another mining town. It was a centre of culture and activity in the Cariboo, with a population of over 1,500.

Cariboo Gold Quartz was successful beyond imagination. Between 1935 and 1943 dividends of over $1.6 million were paid out. From the rich faults of Cow Mountain, 2.7 million tonnes of ore were mined for over $40 million in gold. The town boomed to a population of 4,500 when the Newmont Mining Company opened its equally rich holdings on Island Mountain.

In 1967 Island Mountain closed, its ore worked out, unable to support further digging with gold at $35 an ounce. Wells declined to a low of 200 people. Three decades ago Mosquito Creek Mining Company tried to reach the old Island Mountain drifts from their site. Recent drilling by Barkerville Gold Mines indicates a substantial gold resource that will likely mean the development of new gold mines around Wells.

The population is now dependent on placer mining activity and the influx of summer tourists and is generally recognized as an arts community.

At the east end of town, through what is called Downtown Wells, the foundation of the town is built on outwash from Lowhee Gulch. Tailings here are almost six metres deep.

William Giles of Missouri was known as Jack of Clubs; the lake takes its name from the creek discovered by Giles. High on the lake's south side can be seen washouts from the old Lowhee Ditch, devised by John Hopp to work his company's claims in Lowhee Gulch. In 1907 this 10-mile ditch was dug from Watson Gulch in Lowhee Gulch across this face and up Jack of Clubs Creek to Ella Lake, where a dam was built. The construction took two years, with the Chinese labourers working 10-hour days for 20 cents an hour. The ditch system was eventually 26 miles long, though the term "ditch" is misleading. They were more like small canals: seven feet wide at the top and four feet at the bottom, about four feet deep, with a steady gradient of nine feet per mile. In one of the more notorious disputes over a mining claim and water, Lester Bonner was convicted of blowing up the ditch in several places. He made the mistake of leaving a note: "Hopp—I blew your ditches—L.A. Bonner."

At the end of the lake, Cariboo Gold Quartz Mine and Cow Mountain are on the south, and the old Island Mountain Mine on the north. The lake was longer 100 years ago. Until the time of the hard-rock mines in the 1930s, the lake extended to the toe of the hill on which the town is built. It has been filled at the eastern end by tailings and refuse from hydraulic operations on Lowhee Creek, which runs south, and from the Cariboo Gold Quartz Mine.

12 THE LAST MILE

The Cariboo Road—Barkerville to Richfield

After the Fraser River gold rush of 1858, prospectors followed the river tributaries like spawning salmon to the gravel creek beds of the Quesnelle Highlands. As the miners surged north they found provisions were in short supply, sometimes non-existent. In 1861 starving miners were sent government relief supplies to allow them to escape south for the winter. Although entrepreneurs moved in to fill the need, packing and freighting costs made prices in the mines soar to many times that of goods purchased on the coast. The government realized that in order to see the mines of British Columbia develop as they should, a road was needed.

The Cariboo Wagon Road was begun in 1861, various sections being contracted out under the Royal Engineers. Most of the road was constructed by 1863, but the stretch from Richfield to Barkerville was not completed until 1865. At that time, the road to Williams Creek approached from the south, from Van Winkle by way of Lightning Creek, Summit Rock, Mink Gulch and Richfield, rather than by its present route—constructed in 1885—through Devil's Gulch and Wells. Once the road was complete, supplies could be forwarded by wagons and freight teams

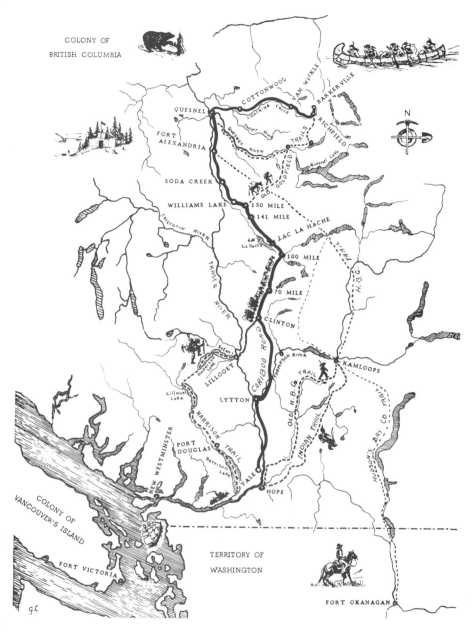

Map showing the route of the Cariboo Wagon Road in 1865. GWEN LEWIS

THE CLAIMS

Noo for claims;
And first a word about their names.
Some folks were sae oppressed wi' wit,
They ca'd their claim by name 'Coo–',
And tho' they struck the dirt by name,
They ne'er struck pay dirt in their claim.
Some ithers made a gae fine joke
And christen'd their bit ground 'Dead Broke'
While some, to fix their fate at once,
Ca'd their location 'The Last Chance;'
There's 'Tinker,' 'Grizzly,'—losh what names—
There's 'Prince o' Wales'—the best of claims'
There's 'Beauregard' and 'Never Sweat,'
And scores o' ithers I forget—
The 'Richfield' and the 'Montreal,'
They say they struck the dirt last fall—
But will they strike it in the spring,
Aye, Sawney, that's anither thing.
—James Anderson

Claim names came from miners' hometowns or the names of partners, loved ones or owners, from descriptions of the claim or the owner's hopes. From the Barker Shaft south to Richfield the claims' names— such as Mucho Oro, Six-Toed Pete, Rising Sun, Perseverance and British Queen—all tell a story. The "Coo–" claim in Anderson's poem, actually Cow Shit, was seen as too coarse, and thus named the Prairie Flower, which refers to buffalo patties.

rather than by the more expensive packhorses or on men's backs. The road brought prosperity to Williams Creek; and to miners whose claims were "proving up," the road meant they had goods and a way to escape and spend their money.

This walk to Richfield through the claims (following the numbered points of interest markers in the "wrong" direction) ends at the courthouse where Judge Matthew Baillie Begbie made his decisions and where, during the summer months, he still holds court.

Barkerville (18)

Barkerville was not established until the end of 1862, following Billy Barker's discovery. By the following year it was rivalling Richfield as the commercial centre of Cariboo.

Diller Claim (17)

Across the creek is the famed Diller claim, which Americans Isaiah P. Diller, James Loring and Hardy Curry staked in September 1860. After months of work the claim proved to be one of the richest in Cariboo. See the story of the Diller claim on pages 68-69.

Black Jack Tunnel

A rough trail crosses the creek to the Black Jack Claim tunnel. The original Black Jack Tunnel followed today's creek bed and was eventually hydraulic-mined. The drift or tunnel seen now is in solid rock and was cut in the 1930s. The Black Jack claim and Burns tunnels took out $675,000 in gold by 1896. With the light of a flashlight or candle, you can walk into the coolness of the tunnel and experience a little of life in the damp underground.

Upstream from the tunnel the careful rock work of miners lines the creek like an ancient fortification or a well tended rock garden.

Stouts Gulch (16)

Edward "Ned" Stout was a California 49er. Born in Bavaria, he was working with his uncle on a Lake Michigan steamer when gold lured him to California and in 1858, to the Fraser River. He came north to Bellingham, Washington Territory, and built two flat boats for the trip to Yale, which he reached in May 1858. At China Bar, First Nations attacked his party. Stout, wounded by nine arrows, was the sole survivor.

After recovering from his wounds, he walked to Cariboo in 1860 and was near Dutch Bill Dietz when gold was found on Williams Creek. Stout's claim did not prove up, so he and two partners staked claims in the valley or gulch running in from the west. Their success encouraged men like Barker to try below the canyon for placer gold.

After mining interest waned, Ned Stout worked as a packer, and then moved to Yale. In 1873 he married Mary Thorpe of Yakima, Washington, and had three children. He is buried in Yale.

A walk up Stouts Gulch leads to several old mining sites, including the great Lowhee pit and what was once referred to as Carnarvon town, now destroyed by modern mining and a possible open-pit gold mine. This road may be closed for mining.

Schoolhouse (15)

During the 1860s the area between Barkerville and Richfield was less defined in terms of town sites. The road was dotted with the buildings of miners and merchants. One of these was Frank Pagden's "Half Way House" at the mouth of the gulch, which opened in 1869, offering the "finest qualities of Liquors, Wines and Cigars." At that time A.D. McInnes had a boarding house and Frederick Rose a hotel further up the gulch near the Taffvale, Jenkins and Mucho Oro claims.

In June 1871 Pagden's roadhouse was converted into a schoolhouse, the location being convenient for children from both Richfield and Barkerville.

Pagden likely left Williams Creek at this time. He moved to Saanich, where he married and took up auctioneering.

Gopher Holes (14)

These "Gopher Holes" are the diggings of the legendary Cariboo gopher, Gopher giganticus Caribooi, which—like the waterwheel Squirrel, the sidehill gouger and the creeping carnivorous conifer—is worth watching for. The more pedantic will insist, though, that the holes are where a miner ran a test lead, believing that gold still remained in rock close to the surface.

Discovery Claim (13)

The Goldfields Act of 1859 specified that claims, except in unusual circumstances or terrain, were to be "100 feet square." The discoverers of a creek were allowed two claims of normal size.

The first claims on Williams Creek were staked here, along

the outcropping of bedrock below the road. Although the creek was named for William "Dutch Bill" Dietz, the Williams Creek discovery claim was registered with the gold commissioner in Williams Lake in May 1862 "in favor of P. Keeman, James Costello and John Metz." In August M. Brown and M.J. Collins were added.

Later a note was entered in the record book indicating that W. Dietz, M. Burns, C. Good, F. Brumiller and J.H. Miller had recorded five claims with Constable H. Hose, who neglected to pass them on to Gold Commissioner Nind. Ironically none was a heavy producer of gold.

Black Jack Canyon (12)

This steep-walled section of canyon was a hazardous place where horse-drawn freight wagons rubbed against pack trains and tempers flared. The gulch below the road was the creek's course when miners arrived. Having been diverted by hydraulic mining, the creek is now only a trickle.

Rerouting of Williams Creek (11)

When facing Barkerville, you will notice a hill rising between the creek's old course, which you have followed through Black Jack Canyon, and the present course. In the 1860s, when the creek's riches were discovered, the hill was part of the larger ridge to the east. The eastern gully where the creek now flows did not exist. Miners discovered that the ancient channel had run to the east before being dammed by glacial deposits, so they removed the entire hillside to get at the gold. The resulting cut was known as the Black Jack Cut, and it eventually diverted the main portion of Williams Creek to the east. A walk along this new creek will take you to many old workings.

Beef and Bacon (10)

The large flat near the road leading to the Richfield cemetery was the site of the slaughterhouse of Messrs. Van Volkenburgh & Company, a partnership developed to supply miners with meat, and reap the rewards. The partnership is described in the Gold Rush Society section under Cattle Drovers.

Abbott and Jourdan Claim (9)

Miners digging along Williams Creek found a layer of hard blue clay they assumed to be bedrock. Above this layer the pay was meagre, so the creek was dubbed "Humbug Creek." Ivel "Long" Abbott, six foot six inches in his stocking feet, and William Jourdan staked a claim here anyway. One day Jourdan headed to town and Abbott decided to dig through the clay. When Jourdan returned, Abbott showed him 50 ounces of gold. The secret was out, and now the Williams Creek rush was really on.

When winter descended, Abbott took his $40,000 share to Victoria, where he lost it all on gambling and drinking sprees. He once entered a saloon and threw $20 gold pieces at the bar mirror until it shattered. Back on Williams Creek his line of credit was soon exhausted, and he lived off the good graces of friends and gamblers who would buy him drinks. Eventually, he wandered up to the Cassiar gold country to try again, but never again did he have the success he did below the hard blue clay on Williams Creek.

The term layer and clay may give a false impression of this feature. In places the layer of rock-hard clay is 10 to 15 feet thick, a considerable deterrent to hand-held picks.

Twelve-Foot Davis Claim (8)

"Twelve-Foot" Davis came by his sobriquet when he noticed that the adjoining claims of Little Diller and Abbott covered 212 feet rather than the legal 200 feet. Davis then legitimately staked the extra 12 feet, from which he sluiced $15,000 in gold. When Davis considered the claim worked out, he sold it to another miner, who produced $12,000. The second owner, in turn, sold it to a Chinese miner who dug deeper and found an additional $25,000 in gold. Davis became famous when he moved north to the Peace River country, still in search of gold.

Richfield Cemetery (7)

The main Williams Creek cemetery is below Barkerville at the site of Cameronton, but here—a short 15-minute walk up this pleasant side road—was the Richfield Cemetery, located close to St. Patrick's Roman Catholic Church. The church was opened July 19, 1868, with Bishop L.J. De Herbomez, D.D., dedicating the building and its bell.

The cemetery was used by Roman Catholics and Chinese. There are no headboards left, only a Chinese memorial plaque and the fenced grave that may be that of Fanny Bendixen.

Known burials here include: James Barry in 1867, Nikel Palsk in 1867, Fanny Bendixen in 1899, Michael Carney in 1868, Colin Chisholm in 1872, Patrick Fitzpatrick in 1968, Michael Hanley in 1875, Honore J. Lions in 1866, William Macartney and Theophile Le Mullard in 1869, Marie Victorie Lauren in 1879, Ah Mow in 1870, Wong Dan in 1931, Wong Wee in 1879, Chang Wong in 1867, and several more unidentified Chinese.

Cariboo Wagon Road (6)

This section of road from Quesnellemouth to Richfield was completed in 1865. Miners had to raise money to extend it into Cameronton and later to Mosquito Creek. Prior to this the only access was over trails.

The *Victoria Weekly Chronicle*, on July 21, 1863, notes that "a ball was given for the benefit of the new trail between the upper and lower towns on William Creek, at Davis and Kelly's new hall in Barkerville (lower town). It was very well attended, a number of ladies being present. The hall was decorated with evergreens and the English and American ensigns were displayed."

Steele Claim (5)

The Steele claim was the richest ground on the creek. When Judge Begbie visited in September 1861, it was producing 30 to 40 pounds of gold a day from a six-foot-thick layer of blue clay 8 to 18 feet below the surface. This claim was often used as an example of rich finds. The New Zealand *Taranaki Herald* quoted the *London Times* correspondent in early May 1862, reporting how development of the mine progressed: "the first day that claim yielded anything was $68 [US]; that of the second day, $170; of the following day, $697; and so on increasing until it reached the astounding sum of $6,579 in a day." From an area of 25 by 80 feet the claim produced $105,000 in two months. By 1896 it had produced a total of $600,000.

Glaciation (4)

The valleys of the Quesnelle Highlands were shaped first by glaciers and then by man and mining. For a century and a half the hills and banks have been scoured and sluiced, eroded and washed until in places the land looks much like it did just after the glaciers receded 10,000 years ago. Now the land is healing itself. After fireweed and other ground-covering plants take root, deciduous trees like willows and cottonwoods begin to grow and soon the conifers return. In a few decades stripped hillsides will once again appear as they did when the miners came.

Richfield (3)

During the summer of 1861 Richfield blossomed from the gravel of the creeks. The resulting town was untidy and unattractive. A visiting journalist described Richfield in 1863:

> The town comprised the ordinary series of rough wooden shanties, stores, restaurants, grog shops and gambling saloons. On a little eminence was the official residence tenanted by the gold commissioner and his assistants and policemen.
>
> In and out of this nest, the human ants poured all day and night, for in wet stinking mud the labor must be kept up without ceasing all through the 24 hours, Sunday included. It was a curious sight to look down the creek at night and see each shaft with its little fire and its lantern, and the dim ghostly figures gliding about from darkness to light, while an occasional hut was illuminated by some weary laborer returning for his nightly toil.

According to the *British Colonist*, on October 14, 1862, the town was named Richfield by Lieutenant Palmer, Deputy Commissioner of Lands and Works. The Williams Creek Grand Jury recommended it be called Elwyntown, after the district gold commissioner, but Palmer thought Richfield more euphonious and appropriate.

The story of Richfield has been poorly told, overshadowed by Barkerville and its heritage status. But for a few short months in 1862 and '63, it was *the* town on Williams Creek, a bustling creek-side array of 63 businesses surrounded by well-paying claims. The town boasted saloons, a bakery, a cobbler's tent, blacksmiths, butchers, a watchmaker, clothing stores, a barber, a bank, barristers, doctors, a surveyor, a dentist, a cigar store, hardware, mining supplies, an auctioneer and more.

The same *Colonist* reporter wrote on August 3, 1863, that Richfield's houses "may be classed as verbs, i.e. they are neither active or passive, but certainly irregular and in some instances defective. The sidewalks are of different grades, and in some parts where a sidewalk would be needed none exist. The hills on each side of the creek . . . are covered in many parts with the tents, shanties, etc. of the mining population."

Richfield had been chosen as the site for government buildings because it was seen as the last of the towns scattered across the Cariboo. It appeared that here, at last, miners might stay for some time, so an administrative complex was built of rough-hewn lumber and logs. But no sooner was the town name confirmed and the buildings completed than Barkerville sprang into existence. By the time the fire of 1868 levelled Barkerville, both towns were in decline.

Government officials decided that even though Richfield was falling down around them, government offices such as the courthouse would remain. As buildings were abandoned they were torn down for construction materials, and miners scratched hopefully at the virgin gravel beneath. Soon little but foundations remained. In 2011 the site was cleared for fire protection and recent archaeological work has uncovered

Judge Begbie's cabin with attached kitchen on the hill about the courthouse.

Williams Creek Gold (1)

Within 30 years of its gold discovery, Williams Creek had produced at the very least $20 million in gold, when gold was $16 an ounce. In dollar value that is about $300 million today, still at $16 an ounce. How much more was found? Perhaps twice the amount recorded, for miners often smuggled gold out to avoid the "monstrous and iniquitous Gold Export Tax" of one shilling and sixpence an ounce.

Richfield Courthouse

The Richfield courthouse stands as a monument to British colonial administration. A supreme court was established here in large part because of the desire that the mainland colony remain a British possession despite massive American immigration. When gold was discovered the British crown moved quickly and established a revised form of British rule in this land where most individuals came seeking wealth rather than settlement, riches rather than order. By the fall of 1858 the Honorable Matthew Baillie Begbie had been appointed first Supreme Court judge for the Crown Colony of British Columbia, the representative of the queen. He was assigned the task of administering British justice in a colony of fur posts and mining camps.

As well as the Supreme Court, county courts were established for lesser cases, and a gold commissioner's court mediated mining disputes, dispensed mining licences and collected duties on gold. This frontier system of justice worked well, in part due to the determination of Judge Begbie. The result was that here—in contrast to lawless California where vigilantes enforced law and order— relative peace reigned. For the most part men went unarmed, and although there were arguments and altercations, robberies and murders, they were few compared to what might have been in a place where desperate men were constantly tempted by extraordinary wealth.

This building is not the original gold rush courthouse built in 1865. This much grander building dates from 1882. When the provincial government took over in 1958, the building had been trashed. Every window was destroyed. Large ornate doors were torn down, thrown in the creek or nailed together to make tables. Two old prospectors, who had wintered in the building, had burned most of the furnishings. A forestry and parks employee said there was probably no other building in Canada that had so many obscenities scrawled on its walls. In frustration a visiting artist had tacked up a sign:

"Through these doors have passed the smallest people in North America. Enter, and join their ranks if you wish, by adding your name to theirs."

Now restored to its 1882 appearance, the building is the site of daily summer court sessions by Judge Matthew Baillie Begbie.

EPILOGUE

I wish I was a boy again,
When the world is young and gay.
A boy among those bully boys
And to-day was yesterday!
The shadow on the dial steals on,
No backward move for me!
You may not know—but my heart knows where
Are the boys of '63.

Where are the boys of '63,
When the "boom" was in Cariboo?
The big bully boys of "roaring camp,"
Rough ready boys and true?

"Some are aged and grey in the mines to-day,
Some back in the "ain country—"
I seek not the old, I ask you where
Are the boys of '63.

The Watties, the Cummings, the Stevenson boys
The Laidlaws, Jamie and Bill,
Thompson, John Bowron, Steel, J. McLauren
Stobo and Fraser and Hill!

"Some will return to Lochhaber no more,"
"Ne'er return to the 'ain countree',"
Peace to the dead, but I ask you where
Are the boys of '63?

— James Anderson,
Tavit Mill House, June 4, 1896

SELECTED BIBLIOGRAPHY

Anderson, James. *Sawney's Letters and Cariboo Rhymes.* Barkerville Restoration and Advisory Committee.

Bancroft, H.H. *History of British Columbia.* San Francisco: The History Company, 1887.

Beeson, Edith. *Dunleavy: From the Diaries of Alex P. McInnes.* Lillooet, BC: Lillooet Publishers, 1971.

Campfire Sketches of the Cariboo. Penticton, BC: Ludditt, 1974.

Cariboo Lodge Number 4. *Spanning a Century with Freemasons of Cariboo.* (n.d.)

Cheadle, Walter B. *Cheadle's Journal of a Trip Across Canada 1862–1863.* Edmonton: Hurtig, 1971.

Gold in the Cariboo. Courtenay, BC: E.W. Bickle, 1978.

Hong, W.M. *And So . . . That's How It Happened.* Quesnel, BC: W.M. Hong, 1978.

Howay, F.W., and E.O.S. Scholefield. *British Columbia from the Earliest Times to the Present.* Vancouver: Clarke, 1914.

Lindsay, F.W. *Cariboo Dreams.* Lumbey, BC: Lindsay, 1971.

————. *Cariboo Yarns.* Quesnel, BC: Lindsay, 1962.

Ludditt, Fred W. *Barkerville Days*. Langley, BC: Mr. Paperback, 1980.

Ormsby, Margaret A. *British Columbia: A History*. Toronto: Macmillan, 1958.

Walkem, W. Wymond, M.D. *Stories of Early British Columbia*. Vancouver: News-Advertiser, 1914.

Weir, Joan. *Canada's Gold Rush Church*. Anglican Diocese of Cariboo, 1986.

Williams, David Ricardo. *The Man for a New Country: Sir Matthew Baillie Begbie*. Sidney, BC: Gray's Publishing, 1977.

Wright, Richard Thomas. *Bowron Lakes: A Year-Round Guide*. Surrey, BC: Heritage House, 1985.

————. *In a Strange Land: A Pictorial Record of the Chinese in Canada 1788–1923*. Vancouver: Greystone Books, 1988.

————. *Overlanders*. Saskatoon: Western Producer Prairie Books, 1985; Winter Quarters Press, 2000.

NEWSPAPERS

Ashcroft Journal

British Colonist

British Columbian

Cariboo Sentinel

Edinburgh News

London Times

San Francisco Call

Scotsman

ACKNOWLEDGEMENTS

WHEN I WENT to Barkerville in 1983 to write the first edition of this book, I was met by special people; Ken Mather, then curator; Ron Candy, conservator; and Judy Campbell, visitor services coordinator, now CEO for the Barkerville Heritage Trust, were among them. They were instrumental in the first edition of this book. Since then there have been a number of people instrumental in developing and telling this story. Dave Jorgenson has helped immensely, always interested in a new discovery, always eager to hike to another site such as Racetrack Flats, and acting as a sounding board for new theories. And it is he who dug up information on the history of the expression Wake-Up Jake. Cheryl McCarthy was always interested in hearing new stories over dinner and a glass of wine. TREAD—the Theatre Royal Exploration and Discovery Group, has also been a part of hiking to and finding lost gold rush graves, towns, ditches and dredges.

Leif and Eva Grandel have kept in touch with many of the Barkerville oldtimers such as the Doodys and freely shared their information, collections and stories over many Swedish dinners.

Achivists virtually all over the world have helped me dig for information, answered questions and pointed me in the right directions. Thanks go particularly to my favourite archives, the National Archives of the UK at Kew, London, which is everything an archives should be, open and welcoming with records freely shared.

The BC Archives in Victoria are always of great assistance and it is here most of the records of BC's gold rush reside.

The National Archives of Scotland were a great help, as were smaller repositories in Wales; Tombstone, Arizona; Idaho, Montana, California, Germany, Austria, and Hong Kong.

Janet Carolyn of the Dollar, Scotland archives and the Dollar Academy was of great help in finding the Anderson story as were researchers Carol Tait and Duncan Hope.

And of course, the staff of Barkerville's archives, curator Bill Quackenbush and archivists Mandy Kilsby and Duane Able are to be acknowledged for digging out information for me for several years.

James Anderson, in Devon, England, the great-great-grandson of Barkerville's important gold rush poet, offered us a room and family stories.

Gethin Matthews, Cardiff, Wales freely shared information on Welsh miners, a generous offer from a fellow researcher.

Appreciation goes to Paul Newman who spent a Saturday with me figuring out how to transfer old Kaypro dbase datafiles to newer FileMaker Pro files so I could once again work with them and build statistics.

My sons, Richard and Raven, have always been encouraging and convincing me to keep telling the stories. Richard and Fiona Tsang-Wright have shared their homes in London and Hong Kong with me while I searched for that elusive record that would tell a better story. And as Dr. Tsang, Fiona has often translated medical reports and inquest reports for me.

Thanks to all the members and directors of the Friends of Barkerville and Cariboo Historical Society who do so much work to enhance Barkerville through fundraising, restoring and maintaining cemeteries and keeping our historic trails open.

A round of applause must go to the volunteer board members

of the Barkerville Heritage Trust who work tirelessly to keep Barkerville one of British Columbia's premier heritage sites.

My appreciation goes to all those Barkervillians who make this creek come alive, both in the 19th century and the 20th; those few who labour with passion and determination, through frustration and the weight of bureaucracy, to keep this piece of BC history alive.

About 50 years ago the late Art Downs, then publisher/editor of *BC Outdoors*, published one of my first articles. He is responsible for my being a writer, so it is appropriate that this book is now published by the company he began, Heritage House, the book publisher most responsible for keeping BC history alive. My thanks to all the folks there, in particular Patrick Helme, Kate Scallion and editor Lara Kordic.

Finally, thanks to Amy Newman, my favourite stage performer, who has shared a grand new adventure with me at the historic Theatre Royal, Barkerville, and enthusiastically travelled the world from Tombstone, Arizona to Mai Po, Hong Kong, and Pitfar, Scotland, digging for our own stories to tell on stage and in this book. I might have done it without you, but it would not have been the life-changing journey that has evolved. Thanks for being there.

INDEX

Abbott, Ivel "Long," 30, 58, 232
Abbott and Jourdan claim, 30, 232
USS *Active*, 24
Adams, Jack, 25
Adams, John, 49
Adams and Pearcy, 204
African-Americans, 54, 56, 103–08, 199
Ah Cow (cabin of), 211
Ah Mow, 184–85, 233
Ah Moye, 88
Ah Sun, 68
Aime, Eude, 94
Alaska gold rush, 27–28
"Albino Annie," 58
Albino Resendes, 58, 111
Allan, Alexander, 52, 118
Allen, Charles W., 117
Allen, Henry, 104
Allen, Janet "Scotch Jenny" (Morris), 58, 82, 84, 223
Americans, influx of, 12, 13, 15–16, 101
Amm, James (aka Ames), 156, 157
Anderson, David, 115

Anderson, James, 114, 115–16, 139, 167, 190, 222; nicknames of, 59; poetry of, 91, 116, 126, 140, 228, 239
Anderson, John, 103
Anderson, Lucy (née Lechmere), 115
Anderson, Marius (cabin of), 211
Antler Creek, 19–20, 24, 28, 35, 53, 60, 101
Asian Exclusion Act, 102
Aurora claim, 117, 176
Austin, Catherine (Parker), 84, 92, 98
Austin, John, 92, 98
Austin Hotel, 98
Australian gold rush, 14, 15, 48, 49, 114

Babbitt, C.H., 223
Bailley, Eliza, 82–83
Baker, John (alias Jean Boulanger), 185
Baker, Louise, 111
Baker, Mary, 111
Baker, W (stable of), 208
Ball, H.M., 153

Ballarat claim, 218, 220–21
Bank of British North America, 136, 138, 158, 164
Barker, Elizabeth (Collyer), 64, 82
Barker, Emma Eliza, 62, 63
Barker, Jane (Lavender), 62, 63
Barker, William "Billy" or "English Bill," 16, 32, 33, 49, 58–59, 61–65
Barker Company: claim, 63, 186–87; flume, 136, 138, 187; shaft, 180–81
Barkerville, 140–41, 166–68; cemetery, 103, 164, 193; fire of 1868, 45, 98, 102, 104, 134–38; flooding and seepage, 132, 216–18; land ownership, 205; lifting of buildings, 187, 194, 196, 216; naming of, 33–34; photograph of, 194–97; population,

House, Charlie, 49, 164, 179
House, Jeanette, 137
House, Joe, 137, 164
House, Margaret (née Ceise), 164, 179
House, Mary, 145
House, Nettie, 78
House, Wesley Charles, 164
House Hotel, 164
Houser, Jeanette (née Ceise), 91, 164, 179, 180
Houser, John, 78, 91, 164, 179
Houser, William (Billy), 179, 180
Houser's House, 179–80
Howman, Edward, 139, 187
Hudson's Bay Company (HBC), 14–15, 16, 33, 101; Brigade trail, 39; store, 138, 165, 166, 196, 216
Hughes, Jack, 25
Hugill, William, 76
"humbug," 16, 30
Hurdy-gurdy dancers, 69, 81, 88–92, 98, 111
Hyda or Haida Annie, 111

Ingots (French immigrants), 93–94
Ingram, Henry, 37, 38, 41
Inland Sentinel, 121
International, 70
Irvine, Isabella, 92

J. Bibby's Tin Shop, 204–05
Jack of Clubs Creek, 44, 156, 225
Jack of Clubs Lake, 26, 27, 78, 225
jail houses, 152
Jane, 105
Jessop, John, 73
J.H. Todd Store, 203
Joe Denny's Saloon, 163

John Hopp Office, 129
Johnson, Alvin, 206
Jones, Dr. (dentist office), 199–200
Jones, Dr. William, 103, 199–200
Jones, Elias, 103, 199–200
Jones, Evan, 66
Jones, Harry, 68, 79, 112
Jones, John, 76, 103, 200
Jourdan, William, 30
Journal of a Trip Across Canada (Cheadle), 41
J.P. Taylor's Drugstore, 161
justice system: jails, 152; law and order, 21–22, 236; murders, 88, 107–08, 185, 193; and prostitutes, 88; and wills, 96; and women, 156

Keeman, P., 231
Keithley, Emma (née Scott), 61
Keithley, Joseph, 61
Keithley, William Ross "Doc" or "Judge," 16, 19, 22, 49, 60–61, 68
Keithley Creek, 18, 60
Keithley Creek (town), 19, 68
Kelly, Andrew, 96, 191, 192–93, 202
Kelly, Elizabeth (née Hastie), 96, 192–93, 202
Kelly, James A., 193
Kelly Hotel, 193
Kelly House, 209
Kelly's General Store, 191–92
Kelly's Saloon, 192
Kellyville, 24
Kelso, James, 76
Kerr Brewery, 169–70
Kibbee, Frank, 138
Kibbee House, 172–73

King, Hub, 145
King, Hubert (house of), 205
Knight, Henry, 104
Knipe, Reverend Christopher, 125
Knott, John, 98
Knott, Johnny, 190, 191, 207
Kurtz, John, 33, 49, 221
Kurtz and Lane claim, 49, 221
Kwong Lee Company, 33, 100
Kwong Lee Store, 138
Kwong Lee Wing Kee Company, 170–72
Kwong Sang Wing Store, 176–77
Kyse, Sam, 73

L.A. Blanc Photo Studio, 198–99
Labouchere, Louis, 14
Ladd, Elizabeth, 90
SS *Lady Seton*, 38
Lai, Dr. David, 162
Lamon, Mme., 83
Lane, Charles, 33, 221
Langell, Ephriam, 92
Langell, Rosa (née Haub), 92
Langevin, Sir Hector, 59
LaSalle, Beech, 155
Laumeister, Frank (Francis), 37, 38, 39, 40, 49
Laurent, Marie, 94, 233
Lavender, Jane, 62
Lawrent, Mme., 83
Lebourdias, Louis, 141
Lechmere, Lucy, 115
Lecuyer & Brun Hotel, 138
Lee, Mrs. Frances, 83
Lee Chong's Store (Museum), 181–82
Lee Chung Laundry, 181
legal system. *see* justice system
Leonidas, 100

ABOUT THE AUTHOR

This latest book by writer/photographer Richard Thomas Wright combines the author's established talent for writing with his love of Canadian history.

Well known as an historical and outdoors writer and photographer, Wright has explored much of this province by canoe, on cross-country skis and by foot, and has spent many summers and winters in gold rush country. For several years Wright was an historical interpreter in Barkerville, creating the character of James Kelso.

He has had 22 books published, including *Overlanders*, the story of the westward Canadian movement to the goldfields of British Columbia and *In a Strange Land*, a pictorial history of the Chinese in Canada. He has written over 500 magazine articles and is an award-winning newspaper columnist

Wright worked as a journalist for several years, first with the *Quesnel Cariboo Observer* and as managing editor of the *Cowichan News Leader* in Duncan, BC. He has worked on several films in the Cariboo country.

He now lives in Wells in the heart of gold country, just five miles from Barkerville, where he continues his writing and photography, and manages Barkerville's Theatre Royal with partner Amy Newman as Newman and Wright Theatre Company. They travel extensively in the off-season researching the back story of gold rush participants.

Richard was the recipient of a BC Heritage Trust Award of Recognition and served on the BC Heritage Trust for several years. He is the founding and current president of Friends of Barkerville, serves on the Barkerville Heritage Trust as a director and is a town councillor in Wells. He has received several awards from the Cariboo Chilcotin Coast Tourism Association, including the 2012 President's Award, recognizing his decades of work in promoting the Cariboo region.

He continues working on books and plays. He has two sons, Richard in London and Raven in Vancouver, and three grandchildren.